Transforming the Law

Transforming the Law

Essays on Technology, Justice
and the Legal Marketplace

Richard Susskind

OXFORD
UNIVERSITY PRESS

*This book has been printed digitally and produced in a standard specification
in order to ensure its continuing availability*

OXFORD
UNIVERSITY PRESS

Great Clarendon Street, Oxford OX2 6DP

Oxford University Press is a department of the University of Oxford.
It furthers the University's objective of excellence in research, scholarship,
and education by publishing worldwide in

Oxford New York

Auckland Cape Town Dar es Salaam Hong Kong Karachi
Kuala Lumpur Madrid Melbourne Mexico City Nairobi
New Delhi Shanghai Taipei Toronto
With offices in
Argentina Austria Brazil Chile Czech Republic France Greece
Guatemala Hungary Italy Japan South Korea Poland Portugal
Singapore Switzerland Thailand Turkey Ukraine Vietnam

Oxford is a registered trade mark of Oxford University Press
in the UK and in certain other countries

Published in the United States
by Oxford University Press Inc., New York

ISBN 978-0-19-926474-2

I dedicate this book,
with all my love,
to my wife, Michelle

Preface

This book is something of a mixed bag. It contains 13 essays that together represent 20 years of thinking about the many ways in which the work of lawyers and legal institutions is undergoing radical transformation through IT. Some of the essays are intensely practical in nature, others are fairly theoretical, while the rest seek to bring theory and practice together.

I was keen to publish this diverse collection for four reasons. First of all, I have been encouraged by colleagues and clients to write formally about some of the new ideas that I have evolved over the last few years. These ideas relate to the Internet, electronic commerce, knowledge management and the impact of these phenomena on lawyers and their clients. They are discussed in Part I. There, I introduce two models that I have developed, both of which are already quite widely in use: the Legal Grid, which clarifies the complex interrelationships between IT, information services and knowledge management within a law firm (Chapter 1); and the Client Service Chain, which explains the ways in which the basic elements of client service are being fundamentally changed by IT (Chapter 2).

Second, I wanted an opportunity to clarify, update and refine the arguments and predictions that I put forward in my book, *The Future of Law*, first published in 1996. That is the purpose of Part II, in which I seek to provide a shortish, easily accessible summary of *The Future of Law* (Chapter 3), an analysis of the impact of my ideas on the future of legal practice (Chapter 4), a summary of likely developments in IT and possible applications in law (Chapter 5), and a reply to criticisms that have been levelled at the book (Chapter 6).

My third reason for wishing to publish this collection was to revisit and republish work that I undertook in the 1980s—in the field of expert systems. Over the past few years, there has been a revival of interest in expert systems in law, especially now that variants of these systems can be delivered across the Internet. I believe that my research and development activities of the 1980s, even though quite theoretical in orientation, are more relevant now than they were when I published on the subject so many years ago. Accordingly, in Part III of the book, I have reproduced a series of papers which are not otherwise easy to find. After an introduction to expert systems in law (Chapter 7), I endeavour to consider these systems from the point of view of jurisprudence or legal philosophy (Chapter 8). I then build on this theoretical analysis by applying my findings to the practical development of the world's first commercially available expert system in law—The Latent Damage System (Chapter 9). My final essay on expert systems is a short case study of what I take to be an instructive failure in the field (Chapter 10).

Finally, I was also eager to look beyond legal practice and gather together some of my thoughts on the broader role of IT in the justice system more generally. This I have done in Part IV, concentrating on the impact of IT on judges, the courts and society. I start with a review of the impact of IT on the civil justice system over the last 25 years or so (Chapter 11). I then suggest how national governments should respond, faced with the task of modernizing their justice systems and given the formidable array of technical options that have emerged over the years (Chapter 12). Finally, I consider, in quite philosophical fashion, the possibility and desirability of the notion of the computer judge (Chapter 13).

As for the target audience of the book, although it is primarily aimed at legal practitioners, academic lawyers, judges, legal policy-makers, legal voluntary workers, law students and information technologists (in all jurisdictions), I hope it is also of interest to a more general readership with no specialist background in the law or IT.

In pulling together this collection, so that much of my work is easily accessible in one volume, I trust that it is not just rationalization on my part to believe that readers might now prefer tackling the field in manageable, modular chunks (separate essays) rather than needing to wade through entire books to grasp the full arguments, as has been required by my previous publications. Indeed, it seems to me, for better or for worse, that the World Wide Web encourages people to read only in relatively concise, digestible modules, always ready to jump off to pursue some linked interests. (It may be that only writers of fiction can sensibly aspire now to having their work read from cover to cover by most of their readers.)

Where the essays have been published before, I have provided the references of the publications in which they appeared. Of those that are republished, some appear with no alterations whatsover, save for minor typographical amendments; others have been updated, in argument and with new references; while still others have been re-worked considerably.

Although the essays cover some quite diverse subjects in and around technology, justice and the legal marketplace, there are nonetheless three running themes that thread through the book.

The first theme is that of the transformative effect of IT. In a nutshell, my expectations of IT and the Internet are that they will fundamentally, irreversibly and comprehensively change legal practice, the administration of justice and the way in which non-lawyers handle their legal and quasi-legal affairs. I am not talking about applying technology in the mere smoothing of some rough edges in the law or to effect some minor streamlining where there are some unpalatable inefficiencies. Rather, I anticipate, in the somewhat regrettable jargon, a complete shift in legal paradigm.

The second theme of the book is my passionate belief that IT can be used to increase access to legal help and, in turn, access to justice. Through the Internet, I argue, non-lawyers will be able to identify and understand their legal rights and duties and be able to pursue their entitlements far more easily than has ever been possible in the past. When I refer to access to justice, I mean more than access to speedier, cheaper and less combative mechanisms for resolving disputes. I am also referring to the avoidance of disputes through better understanding of the law and to readier and more widespread appreciation and harnessing of the benefits that the law can confer.

In a just society, like situations are treated alike under the law (this is formal or procedural justice), the laws and the consequences of their application are equitable and fair (this is a form of substantive justice) and the benefits (rights) and burdens (duties) created by the law are evenly spread across all members of a community regardless of their wealth or status (this is a form of distributive justice). One of my aims is to show that the Internet, by making the law and legal processes more widely and readily accessible, can at once be used to promote formal, substantive and distributive justice.

With greater access to legal help, does this mean, as I am sometimes asked, that the Internet will give rise to a more litigious society? There is a danger here of confusing the behavioural and psychological issue of litigiousness, which I take to refer to a strong tendency towards, or preference for, the (often aggressive) pursuit of disputes, with the quite different notion of having improved legal facilities in place. It surely does not necessarily follow from the fact that people are better informed about the law and their rights that they thereby become more combative or confrontational. Being forewarned about the law may pre-empt disputes and even if there are more disagreements requiring settlement, earlier awareness of legal ramifications can allow these to be addressed before unnecessary escalation. Further, online techniques are emerging to handle such situations using methods that are less intense, lengthy and formal than today's dispute resolution processes. Another desirable effect is also conceivable—that more widespread understanding of the law and access to legal remedies may deter unscrupulous individuals (such as some landlords) from pursuing unlawful or exploitative courses of action. In the past, they may have behaved as they wished regardless of the law, secure in the knowledge that those to whom they were causing suffering were deterred from taking action precisely because of the complexity or inaccessibility of the law and the courts.

If the Internet can lead to less confrontational handling of disagreements or to dispute avoidance or to a reduction of exploitation, then I, for one, will sleep easier.

My third and final running theme is that of knowledge management, a term that is very much in vogue today. Leaving the label aside, almost all of my work has focussed on the use of IT to capture, preserve and disseminate legal knowledge and expertise, so that legal guidance is more widely available and easily accessible. During the 1980s, this motivation was at the heart of my work (and that of many others) on expert systems—I was exploring the possibility of eliciting expertise from human beings and embodying it in computer systems so that it could be accessed by non-experts. Knowledge management was central also to the ideas presented in *The Future of Law*, in which I argued that online legal guidance derived from the knowledge of practising lawyers, delivered across the Internet, will come to be the dominant source of legal assistance in the future.

The architectural solutions that I embraced in these two phases of my work were, of course, quite different. For expert systems, I had in mind the use of rule-based programming tools into which very formal representations of primary sources (legislation and case law) would be cast. For online legal guidance systems, the World Wide Web became my preferred delivery vehicle, carrying much less formal models of the law—practical, punchy, jargon-free renditions of the law as articulated by legal specialists. But whatever the underlying technology and knowledge models, the aim was the same—to spread knowledge and expertise using IT.

In this light, it can be seen that those who say that expert systems are now dead are, to some extent, missing the point. If we define expert systems architecturally, then it is true that comparatively little progress has been made on the commercial exploitation of rule-based systems since my work in the 1980s. However, if we take a wider view, a functional perspective, that expert systems are all about making scarce expertise and knowledge more widely available and more easily accessible, then the spirit is alive and well because that is what many contemporary and highly successful online legal services are all about.

Hundreds of friends, colleagues and clients have helped me over the last two decades. Invidious though it may be to single out just a few of these for express thanks, I feel so indebted to a small group of individuals that it would be entirely remiss of me not to acknowledge expressly those who, I feel, made a very major impact on my work. Without prejudice (as lawyers would have it) to the generosity of those not mentioned, I do therefore want to mention, by name, the members of that small group.

My interest in computers and law was kindled in 1981, while an undergraduate at Glasgow University. My mentors then were Robin Downie and Tom Campbell, both philosophers. If there is any structure, rigour and coherence in my arguments, it is largely down to them.

My work on expert systems spanned the best part of the 1980s, during which time, in quite different ways, I was helped enormously by Colin Tapper, David Gold, Neil MacCormick, Jon Bing, Phillip Capper, John Barney and James Tucker.

In writing the *The Future of Law* and many related publications, I drew heavily from my experience of working at the London-based, international law firm, Masons. At that time, Martin Telfer, John Bishop, Iain Monaghan and Chris Dering greatly helped to clarify my thinking.

In relation to my work in advising on the use of IT in courts, I have been hugely fortunate in having the support of a remarkable triumvirate of venerated judges—Brian Neill, Mark Saville and Henry Brooke. In different ways, each has encouraged and inspired my work on the computerization of the courts; and each has worked tirelessly in modernizing the English courts. Their contribution to the exploitation of judicial and court technology cannot be overstated.

With regard to my latest work, as presented in Part I of this book, I am immensely grateful to Matthew di Rienzo, Elizabeth Broderick and Tony Williams, each of whom challenged the models I developed and unquestionably led me to vital revisions and refinements.

Over and above those who contributed to particular phases of my work, I have benefited also from general support over the years from Alan Paterson, Ian Lloyd, Christopher Millard and Richard Hart.

I must also acknowledge the support of various institutions and organizations that have variously employed, housed, supported or engaged me—the Programming Research Group of the Oxford University Computing Laboratory, Ernst & Young, Masons, the Lord Chancellor's Department, Clifford Chance and the Centre for Law, Computers and Technology at the University of Strathclyde.

In the preparation of this particular book, I have been motivated, cajoled and chased, but always with admirable tolerance, by a fine team from Oxford University Press. I extend my particular thanks to Christopher Rycroft, Rebecca Allen, Jan Miles-Kingston, and Dominic Shryane.

Over and above the range of professionals who have helped me, I have had the enormous benefit of the unstinting backing of devoted parents and of Alan, a hugely supportive brother.

My wonderful children—Daniel, Jamie and Alexandra—deserve particular mention. Without them, my study, in which much of this book was written, would have been entirely free of dirty socks, cake crumbs, sweet wrappers and all manner of other detritus, and I would not have had to compete with their own, near-obsessive usage of the Internet. But I would not have wanted my working environment any other way. I am blessed with fantastic kids, whose energy, enthusiasm and talent are a joy to behold. No writer could have finer sources of inspiration.

Finally, I must express my profoundest gratitude to my wife, Michelle, to whom this book is lovingly dedicated. With supererogatory forbearance, and with greater confidence in me than I have in myself, she has ceaselessly supported me over the last 20 years, through both fair and foul weather. I cannot thank her enough.

October 2000   Richard Susskind
Radlett, England

Preface to Paperback Edition

When this book was first published, in late 2000, our world was enjoying relatively stable geopolitical conditions, buoyant major economic markets, a thriving and evolving professional services sector and, of course, the excitement and apparent profitability of the dotcom movement. Much has changed.

Although the substance of a law book might be thought to be relatively sheltered from global concerns of security and commerce, the subject matter of this book—the impact of IT on lawyers and the administration of justice—cannot be isolated from such factors. Indeed, the book's analysis, predictions and recommendations to a large extent depend on a range of wider assumptions, including prevailing social and economic conditions, the nature of professional services, and the influence of current and emerging technologies.

Accordingly, while I remain convinced of the force of the central arguments and claims laid out in the following pages, it would be remiss of me, in this preface to the paperback edition of the book, to ignore the undeniable changes that our world has endured since its publication almost three years ago.

Our turbulent world

Geopolitically, the horrors and tragedies of September 11 2001 destabilized our world fundamentally. The human costs, individually and collectively, of the loss of life and of the associated emotional and psychological damage, are incalculable. No aspect of our social and economic lives was left untarnished by that day and its ramifications and effects are still far from understood. Commerce and industry were radically affected, adversely reducing production and palpably undermining the confidence and performance of the markets.

The subsequent efforts to counter terrorism and the recent military action in Iraq have further diluted assurance and conviction in the markets. It seems unquestionable that terrorism, the shadows it casts and the fear it engenders, has contributed, in part, to the current economic recessions in many states and to the less dramatic downturns in others.

In the smaller world of professional services, the last few years have also witnessed events that were all but inconceivable when I submitted the original manuscript for this book. Uppermost in my mind here is the rapid collapse of Andersen, following the revelations that constituted the Enron scandal. It is still hard to accept that the activities of an allegedly errant team of auditors in one city in the USA could precipitate within a few months the sudden death of a global professional empire whose brand had previously been amongst the strongest in the commercial world. Nonetheless, Andersen went down, and with its demise came also the implosion of its law firm, Andersen Legal, a vast worldwide network that, at the time of meltdown, had developed advanced plans for radically streamlining and overhauling legal service, relying very much on imaginative uses of IT. These plans also died. At the same time, the promise of multi-disciplinary professional service, of which Andersen had been the most compelling advocate, also suffered a body blow which, although not fatal, will require some considerable period of convalescence.

On the technology front, closer to the heart of this book, the dotcom bubble has inflated and burst since the first appearance of this book. It is not easy to capture in retrospect the enthusiasm, energy and optimism of the dotcom movement but we can be sure that we were witness to a remarkable phenomenon, even if it was substantially misconceived or, at least, ill-timed.

What are the effects of these various, disruptive events on the field of legal technology, on the substance of this collection of essays? It is beyond my sphere of competence to comment authoritatively on international relations, military strategy and global economic conditions. On these matters, I want to say nothing more directly than that they seem collectively to have given rise to a commercial environment in most leading economies that is less active, adventurous and entrepreneurial than that which prevailed three years ago.

The short term for law firms

In turn, most major commercial law firms, reflecting the wider conditions of industry and commerce, have followed this trend; and their caution and conservatism has led to a more measured approach to IT and e-commerce. In the short term, it follows, I suggest, that law firms are set for a period of consolidation with their legal technologists and technologies. In these tougher times, lavish IT budgets are improbable, and hard-nosed managers everywhere are likely to focus on squeezing the most out of existing systems. And so they should. Lawyers have spent handsomely on IT in recent years and ought, in any event, to pause now and take stock before jumping to the next e-fad. They should be looking at their practice management systems, document management systems, intranets and licences for software and thinking hard about how best to secure far greater returns from these technologies. Equally, with an eye to risk management, many practices should devote energy to bringing their e-mail under control. Although the days of the paper-based master file have gone, this need not lead to the chaos in so many firms of delivering key advice to clients in e-mails but then storing these indiscriminately and often, it seems, irretrievably in innumerable 'sent' folders—on networks and on hard discs of different laptops, few of which are systematically backed up. Admittedly, e-mail is a moving target. While managers will seek to contain it, lawyers will increasingly want to pick up their e-mails on the move, through mobile phones, personal digital assistants or laptops. The technologies are available to make this happen, so the average lawyer will soon be 'always on', permanently connected. Thus the e-mail neurosis will continue to be fed, with no refuge from its intrusions.

Looking beyond this modest, short-term approach to legal technology, I thought it would be appropriate in this preface to reflect again on what is likely in the medium term, over the next three to five years. (I will say little about the long term, standing resolutely, as I do, by my ideas as presented in Chapter 3, an essay that summarizes the main theses of my book, *The Future of Law* [1].)

My starting point is the dotcom phenomenon, a sober understanding of which serves as a useful backdrop to my discussion of two further topics: the increasing role of clients in determining law firms' IT strategies; and the three most significant emerging technologies.

The dotcom phenomenon

In mopping up after the burst of the dotcom bubble, Internet commentators have fallen into two groups. One has argued that e-commerce was an over-hyped, transient fad, while the other maintains that its impact will yet be massive and transformational. A leading exponent of the first group is John Cassidy, a journalist, in the mould of Minerva's owl, whose views are clearly sign-posted in the title of his book of 2002, *dot.con: the greatest story ever sold*.[2] Cassidy relentlessly reveals the fervour, greed and 'irrational exuberance' of many dotcom investors and managers. Ironically, however, his own hype in debunking e-commerce is often as irrationally exuberant as the dotcom fiends he seeks to expose. Contrast the management editor of *The*

[1] Oxford University Press, Oxford, 1996. (Paperback edition, 1998.)
[2] Penguin, London, 2002.

Economist, Frances Cairncross, a sober adept of the second school, whose book, *The Company of the Future,* at once acknowledges that the profitability of e-business was grossly overstated but maintains that its long-term significance for business was not. Indeed, she argues, with lucid conviction and compelling evidence, that the Internet may well be the single most profound force shaping tomorrow's businesses. She puts it succinctly in the preface to her book: 'No manager should be deceived by the 2000–2001 collapse of technology companies and stocks into thinking that the influence of technological change has been exaggerated. Its profitability was grossly oversold but not its significance. That will take time fully to emerge . . .' [3] I agree wholeheartedly with Cairncross in this regard. I still maintain that, in the long term, the Internet will facilitate an elemental change in the way we communicate, and so in the way we live, a shift as far-reaching as that occasioned by the advent of the printing press. Cassidy and his school do powerfully expose the excesses of the dotcom movement but they surely neglect the profound impact that the Internet continues to have and is yet to exert.

In the world of law in this connection, the pragmatist might therefore ask—what is the significance of the death of many legal web sites over the past few years? Disappointing though it may be for lawyers who hanker after the ways of the past, I am at pains to stress that there is no serious evidence that the Internet is on the way out. On the contrary, electronic mail, the World Wide Web and collaborative working are firmly entrenched in many firms and are incontestably here to stay in some form or other.

But there are vital lessons to be derived from the false starts. In the first instance, we can discern a pattern in many failed legal web sites of entrepreneurial and confident individuals, piling into an immature marketplace, often with no serious experience of legal technology but suffused with the land-grab, gold-rush spirit of the dotcom movement. Indeed we can see here, in microcosm, the shortcomings of the entire dotcom phenomenon— the prospect of immediately securing unimaginable wealth created a frenzy of business activity without apparent regard for conventional management disciplines, such as watching the cash flow or caring about trifles like turning a profit.

Legal historians will no doubt regard the demise of most legal dotcoms as a quaint yet brief distraction and will focus instead on the success stories which will have come to change the entire legal landscape. These, I believe, will fall into two broad categories: conventional legal businesses (law firms and publishers, largely) that establish a variety of online facilities and

---

[3] Harvard Business School Press, Boston, 2002.

services to complement their traditional offerings; and a few determined entrepreneurs with innovative legal services, only a fraction of whom, whether by floating or selling, will enjoy huge but well-deserved profits. For managers, I believe there is a clear lesson: these old and new businesses have it in common that they are focused, tightly managed and do not expect immediate returns. They are committed to the long-term sustainability of their ideas and not just to quick financial gain.

Another lesson emerging from the recent, tumultuous times for e-commerce is that most organizations will find success in the new economy not by devotion exclusively to the Internet but by creating a blend of online activity and traditional presence. In the retail world, this is often captured in the suggestion that businesses must sustain a balance of 'clicks and mortar', of online service (mouse clicks) and physical premises. I now argue that the emphasis for lawyers and other professionals should instead be on 'clicks and mortals'—on combining online and traditional human service. (Indeed I intend this to be the title of my next book.) The biggest challenge here is for lawyers honestly to identify those situations in which personalized, human service is genuinely needed and adds relevant value that online service cannot simulate or better. In the future, high-powered human service will still be in demand but routine and repetitive interactions with clients will be handled online.

One telling gauge of the level of ongoing Internet activity in the legal world, from my own perspective, is the level of communication I receive in respect of my regular 'online' column in the law section of *The Times*. To encourage feedback and in the hope of learning about interesting new initiatives, I include my e-mail address at the bottom of each column (one every three weeks approximately). Keen for exposure, many people write to me with tales of new systems, services and ideas. I have not found, since the dotcom demise, a marked reduction in such communication. Indeed, leaving aside the extreme and the farcical e-mails (and there were quite a few of these during 1999/2000), the level of traffic has been relatively stable. This reflects, in my view, a maturing legal technology market in which legal web sites, for example, have become mainstream rather than unusual.

However, the content and functionality of such sites is changing. Law firms and legal publishers alike are continually enhancing their offerings, so that the quality and utility of the online facilities is increasing steadily. Another shift I perceive is the far greater interest and involvement by clients.

The role of clients

Chapter 1 of this book details a wide variety of Internet-based systems and services that law firms might provide to their clients — for example, to enable clients to monitor, manage and progress work being undertaken for them or even to provide clients with online legal advice and documents. Many legal businesses now offer such systems, mainly through their own web sites. As I point out, however, exciting though these first generation applications may be, those clients who instruct many law firms (and some organizations engage hundreds), tend to find it unacceptable to have to log on to the many different systems set up by the different law firms for each piece of legal work with which they are involved.

Until recently, it is fair to say, the direction of client systems has been determined by the law firms. Before 2001, most clients were rather passive recipients of whatever systems law firms saw fit to bestow upon them. In a sense, the 'inmates have been running the asylum' (to borrow and adapt the title of Alan Cooper's splendid book [4]).

This approach to client systems is changing rapidly. Soon, law firms will be driven in their IT by the preferences of clients. In fact, in-house lawyers are already becoming ever more influential in the direction of law firms' IT strategies. These clients are becoming much more knowledgeable about the benefits IT can bring and ever more determined that the systems used by their advisers add genuine value. And so, in the past couple of years, clients have begun to say, for example, that instead of visiting many different sites, they want to monitor their entire matter load and receive other forms of online legal guidance from one single, online location.

There are strong analogies here with e-mail just five years ago, when clients rightly bemoaned the need to log on to numerous different systems every morning. This was manifestly unpalatable and the answer was the now taken-for-granted universal mail-box, into which all e-mails generally come today, irrespective of the systems from which they have been sent.

Client sites will soon need to be as integrated as contemporary e-mail. If a particular client has three deals and four disputes being conducted by seven different firms, it should not need to visit seven different sites to monitor progress. Instead, they should have the information about all seven, distilled and available to it on one site, sitting perhaps on the client's Intranet or on some dedicated master site or exchange. This will be immeasurably more

---

[4]   *The Inmates are Running the Asylum* (SAMS, Indianapolis, 1999).

convenient than jumping about a series of unconnected sites. Equally, if a client is involved with, say, an acquisition and wants to conduct research on the topic using online facilities offered by its external law firms, then it should not need to navigate around a set of separate web sites but should be able to access the different offerings from one central point of departure.

How do we get from here to this utopia of integration? For a while, the various firms with first generation systems have been jostling at some putative starting line, each arguing to clients that their tool should become the standard. One dimension of this initial skirmish has been rather melodramatically termed 'the battle of the deal-rooms' although it has hardly moved clients.

One promising new tack was promoted bullishly by LawCommerce in the US in mid-2001.[5] Their aim was to create a worldwide standard for deal rooms, a common technology platform. The venture was strongly backed by various heavy-hitting law firms around the world, which therefore recognized that no matter the strengths of their own offering, they had to inter-operate with other systems in the market.

In the event, despite its good intentions, I do not think that this initiative has wholly succeeded; and certainly not in the UK. When it was announced, I predicted publicly that there would be competition. I pointed out that some senior in-house lawyers felt they should be setting the standards; various investment banks and accountants also had strong views and vested interests; while an array of technologists would be keen to promote dedicated private networks. Meanwhile, I said, there would also be software developers offering cheap and cheerful off-the-shelf solutions, which might quickly reach the mass market, meet the worry about affordability and even become standards themselves. Standards for the inter-operability of deal rooms, I suggested, would therefore be likely to ooze into the marketplace from all directions, bringing to mind the old, ironic IT quip that the great thing about standards is that there are so many to choose from.

There have been two especially significant developments which have rather echoed my expectations. One is the development, by BAT (British American Tobacco) and Ford Motor Company, of the Anaqua system, while the other is the very recent establishment of a legal technology group of investment banks in London. I thought it would be useful to say a little about each by way of update.

In 2002, BAT launched an Internet-based service, developed with Ford, called Anaqua. At the time, this brought to the market a new way for major

---

[5] See www.lawcommerce.com

clients to be served by their professional advisers.[6] For any particular case or project within the intellectual property function of BAT, Anaqua provides a dedicated web site. Such a web site is conceived as the focal point for the conduct of all work—as an electronic master file containing relevant documentation from all sources and as a communications centre through which providers and their clients must interact. As the nerve centre for any given deal, dispute or initiative, Anaqua thus enables users within BAT to retrieve all documents and files, monitor invoices and costs, generate and file tailored reports, send and receive e-mails that are automatically attached to the appropriate site and, more generally, manage the flow of individual matters. More, there is an asset management utility, a conflict tool, a linked knowledge management module, and a facility to enable intellectual property owners and their lawyers to assess the suitability of disputes for early settlement.

From the professional provider's perspective, an Anaqua site functions at once as the repository into which their advice and progress reports must be sent as well as an online tool to which they also have access (a suitably sanitized version of the internal site).

The driving force behind Anaqua was a passion for closer and more effective collaboration between BAT and Ford and those with whom they worked, including their lawyers, domain name managers, patent agents and inventors. The system brought all diverse strands of work and advisers under the one virtual roof.

While the first version of the service was designed for the intellectual property functions of BAT and Ford, it was said that Anaqua could easily be extended to operate wherever teams of advisers are working on complex projects.

Online tools for collaboration were not new at the time of the launch of Anaqua. Aside from generic services that were launched in the mid-1990s, several English-based law firms, from early 2000 onwards, had taken the lead in the legal marketplace by launching specifically branded sites. These first-generation systems were generally well received by clients, although they were regarded as the first and not the last word in improved communications. In particular, as just noted, those who instructed many law firms found it unsatisfactory to have to visit the many different sites of their many advisers. Instead, clients said they wanted to handle their entire matter load from one single, online location. This is precisely what Anaqua offered. The centre of gravity becomes the work—and convenience—of the client; and not that

---

[6] See www.anaqua.com

of the lawyer or other professional. Here lay the fundamental shift. Thus, the second-generation system became a reality.

But where did this leave law firms that had already invested in their own client systems? In short, the far-sighted firms were well placed. If they had anticipated the second generation, the firms could comfortably accommodate Anaqua as one of a variety of online facilities to which they were happy to commit. Further, the firms that were providing access to their own services should have found it easiest—technically and culturally—to feed the relevant files into Anaqua-type environments. That said, the opportunities for law firms to gain competitive advantage simply by offering online communication or collaboration were clearly seen to have diminished.

Interestingly, BAT added an extra edge with Anaqua by making it unambiguously clear that its use by their professional providers was to be non-optional. Here was the message—if you want to advise BAT's intellectual property function in the future, you must use Anaqua. Full stop. Rarely in this field, if ever, had an injunction been so starkly formulated. (No exception was therefore to be made for partners in law firms who were not sure if the Internet was a good thing.)

To cap it all, it appeared to be the intention of BAT and Ford to make the system freely available to any company that wished to use it. It still remains to be seen whether Anaqua will emerge as the industry standard for which many in the online deal-room community have clamoured over the past two years. But what was crucial, in historical terms at least, was that a sophisticated tool was to be made widely available at no cost, a system whose use would require many firms comprehensively to re-visit many of their working practices.

News of the second significant development in the world of client systems was emerging as I was writing this preface. In what appears to me to be the most notable development in legal technology of 2003, a group of major global investment banks has set up a legal technology group dedicated, as I understand it, to the development of IT standards and systems to support their in-house legal departments. Together, these banks have called upon a small group of leading City law firms to help them. Their first initiative seems to be to develop an information and knowledge portal—a single point of access for in-house lawyers, through which they will enjoy easy and direct access to the combined body of knowledge and information resources of the participating firms.

This makes sense. Each of the law firms involved already provides a variety of information and knowledge resources to clients. Some of these are online services, for which subscription fees are levied; while others are made available at no charge, including news flashes and updates, analyses of legal developments, practice notes and even some precedent documents. From the clients' point of view, it would be a major step forward simply to have all current materials available in one online location. However, once that mechanism is in place, it is likely that law firms will begin to compete in this new electronic legal marketplace in seeking to provide the most useful and valuable resources.

Naturally, there will be some reluctance on the part of some firms to engage, not least because solicitors worry about giving away their 'crown jewels'. Nonetheless, this hesitancy will be overridden by stronger emotions —bettering the competition and being seen to meet the needs of major clients. The potential influence of this new group can hardly be overstated. Together, their annual spend on external law firms is said to extend to hundreds of millions of pounds in the UK. Leading firms will find it hard to resist their demands.

One major stumbling block that I can foresee is in the process of developing the standards and technical platform for the portal. The best technique, I feel, is fairly obvious—a hub (or in the now unfashionable jargon of two years ago, a business-to-business ('B2B') exchange) which is at once a one-stop shop for clients and at the same time a single pot into which law firms will be able to input their materials for all their clients. (Just as clients do not want to have to visit numerous web sites in their search for information and knowledge, then, similarly, law firms will not want to have to transfer their offerings in different formats or to different locations for different clients. Here we can see a shortcoming in the Anaqua approach—if it became a standard, then that would work well but if other organisations launched similar but distinct systems, then this would make life oppressive for law firms seeking to feed the likely plethora of systems.) The obstacle I fear is that law firms are asked to collaborate in designing and developing the system. This would be a gross error—law firms find it difficult to collaborate on IT matters and such a project would, as likely as not, suffer from interminable delays and debate.

Far better would be for the hub to be provided by a third party. And, in my view, the strongest candidates here are large legal publishers, with experience of implementing major systems, with expertise in security of systems (a pivotal issue), and the added advantage of having their own content (for example, databases of legislation and case law) to add into the mix. Involvement of such a third party could also lead to more rapid adoption of the hub by the rest of the legal community—by other firms, non-banking clients, the courts and even other professional service providers. Ideally, there should be one hub only—internationally. I suspect that this vision will not be achieved through the construction of one monolithic system. Rather, I can imagine a basic platform, supported by agreed standards—a virtual legal (or professional services) hub, in effect.

Again, as with Anaqua, it is too early to say if this initiative of the banks will be a definitive next phase in the world of legal technology. What is crucial is the trend that both ventures embrace—the move towards a single online port of call for clients. This is all but inevitable. And if Anaqua or the banks' initiative do not take hold, then another similar scheme surely will.

Significant emerging technologies

Aside from the virtual legal hub, there are three other emerging technologies to which I feel I must draw attention in this update. I find each enormously exciting and I take the view that the techniques involved have now come of age. They are all anticipated in the chapters of this book but only now, I believe, are they of immediate and radical commercial potential. I have in mind e-learning, document assembly and handheld systems. In the remainder of this preface, I say a little about each.

E-learning

Of all emerging information technologies, none perhaps holds greater potential for the legal world than e-learning, a term used to refer to a specific set of IT-based techniques that support the transfer of know-how, insight, experience and expertise.

Perhaps the most ambitious current commercial offerings in the world of legal e-learning are multi-media presentations on topical areas of law, delivered by leading experts in the form of 'web-casts'—extended online video clips accompanied by slides and text. Sometimes, these are packaged as CDs and loaded onto organizations' local intranets but, in due course, with the advent of broadband, such services will be available online. I have been experimenting with these techniques with students at the Glasgow Graduate School of Law.[7] There, with the assistance of Paul Maharg and Scott Walker, I have produced several hours of web-casts (renditions of the first two chapters of this book). These are available on the law school network and students are able, essentially, to attend a virtual tutorial—watching and listening to

---

[7] www.ggsl.strath.ac.uk

me via their computers. Research so far suggests that the technique works well and while it is, no doubt, better for me to be there in person, it is considerably better than my not attending at all.

Meanwhile, my colleagues at the University of Strathclyde, Ian Lloyd and Moira Simpson, continue to enjoy success with a different species of e-learning—distance learning.[8] The Ll.M degree in IT Law, as introduced in Chapter 5, is available entirely by distance learning. It began in 1994 with five students. Today, 159 students from 36 countries are enrolled. The flexibility of distance learning techniques—especially its availability at all hours—has led many commentators and trainers to take a step back and reflect on the very nature of learning and training. Some have concluded that traditional, *just-in-case* training is often inherently inefficient and so have worked on the development of what I call *just-in-time* training. The latter type of facility is a resource which should enable lawyers, when confronted with subjects beyond their range of knowledge, to be able to go online and benefit from immediate insight to relevant knowledge, to instant training sessions—maybe video clips from acknowledged specialists. This contrasts with traditional just-in-case education, whereby lawyers are exposed to new developments, through face-to-face sessions with trainers, often at hotels or conference centres, equipping them with insight and knowledge that they *might* need at some future stage.

E-learning can thus be seen to extend beyond distance learning and online training into the topical and yet substantially unfulfilled discipline of know-ledge management (which purports, as Chapter 1 explains, to provide tech-niques for capturing, sharing and re-using knowledge within organizations). To date, most lawyers have been disappointed with their knowledge sys-tems, which have often been no more than large, inaccessible electronic store-rooms of documents. With e-learning comes a more powerful and intuitive way of offering insight into the knowledge of experts—not simply by using text (as in the dominant medium for traditional knowledge manage-ment systems) but by harnessing multi-media (through exposure to image and sound as well). Or, in the language of Part II of this book, echoing the ethos of expert systems work, legal e-learning is another way of using IT to make scarce expertise and knowledge more widely available and easily accessible.

Classroom training, as it were, will always have its place (if only for atten-dees to network in the social sense) but distance learning will make training materials more widely available and accessible; just-in-time training will

---

[8] www.law.strath.ac.uk

ensure that lawyers and their clients, while working, always have training resources at their fingertips; and knowledge management will ensure that legal communities harness and share their collective wisdom and experience.

Document assembly

Automatic document assembly is a technique that is mentioned in many of the chapters of this book. I point to it as a type of expert system in law (itself a branch of artificial intelligence and the law) that is of considerable commercial potential. Since the original publication of this book, there have been two interesting developments.

It may be helpful to take a step back or at least to one side. It should be gleaned from Part II of this book that there are two main ways to make computers do clever things. The first is to build a body of human expertise especially for some task and to offer access to this knowledge through some system. Historically, most automated document generation work has fallen into this category—crudely, a complex decision tree with standard chunks of text is compiled by skilled lawyers and dropped into an off-the-shelf package.[9] The resultant systems ask users questions and automatically produce tailored documents (from wills to loan documentation), based on their decision trees. But developing the trees is a formidable task. This is where the second kind of clever computer might come in—these are systems that themselves can actually produce something impressive and apparently intelligent as output without all the difficult, intellectual work up front. The first of the interesting developments to which I alluded is that a small London-based software company, Business Integrity, has chosen this second path for its DealBuilder system, which takes existing precedent documents and, using artificial intelligence techniques, semi-automatically converts these standard forms into templates upon which automated generation can work directly. [10]

The second development is a related one and that is the emergence of online document assembly systems developed by professional firms for their clients. For example, and indeed using DealBuilder, Linklaters became the first major law firm to offer an online automatic document-drafting service for clients. The system is known as Term Sheet Generator, was developed by the firm's banking practice and was successfully piloted with clients before

---

[9] For example, HotDocs (www.capsoft.com) or Rapidocs (www.rapidocs.com).

[10] www.business-integrity.com

[11] The system is part of the firm's Blue Flag suite of online services (www.blueflag.com), as mentioned in Chapter 1 of this book. Linklaters is a client of mine but I can claim no personal credit for this innovation.

formal launch.[11] It enables banks, after completing online questionnaires, to generate polished term sheets automatically, speeding up this process, it is said, from hours to minutes. Term sheets are documents that summarize the terms and conditions upon which banks are willing to provide finance. Today they are drafted by banks. Accordingly, the system does not automate a task undertaken by Linklaters. Instead, to adapt an old popular advertisement for lager, the system enables the firm to reach parts of its clients that other firms cannot. The crucial difference between past deployments of document assembly and Linklaters' approach is that the firm is providing an online facility for clients and not using it here as an internal efficiency tool as has been the way in the past.

Another document assembly system, but one which also offers a glimpse of the promise of multi-disciplinary online service, is 'beprofessional', the product of a joint venture between the accounting giant Deloitte & Touche and City law firm, Berwin Leighton Paisner.[12] This is an Internet-based service that offers help in various areas of tax and law. It provides practical guidance for small and medium-sized businesses and automatically assembles documents online (including formal agreements) that are tailored to users' individual requirements. Its main services are in the fields of employing staff, managing staff, tax compliance and share options. The system is easy to use and technically impressive, especially its online document generation features, its real-time session maps (which echo early work on expert systems) and its production of formal documents in 'pdf' format. The considerable body of content is made accessible by being built, not in accordance with conventional textbook headings, but around the real-life circumstances facing clients.

Within a few years, online document assembly systems, such as those just outlined, will be commonplace.

Handheld systems

I often jest that most meetings on IT strategy in law firms degenerate into discussions of handheld devices. For many years, gadget fiends' enthusiasm for such machines could comfortably be dismissed as technical gimmickry, IT for its own sake; and frequently a male obsession. (I plead guilty to being a fan.)

More recently, however, as it became possible for these devices to be

---

[12]   www.beprofessional.com. Deloitte is also a client but once again I claim no credit for the development of the system in question.

synchronized, using cradles, with desktop machines sitting on firm-wide networks, their genuine practical import has come to be recognized even by technophobes. And more recently still, a new wave of handheld machines has arrived—the mobile phone that is also a PDA (personal digital assistant). Until then, the hi-tech legal worker who had wanted a full range of facilities had to carry two little (incompatible) boxes: the mobile for telephone calls and text messaging; and the PDA for electronic diary, contact database, word processing and spreadsheet work. The latest machines bring all these facilities together in one unit that offers Internet e-mail and often web browsing as well. Before long, most of these machines will enjoy speeds of access to the Internet similar to desk-top connectivity today.

In the United States, one particular handheld machine seems to have taken the corporate and professional services market by storm—the Blackberry machine.[13] Indeed, at many if not most business meetings in the US today, participants now come armed with their Blackberry machines. Every minute or so, these Blackberry users peer into their neat black boxes to see if new e-mail has arrived or if there are updates to their diaries. These machines are always connected to their owners' corporate IT networks and they automatically synchronize with them without the need to log on. So pervasive are these mobile machines that, it is said, one US investment bank has a notice above its urinals declaring that the costs of repairing a dropped Blackberry will not be reimbursed!

Blackberry machines are now coming to be challenged by Microsoft Windows-based systems. Whatever system is in play, however, and without denying that they are truly remarkable, serious thought must be given to their use, so that they emerge as invaluable connectivity tools rather than intrusive distractions. Law firms may report that their users deliver more chargeable hours when armed with their handhelds but the quality of their private lives may be diminishing commensurately.

Another application of handheld machines is for legal research. In early 2002, for instance, the Supreme Court of Israel began using the first searchable database of Israeli law to run on the popular Palm range of handheld machines.[14] This convincingly demonstrated how users can be given instant, mobile access to significant bodies of legal materials and can comfortably search, browse, view footnotes and even add their own comments. This application is no doubt a forerunner of numerous legal applications that are likely to emerge soon for these pocket-sized computers.

In short, handheld machines are becoming more powerful and flexible

---

[13] www.blackberry.com   [14] www.palmdinet.co.il/english

as each month goes by. With improving processors and greater storage, alongside folding keyboards, fabric screens and permanent connection to the Internet, the mobile lawyer will surely be fully equipped when in possession of a box no bigger than a pack of cards. As ever, the field of legal technology continues to challenge and excite.

Richard Susskind
19 May 2003

Contents

Part I

Legal Service in the New Economy

1

Legal Electronic Commerce

One of my main purposes in writing *The Future of Law*, which was first published in 1996,[1] was to suggest to the legal world that it was on the brink of a seismic shift. I claimed that information technology generally, and the Internet in particular, were about to precipitate huge changes in legal practice and in the administration of justice. I suggested that we were at the start of a 20-year period of upheaval, after which quite different forms of legal service and legal process would emerge.

In the two years that followed the publication of the book, I had the opportunity to present my ideas in person to thousands of lawyers around the world—at seminars, workshops and conferences. The question-and-answer sessions that followed my talks were particularly illuminating for me. The running theme of those who offered views during that period was that of incredulity—not a denial that the Internet would have a substantial impact on the business and domestic lives of all, but a disbelief, or at least a considerable doubt, that the online revolution would really extend into the legal domain. To be sure, in every audience there were enthusiasts who were exasperated by their colleagues' scepticism but, generally, lawyers expected adjustments at the periphery of their world rather than the fundamental transformations that I was predicting.

From 1999 onwards, however, the mood of most meetings changed perceptibly. It was by then clear that some of my predictions, which but two

[1] Oxford: Oxford University Press, 1996. (A revised paperback edition was published in 1998.)

years previously had seemed science fictional, were already coming true. For example, whereas pervasive use of e-mail by law firms as a central means of communication with clients had seemed improbable to many in 1996, just over two years later most lawyers recognized that a shift had occurred—swiftly, uncompromisingly and not necessarily at their own instigation. Likewise, many firms had embraced Intranet technology and had offered universal access to the World Wide Web for their fee earners—developments that were barely conceivable twenty-four months previously. In light of these undeniable developments, coupled with a variety of high-profile innovations by major law firms (most notably Linklaters with its Blue Flag services and Clifford Chance with NextLaw[2]), my hitherto more radical ideas rapidly became more tolerable. For example, my suggestions that IT might play the definitive role in communications between lawyers and their clients, and that legal advice might be delivered through online services, became topics of serious debate.

A revelation for me, from around the beginning of 1999, was the new, dominant theme in the discussion sessions that followed my talks. The scepticism gave way to genuine interest and, crucially, the posing of one central question—how should our firm respond to the Internet revolution? Lawyers were now less interested in the theory and principles and were becoming more practical and action-oriented. At the same time, I became conscious in my own work that I had not made the numerous issues, concepts and developments sufficiently clear to allow senior managers to plan confidently and decisively for the challenges of the future. Accordingly, I set about developing some models to help decision-makers and enthusiasts alike to think more systematically, and yet still practically, about the new phenomena engulfing the law and legal practice.

In Part I of this book, I introduce the two models which seem to have worked best with clients and colleagues over the past two years or so. The first, the subject of this chapter, I refer to as 'The Grid'. The second, as set out in Chapter 2, is the 'Client Service Chain'.

1. The Grid

In the past, when introducing or explaining ideas to lawyers, I have not been a fan of the use of charts, diagrams or graphs. By training and disposition, it

---

[2] See www.blueflag.com and www.nextlaw.com

had seemed to me, lawyers preferred to digest new concepts through immersion in words, the tools of their trade. In developing The Grid, however, I found a model to which most lawyers seemed strongly sympathetic. I am pleased to say that The Grid is coming to be used by specialists in IT and law across the world, as well as in government and industry in the UK.

My approach here is, first, to introduce a generic version of The Grid and then to focus on a legal variant of it, providing an in-depth commentary and detailed analysis of its use in law.[3]

My main aim in publishing The Grid is to help explain and clarify the complex and often confusing interrelationships between the concepts of IT, information, and knowledge. Moreover, I also intend that The Grid should bring sharply into focus the differences between the use of IT, information, and knowledge within an organization as opposed to its exploitation beyond. The Grid also serves another purpose, that of providing a tool to help those involved with strategic planning. Proposed IT and knowledge-management strategies, for example, can be plotted onto The Grid as part of a strategy-development process; and, as I will show, competitors' positioning can similarly be mapped and then compared using The Grid.

Figure 1.1 shows the basic generic version of The Grid. It consists of two axes, which intersect to create four quadrants. The horizontal axis is perhaps best introduced by reflecting on our common usage of the term 'IT'. It is revealing that when most of us talk of 'IT', we invariably have the 'T' in mind rather than the 'I'. Indeed, our shorthand for IT is often 'technology'. Very

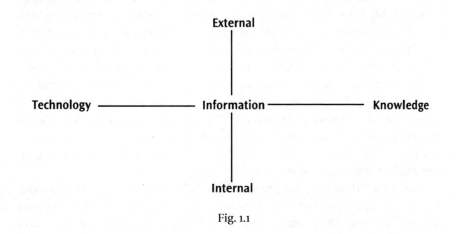

Fig. 1.1

[3] I am grateful to Tony Williams, Matthew di Rienzo, Stuart Popham, Brian Collins, Susan Hall, and John Barnard, each of whom made helpful observations as I evolved The Grid.

rarely, do we find people using the word 'information' to denote the concept of IT. It might even be said that we have come to be obsessed with the technology alone, with the enabling systems and the underlying technicalities.

And yet, the bare technology itself is no more than 'plumbing'. Following this metaphor, the technology provides the pipes, tanks, and pumps but is indifferent to that which is flowing within the systems. However, it is surely the content—the data, information, and knowledge—that is captured, stored, transmitted, analysed, and applied by the technology that is really what is of value when it comes to IT. The mere plumbing on its own—the machines, cables, and operating systems—are of little inherent value in themselves.

The horizontal axis of The Grid seeks to reflect the spectrum of concepts embraced by the term 'IT'. This follows my earlier thinking, as articulated in *The Future of Law*, where I developed what I termed there the 'legal information continuum'.[4] At the left-most side of the axis is the label 'technology', referring to the basic plumbing. At the other extreme, is the term 'knowledge', which, in ways revealed throughout this book, can be taken to be one of the most valuable, powerful, and useful types of content that can be processed by technology. As computer systems become capable of making human knowledge available online, then we move into a whole new era in the world of IT.

In crude linear terms, the evolution of IT can be regarded as a movement across this horizontal axis. In the beginning, there was the bare technology, capable of basic and then increasingly sophisticated numerical processing. From number crunching, the field developed into data processing, which enabled the manipulation of all manner of unstructured and unanalysed data. Then, with more sophisticated technologies, came the era of information processing, characterized by the manipulation of data that had somehow been subject to human analysis, such that it was genuinely informative in its own right. From there, we have been moving gradually towards the application of a variety of techniques for the management of knowledge using technology. This evolutionary path is reflected on The Grid, not just with technology and knowledge placed at the respective poles, but with 'information' situated in the middle.

As for the vertical axis, the underlying idea here is more straightforward. The southerly point on the axis is labelled 'internal' to denote, when overlaid upon the horizontal axis, the internal application of technology, information systems, and knowledge services within an organization.

---

[4] *The Future of Law*, n. 1 above, pp. 85–91.

As will become clearer below and in the chapter that follows, many current and future uses of IT, information systems, and knowledge services will involve sharing these systems with, or extending them to, organizations or individuals beyond the originating companies, firms, or bodies. These applications of technology, information systems, and knowledge services can be said to be external and, in the diagrammatic terms of Figure 1.1, are positioned above the line. In summary, then, the vertical axis seeks to distinguish graphically between the exploitation of technology, information, and knowledge within and beyond an organization.

In intersecting, the two axes create four quadrants (each labelled in Figure 1.2). The main idea of The Grid is that each quadrant represents a category of exploitation of IT, information, or knowledge, as the case may be. In summary, in so far as the generic version of The Grid is concerned, the quadrants represent the following categories:

- bottom-left: internal use of technology;
- top-left: external technology links;
- bottom-right: internal management of knowledge; and
- top-right: provision of access to knowledge.

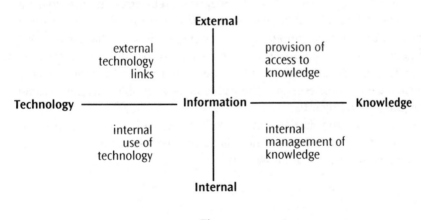

Fig. 1.2

These four categories are explored in greater detail below in the specific context of a legal version of The Grid. But before moving to that discussion, two general points should be noted.

First, like all models, The Grid is a simplification of reality and does not purport to capture all relevant complexities and subtleties. The scholar or purist could find numerous difficulties with The Grid. For example, the many distinctions implicit in the horizontal axis are often the subject of fierce, academic debate, such that the difference between information and knowledge could of itself be the subject of a major conference. At the same time, it might be said that the label 'data' should occupy the position allocated by me to 'technology', thereby reflecting a more coherent range of phenomena across the spectrum. This is, however, an illustration of where I have been pragmatic in creating The Grid. The reality is that most lawyers on whom I tested versions of The Grid have found it considerably easier to understand when 'technology' is placed at the left-most extremity. Given that my purpose is to promote general understanding, and not necessarily to defend a coherent epistemology, I have preferred the more readily understandable to the intellectually elegant. (Similarly, in relation to my selection of 'knowledge' at the right-most end of the horizontal axis, I could have placed 'expertise' or 'wisdom' there to convey a sense of the most highly distilled knowledge but, having tested these alternative terms with lawyers, I found that they caused greater confusion than the more readily understood 'knowledge'.)

My second general point about The Grid is that it can be used in many different contexts. For example, in my work in advising national governments, I replace the label 'external' with 'citizen' thereby stressing the possibility, and indeed the desirability, of government systems reaching out to those in whose interests government exists—namely, citizens themselves. When working with retail organizations, I make a corresponding change: this time from 'external' to 'consumer'. (I have also tailored The Grid for use with in-house legal departments and their clients; law schools and their students; and judges and litigants.)

For law firms, the change that I make to the north-most point on The Grid is from 'external' to 'clients'. And it is to that specific version of The Grid, as applied to law firms, that I now turn.

2. The Legal Grid

Figure 1.3 shows The Grid, as adapted for legal purposes. In broad terms, the space above the horizontal axis ('above the line'), refers to technology, information systems, and knowledge services to which clients have access, whereas everything below the line refers to internal technology, systems, and services within a law firm. While my treatment of The Legal Grid in this

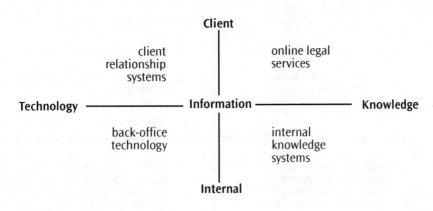

Fig. 1.3

section has the law firm in mind, my arguments can easily be adapted to apply to other types of legal-service providers.

On The Legal Grid, the four quadrants represent four broad categories of systems, as follows:

- bottom-left: back-office technology;
- top-left: client relationship systems;
- bottom-right: internal knowledge systems; and
- top-right: online legal services.

In Figure 1.4, examples of each category of system are presented to give a flavour of the scope of each quadrant. Later in this chapter, I discuss in some detail the profound business implications of the second, third, and fourth quadrants. For now, my initial purpose is to introduce all four.

In the bottom-left quadrant, which represents back-office technology, we can place not just basic technology, such as hardware, networks, and operating systems, but also the fundamental databases, which to a more or less structured extent, are operational in all substantial law firms. I have in mind here:

- document management systems (for the storage, management, and retrieval of word-processed documents, and, in principle, all other files);
- practice management systems (holding accounting, financial, billing, and time-recording information);
- human resource management systems (in which data about individuals are held);
- marketing systems (containing information about clients and potential clients); and
- standard office systems (including electronic mail and electronic diaries).

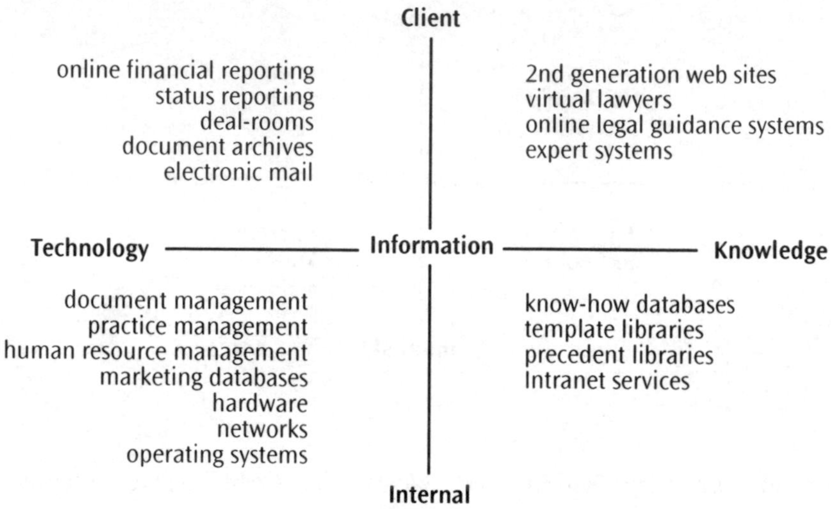

Client

online financial reporting
status reporting
deal-rooms
document archives
electronic mail

2nd generation web sites
virtual lawyers
online legal guidance systems
expert systems

Technology —————————— Information —————————— Knowledge

document management
practice management
human resource management
marketing databases
hardware
networks
operating systems

know-how databases
template libraries
precedent libraries
Intranet services

Internal

Fig. 1.4

In an ideal world, these basic systems cohere and interoperate seamlessly and so function like one large database. In the real world, they tend to be wildly incompatible, with each type itself often made up of smaller non-interoperable component parts. Whether coherent or incoherent, however, these systems do fall into the category of what I call back-office systems and sit in the bottom-left quadrant.

Turning now to the top-left quadrant, where client relationship systems reside, a useful way to grasp their significance is in the context of an entirely different service. Consider the world's leading parcel delivery services. As a matter of course, it is now possible for senders or recipients to go onto the Internet and determine where any particular parcel might be (for example, in transit or in a warehouse pending delivery). When I speak to clients of law firms, and ask them what they expect of their legal advisers' use of techno-logy, they often ask for a similar kind of service. Crudely, they want to be able to gain access to the data or information held within many of the systems of the law firms that advise them. For example, they would like online access to accounting and financial information, as held in firms' practice manage-ment systems or to archived documents, as stored in the law firms' docu-ment management systems. In a sense, they want to be brought under the same 'virtual roof' as their legal advisers and to have easier and direct access to certain types of information without necessarily having to speak directly to the lawyers themselves.

With regard to the bottom-right quadrant, representing internal know-ledge systems, a variety of systems fall into this category. Historically, many law firms have developed 'know-how databases', which often are no more than electronic storerooms of potentially relevant materials, such as press cuttings, journal articles, and bibliographical lists. In the mid-1990s, these materials were frequently indexed and made searchable by computer, although often only by librarians or information staff. Also in the internal knowledge systems category are precedent documents (with commentary), templates, standard forms, and practice notes generally. More recently, these and other materials have become accessible within organizations using Intranet technology—materials are made available on the equivalent of an internal Internet. Leaving the particular technologies to one side, the crucial point here is that attempts are made to capture and reuse internal knowledge within law firms.

The fourth quadrant, the top-right block of The Legal Grid, represents online legal services. To understand this quadrant, it is helpful to step back. In the past, when most non-lawyers needed legal help, the main way in which this was obtained was through direct consultation with lawyers—a face-to-face, one-to-one, consultative, advisory service, usually delivered on an hourly billing basis. Lawyers were the interface between non-lawyers and the law. More recently, however, with the emergence of the World Wide Web, it has been possible for clients to gain access to increasingly sophisticated online facilities. Where the first wave of legal web sites were no more than brochures online, a second wave has emerged from which useful legal infor-mation can be obtained. We are now seeing a third wave of sites from which legal guidance and legal advice can be delivered. These services belong in the top-right quadrant. Whether one calls them online legal services, 'virtual lawyers', or legal advice systems, they are online resources that contain the knowledge of lawyers which no longer needs to be accessed exclusively by traditional human consultation. Positioning in the top-right quadrant has nothing to do with whether or not any charges are being levied for access to the knowledge. It is the fact of online provision that is determinative.

The Legal Grid can also be used to highlight and clarify the business impact of systems to be found in each quadrant. This is shown in Figure 1.5. It can be seen that I am suggesting, in respect of the bottom-left quadrant, that there are three basic purposes of back-office systems. The first is an operational one—keeping a law firm's basic systems going. Without elec-tronic mail, word processing, and accounting systems, for example, most law firms would crumble within days. The second purpose flows from the first and relates to risk management. Firms invest in back-office technology not to secure strategic advantage but to avert the risks of being left behind or of creating undue dependence on operational systems. Thirdly, the business purpose of back-office systems is to provide a robust infrastructure, a platform and foundation upon which systems in the other three quadrants can rest. The importance of this cannot be overstated because many client relationship systems, in particular, rely for their smooth operation on sound, robust, and reliable back-office systems.

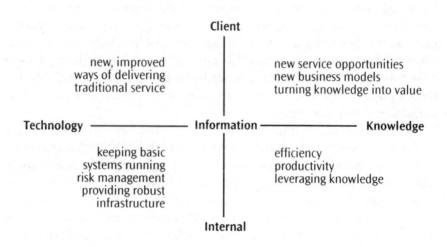

Fig. 1.5

The business purpose of client relationship systems, belonging in the top-left quadrant, is quite clear—it is to provide new ways of delivering traditional legal services. The systems in this category, as discussed more fully later in this chapter, do not change the fundamental nature of the consultative service but enhance the way in which that service is delivered.

From a business point of view, the purpose of systems in the bottom-right quadrant, internal knowledge systems, is to improve efficiency and productivity. If, as is hoped, much of the collective experience and know-how of a firm can be captured and reused, then this should give rise to considerable improvements in efficiency and productivity. With knowledge systems in place internally, there follows the possibility of establishing a business model that depends on the leveraging of knowledge, as distinct from the leveraging of human lawyers which has characterized the business model of so many firms in the past.[5]

---

[5] On knowledge leverage, see Thomas Stewart, *Intellectual Capital* (London: Nicholas Brealey, 1997), passim, esp. p. 135.

As for the top-right quadrant, representing online legal services, here the business purpose is to provide new service opportunities altogether, new ways of packaging and selling legal knowledge, expertise, and insight. In a memorable extract from its mission statement, KPMG, the global accounting and consultancy firm, talk of their commitment 'to turn knowledge into value' for the benefit of their clients. This superbly captures the aspirations of systems and services in the top-right quadrant. Fundamental new business models are envisaged here, whereby legal knowledge is transferred to clients, not in the traditional one-to-one, consultative, and advisory fashion, but through the provision of legal experience embodied in online knowledge systems.

It is crude but perhaps helpful to suggest that systems that reside above the line (above the horizontal axis) tend to be devoted to the provision of better service, whereas systems below the line focus on the more cost-effective delivery of legal service. Here we have the two main ways in which competitive advantage can be achieved—by delivering better service or delivering cheaper service. It is a fundamental question of strategy for any law firm to determine whether or not it prefers its investment in technology to give rise to improved or less expensive service.

When one delves a little deeper, however, it transpires that the position is more subtle than this. It will become apparent from my arguments later in this chapter that I believe clients will soon request, and later demand, that firms have a top-left capability, that is, that they can provide a range of client relationship systems. If indeed this becomes commonplace in the legal market, as common indeed as the basic back-office systems of the bottom-left, then it may well be that, in due course, there will be no competitive advantage derived from any systems to the left of the vertical axis. In other words, law firms will simply be expected to have basic technology and data-processing systems in place, whether for internal or external access.

In that event, it may transpire that competitive advantage can only be attained through the deployment of systems that sit to the right of the vertical axis, that is, from systems and services that embody legal knowledge (again, whether for internal efficiency or external client-access purposes). Intuitively, this seems likely, for surely lawyers should derive competitive advantage in their marketplace not from the raw technologies that they use but from their ability imaginatively to apply their most valuable resource—their knowledge and experience.

The Grid has also helped me to explain two buzzwords prevalent in management jargon today. I refer here to the notions of 'electronic commerce' and 'knowledge management'. As can be seen from Figure 1.6, both of these

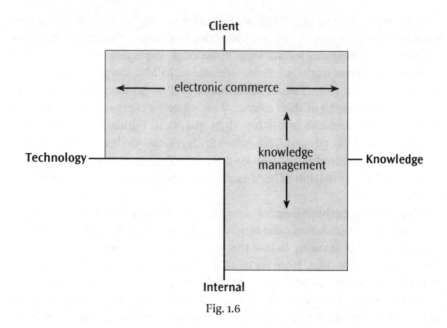

Fig. 1.6

concepts can be mapped neatly onto The Legal Grid. Electronic commerce, it seems to me, belongs above the line. In law, as elsewhere, electronic commerce is about the use of Internet technology (in the main) both to improve and enhance current working practices and business models (top-left) as well as to give rise to entirely new forms of products, services, and commodities (top-right).

Knowledge management, I believe, refers to all systems to the right of the vertical axis, whether internal or external. Not long ago, knowledge management was thought to be a matter of internal process only. As I said earlier, the goal was to increase efficiency and productivity by capturing, preserving, and reusing the collective expertise of an organization. However, with the advent of the Internet, it is possible for this knowledge to be shared with others beyond the originating organization, and indeed to be made available on a variety of commercial bases. Accordingly, knowledge management has been extended to embrace not just the bottom-right but the top-right as well.

I find it fascinating to note that it is in the top-right quadrant, the home of online legal services, that electronic commerce and knowledge management overlap. It is here, I believe, that the real revenue opportunities will arise. It is here that the transformation of law will occur. Just as the top-right was the focus of much of *The Future of Law*, it is a prime concern of this book as well.

In this introduction to The Legal Grid, I find it at once instructive and yet depressing to note that most law firms' current budget for IT allocates about 95 per cent of expenditure below the line and a mere 5 per cent above the line. As a strategy for legal electronic commerce, this seems to me to be meagre.

Using The Legal Grid now to capture the level of technology exploitation in most major law firms (by which I mean, for this purpose, the world's top 250 law firms), the extent of exploitation and investment by most firms in 1995 is captured in Figure 1.7 in which the shaded area suggests overwhelming investment in back-office systems, in the bottom-left quadrant. This state of take-up coincides with a regular and heartfelt complaint that I heard expressed by innumerable partners of law firms around the world in the early 1990s—in exasperation, they would invite the managers in their law firms to explain precisely what benefits had accrued from their considerable investment in technology (hundreds of thousands, even millions, of pounds in back-offices systems). The answers were usually fudged but the reality was, at that stage, that no serious benefits had yet begun to accrue. But how could they have done? It was as though plumbing and pipes had been installed but no water was yet flowing. Unless and until the systems are developed so that they reach out into the other three quadrants—to enhance client relationships, to improve internal knowledge management, or to provide new forms of legal service—it is hardly conceivable that any serious

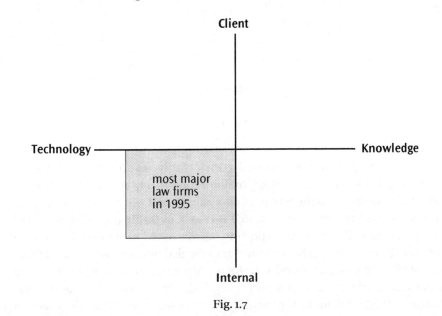

Fig. 1.7

business benefits can be realized. In 1995, therefore, in technology terms, the world's leading law firms were all dressed up but with nowhere to go.

Moving forward about two years to 1997, some significant changes were becoming apparent in the leading firms, as shown in Figure 1.8. The back-office systems remained similar but we saw the beginnings of activity in the top-left, in the arena of client relationship systems. The sliver of shaded area in the top-left in Figure 1.8 depicts electronic mail traffic between law firms and their clients, not for social purposes but for the conduct of legal business. Meanwhile, in the bottom-right quadrant, the utility of know-how databases was becoming acknowledged, even if their access was restricted to internal information specialists.

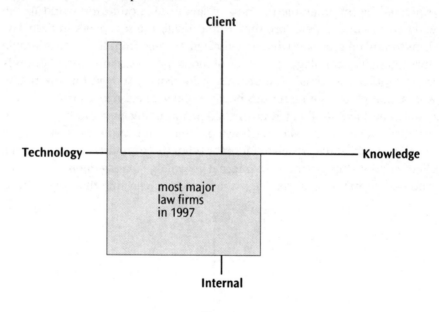

Fig. 1.8

In 1999, the picture had changed considerably, as shown in Figure 1.9. Again, the back-office technology remained relatively stable. However, we saw major leaps in client relationship systems, not only a vast upsurge in electronic mail (on average, a 20-fold increase in traffic over that period of two years) but also in online reporting, as discussed more fully in the next section of this chapter. The bottom-right was also burgeoning, as most firms installed Intranets and found genuinely easy and intuitive ways of storing and sharing information internally (even if they were not yet culturally prepared for this). And, in the top-right, a variety of firms produced their second

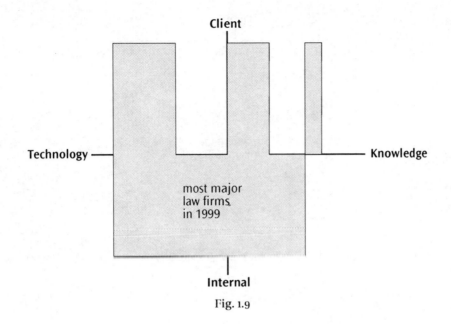

Fig. 1.9

wave of web sites, offering useful practical updates and substantive legal information, while a few (represented by the right-most shaded area) even launched online legal advice systems.

At the time of writing this chapter, in June 2000, I can safely say that I have seen more progress in the last two years of my work in the field of IT and law than in the previous eighteen. It is, therefore, with some confidence, that I suggest that the profiles of the most successful law firms by 2005 will look like Figure 1.10—active and full participation in all quadrants.

3. The Three Crucial Quadrants

My purpose now is to offer some further, more detailed comments on the challenges arising in what I take to be the three crucial quadrants of The Legal Grid—the top-left (client relationship systems), the bottom-right (internal knowledge systems) and the top-right (online legal services). I am not suggesting that the bottom-left is not important. On the contrary, as I stressed earlier, these back-office systems will frequently provide the foundations upon which developments in the other three quadrants are built.

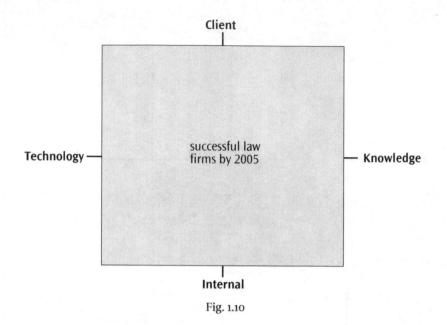

Fig. 1.10

Indeed, I would suggest that one of the most formidable challenges facing any law firm over the next two or three years is to move from what I invariably find are a collection of broadly incompatible and incoherent back-office systems to a seamless set of (at least) interoperable systems (including practice management systems and document management systems, as well as the other categories noted in the bottom-left quadrant of Figure 1.4).

More specifically, I recommend that wherever possible—on acquisition or development of new systems, or on enhancement of existing systems—firms should strive to render their major underlying information systems *unified*, that is, the different back-office systems should be capable of actually operating alongside one another and sharing one single body of data (with, for example, globally unique means of identifying people, clients, and matters). Failing this, the different systems should at the very least be *interoperating*, that is, they should be able to operate alongside one another even if they cannot share one single body of data. Having articulated that huge task, I will say little more about back-office systems in this book, leaving the practicalities to specialist information systems consultants and systems integrators.[6] Instead, I will focus, in this section particularly, on the other three quadrants, occupation of which I am suggesting will be essential for any successful law firm in the coming five years.

---

[6] A useful primer on the management of back-office systems (and other aspects of IT in legal practice) is John Irving's *It's Legal* (London: Bowerdean, 2000).

Client relationship systems (top-left quadrant)

Over the past three years, while preparing presentations to many law firm partnership conferences, I have had cause to read a number of client satisfaction surveys. These have usually been prepared by external consultants, whose aim has been to determine systematically, from a selected sample of clients, the level of satisfaction with the service delivered by the law firms in question. While many of these studies differ in detail, I have found a common trend—clients rarely complain about the quality of legal work or the level of knowledge of the lawyers advising them; but they frequently express concern about the mechanics of the working relationship between client and firm. More particularly, it is often said that there is a poor level of communication. Thus, I often read that lawyers appear to be pathologically incapable of returning phone calls promptly; they often fail to keep clients apprised of progress; when bills arrive, they are regularly larger than has been expected by clients; and, generally, clients complain that they do not feel that they know what is going on.

At the same time, advising at board level in a number of organizations, I know that many chief executives of client organizations are worried about the rigour with which their external lawyers are being managed. They are not always confident that their senior in-house lawyers are able to control the many law firms working for them.

I believe that these client satisfaction surveys and the misgivings of top management point in the same direction—towards the need for improved, streamlined, and regular information flows between law firm and client. I mentioned earlier that clients tell me that they would like to log onto law firms' systems to check progress much in the way that we can monitor the progress on the Internet of a parcel being sent across the world. This gives rise to what I call 'first generation' client relationship systems. These enable clients to gain access to information about the work being undertaken for them directly, on the Internet, without needing to speak to their lawyers on the telephone or meet on a face-to-face basis. I believe, within two years (by 2002), that any law firm that does not provide such services will put itself at a considerable competitive disadvantage. As I suggested earlier, I do not think, in the medium term, that having these systems in place will offer competitive advantage for law firms. Instead, they will come to be basic tools of the lawyers' trade. At this stage, I have identified eight different (although often overlapping) categories of first generation client relationship systems:

1. *Status tracking systems.* These enable clients to monitor the status of any matter being conducted on their behalf so that they can determine, for

example, what the latest activity has been, on whom the next responsibility falls, or the basic milestones and deadlines for the matter in question.

2. *Financial reporting systems.* These offer clients the facility to find out, in respect of any particular matter, how much time has been recorded, what bills have been rendered so far, the level of outstanding work in progress, the charge-out rates being applied, and other related financial information.

3. *Contact systems.* So that clients are able to determine the identities, qualifications, and experience of lawyers working on any particular matter, these systems make that information easily available, alongside the ability to search for suitable practitioners for particular classes of work.

4. *Virtual deal rooms and virtual case rooms.* These are online, secure sites for the posting and accessing of documents pertaining to any particular deal or dispute.

5. *Online archives.* Developed for particular clients, these provide an online collection of all advice, documents, agreements, and other work produced for that client, held in one indexed and easily accessible repository.

6. *Online instruction.* This is a facility to enable law firms to be invited to begin work on new matters without cumbersome, face-to-face procedures or exchanges of formal letters.

7. *Case/matter management services.* A form of project management facility, and often embracing many of the above categories of client relationship system, these enable clients to monitor the flow of individual matters or to assess the collective workload being undertaken by a particular firm.

8. *Client relationship sites.* These are online sites dedicated to the particular relationship between one client and one law firm, being a first port of call for the client wanting access to any of the firm's services.

In technical terms, the crucial point to notice about these first generation systems is that they will be located either as a secure site on the World Wide Web, or as an 'Extranet' service (that is, a part of a law firm's Intranet that is made available, under secure conditions, to a particular client—see Chapter 4).

The shift towards second-generation client relationship systems, in my view, will come about largely as a matter of convenience for the clients themselves. When advising clients, as opposed to law firms, I feel bound to point out that for those clients who instruct many law firms (and some corporations instruct literally hundreds), it is not sufficiently handy for these clients to log onto innumerable separate systems, in respect of each matter or each law firm in which they are interested. Instead, they should want the sum total of law firms' client relationship systems to be integrated and made available to them, either as one dedicated master site, or perhaps sitting on their own Intranets. In either event, rather than visiting many different sites, clients should be able to monitor their entire matter load, as well as their panel of external lawyers, from one single online location. Thus, if a particular client had three deals and four disputes being conducted for it by seven different firms, for example, it would not need to visit seven different sites, but would have the information about all seven, distilled and available to it on one site. Not only would this be more convenient, it could also be designed so that clients could undertake comparative analysis (assessing, for example, the relative productivity and efficiency of the various firms currently acting for them), as well as integrated calendaring (so that, for instance, an in-house lawyer could have a consolidated list of all tasks for a particular week in respect of all the matters being conducted by his or her entire panel of lawyers).

The main, current focus of law firms who are exploring and exploiting client relationship systems is on first generation systems. A fascinating question for the legal marketplace is whether the basic systems to support second-generation client relationships systems will be provided by law firms; by other players in the emerging legal marketplace, for example, publishers, accountants, or ASPs (application service providers); or even by other entrepreneurial enterprises who find exciting commercial opportunities arising from transforming the way in which clients manage their law firms.

Internal knowledge systems (bottom-right quadrant)

I often refer to the successful development of internal knowledge systems as the Holy Grail of legal technology. No one seems to doubt that, if they were well implemented, such systems would be of immense value. But successful implementation seems to elude the overwhelming majority of firms.

It is worth pausing to reflect on why this is such an important issue. In the first instance, the collective knowledge, and experience of a law firm is of immense commercial value for it is the knowledge, experience, and expertise of a firm's lawyers that clients are actually happy to pay for. In most cases, it is precisely because a lawyer or law firm is perceived to have expertise lacking in the client that the law firm is consulted at all. The lawyers in question have been recognized to have the experience, track-record, and insight to help a client with some given set of circumstances. And yet, in most law firms, the knowledge of the finest practitioners is not formally captured. Instead, it is locked in filing cabinets, lost in the ether once delivered to clients, or held in the heads of specialists, all of whom eventually retire or leave.

Even in the world's largest and finest law firms, the large number of partners and lawyers does not lead to correspondingly formidable internal knowledge sharing. The reality, all too often, is that firms operate as large coincidences of sole practitioners rather than as coherent teams of knowledge specialists working in a learning environment. In summary, there is leverage of human lawyers (when, for example, one partner has five assistants working for him or her) but there is, as yet, little leverage of knowledge. There is insufficient management of knowledge as a resource that of itself can help yield enormous business benefit.

Within and beyond the legal profession, those who have given serious thought to knowledge management recognize that the ready availability of relevant knowledge (not just libraries, but distilled, usable know-how and guidance) will lead to improved client service, whereas the absence of knowledge systems will lead to competitive disadvantage. If knowledge is indeed so central to client service, then it must surely be nurtured and exploited systematically—internally and externally. This in turn calls for *knowledge management*—the organization and deployment of knowledge as an identifiable activity and responsibility. In turn, for internal purposes, the effective management of knowledge should:

- ensure that collective experience is available within an organization;
- discourage duplication of effort within the firm;
- encourage valuable work to be recycled and not disposed of; and
- ensure consistency of service.

When lawyers reflect upon this, they quickly come to accept the potential power of internal knowledge management. If knowledge can indeed be leveraged, then there arises the twin possibilities of manifestly improved service coupled with much greater profits. So what has gone wrong in the past? Why have lawyers failed to exploit this opportunity?

I have come to recognize six difficulties. First of all, many lawyers do not recognize that they are in the business of knowledge management. This is not language that they readily understand. I find it helps here to provide evidence; to point to some of the knowledge management activities that lawyers might recognize within their firms. I have in mind:

- *Creating knowledge*—through innovation, research, by training and learning, or in the course of client work.
- *Importing knowledge*—through the recruitment of people or access to external knowledge systems.
- *Capturing knowledge*—from work product, from filing cabinets, and from the heads of leading specialists.

- *Maintaining knowledge*—ensuring that the latest knowledge is continually being captured and that dated knowledge is removed from systems.
- *Providing access to knowledge*—putting knowledge at the fingertips of all lawyers, increasingly through IT.
- *Integrating knowledge into daily practice*—ensuring that knowledge facilities (including 'group-working') are usable and actually used in practice.
- *Knowledge-inspired changes to work processes*—when greater understanding or analysis of knowledge leads to shifts in the way service is delivered.
- *Knowledge transfer and knowledge sharing*—encouraging wider access to knowledge, internally and externally.
- *Selling knowledge through professional service*—delivery of service in the traditional way, through one-to-one consultative techniques (at meetings or through documentation).
- *Packaging knowledge*—presenting knowledge as a product, either for external sale (for example, online services such as *NextLaw*[7]) or for internal use (for instance, as procedure manuals or methodologies).

It is clear that knowledge management is pervasive within law firms, even if it is not explicitly recognized as such or not done well.

Second, law firms tend to have what I call an 'information non-sharing culture'. Whether for fear of having their work product criticized or by dint of distrust of colleagues' ability to reuse their work, many lawyers are reluctant to share their knowledge. This reluctance is bolstered by appraisal systems that value individual over team performance. All of this is in stark contrast with other outstanding professional services organizations, such as McKinsey, who say explicitly that their success depends on their ability 'to stand on each other's shoulders'. At McKinsey, it seems to me, they have a publishing culture, whereby consultants compete to have their work product for clients published internally—as illustrations of best practice, as guidance for future similar engagements and, I suspect, as maintenance of continuity with the strong academic backgrounds from which most of their consultants come. Law firms would do well to mimic the information sharing culture of McKinsey and other top ranking strategic consulting firms.

A third difficulty with internal knowledge management has been a general lack of commitment to, and involvement with, knowledge management from the top of organizations. It is rare to hear a senior partner, or managing partner, of a law firm extol the virtues of knowledge management. But if top

---

[7] www.nextlaw.com

management is not leading by example, or not insisting, for instance, that contributions to collective knowledge are acknowledged in annual appraisals, then the prospects are bleak. If business managers within law firms do not continually reinforce the message of the huge potential for leveraging knowledge, or urge their fee earners to think not just of serving clients but of contributing simultaneously to their collective 'institutional memory' then progress will continue to be modest.

Fourth, most law firms have failed to recognize the overlap between internal knowledge management on the one hand and training on the other. In structural and organizational terms, this has tended to lead to two distinct functions within law firms—one organizing know-how and the other responsible for training. Yet knowledge and training are two sides of the same coin. The substance of any practical training course, for example, will be the provision of valuable know-how that should be available, not just in formal training sessions, but on firms' Intranets as well. Equally, the materials currently being loaded onto Intranets could be brought to life so much more powerfully by being introduced in the context of internal training programmes, perhaps using the power of multimedia, including video clips by experts, well illustrated in the context of 'on-the-job' or 'just-in-time' training—the availability of training resources to support lawyers as and when new challenges arise. Such resources, if online, are a clear mix of genuine know-how and training material.

The world's leading accountancy firms have training and knowledge capabilities that would put many medium-sized universities to shame. They are creating virtual learning environments in which training and know-how are integrated and Intranet technology provides the basis of delivery for both. As ever, law firms have much to learn from the global accounting practices.

A fifth difficulty that I have noticed with internal knowledge systems is the desire of managers to impose one approach to knowledge management across an entire firm. This has been a big mistake. Most firms provide a wide range of services. Often the service lines constitute quite different types of business venture. In turn, a knowledge system that is well suited to one practice area within a firm may well be entirely inappropriate for another. For example, in major international practices, the thrust of many finance practices today is towards standardizing, systematizing, and even productizing their services. It is recognized that much of their work can and should be organized as a type of production line, even supported by standard methodologies for certain types of deals. The knowledge systems required to support such practices tend to be sophisticated, very much towards the knowledge end of the horizontal axis on The Legal Grid. Sophisticated finance practices are looking, therefore, at advanced technologies such as expert systems and document assembly systems as a means of packaging their knowledge.

In contrast, a litigation practice can forcefully argue that its need of substantive legal knowledge systems is quite different (although they may undoubtedly need sophisticated document management systems for handling evidential materials or project management systems to help run and control any particular case). The commercial litigator will find it more difficult to package the substantive knowledge upon which he may rely in as systematic a form as his finance colleagues achieve. Even then, however, the specialist litigator—for example, the construction litigator—may indeed be able to develop standard models for the pursuit of certain typical sorts of action. Nonetheless, the enabling technologies upon which the litigator will rely will be positioned nearer to the centre of The Legal Grid than those of the finance lawyer.

Tax lawyers will have quite different needs. They will tend strongly to resist the commoditizing of their knowledge but will insist instead on having a full range of primary source materials (legislation, regulations, and case law) at their fingertips and easily accessible online. Thus, their knowledge systems will also sit a little to the right of the vertical axis on The Legal Grid.

Finally, corporate lawyers may tend to say that their work is less capable of commoditization than their finance colleagues and that every deal they broker is quite different. They may go on to claim to have information and knowledge needs more akin to the tax lawyer. In practice, the uniqueness and artistry of the corporate deal-maker is often exaggerated. I believe that substantial parts of corporate work can be systematized and reused and that those corporate law firms that recognize this may enjoy considerable success from exploitation of the technologies towards the right hand side of The Legal Grid.

The sixth and final difficulty I have noted in relation to internal knowledge systems flows directly from the fifth, but is worth articulating separately. In summary, lawyers have failed to recognize that there are many different enabling techniques and technologies available to support the internal management of knowledge. The apparent passion that many law firms have had for particular software packages (not even categories of systems) has been severely prejudicial to successful knowledge management.

To give a flavour of the range of systems, I have mapped five (abbreviated) categories of knowledge system onto their appropriate place in the top-right quadrant of The Grid, in Figure 1.11. Consistent with my previous description of the horizontal axis of The Grid, the techniques become increasingly sophisticated as they move from left to right. A fuller list of categories of systems is as follows:

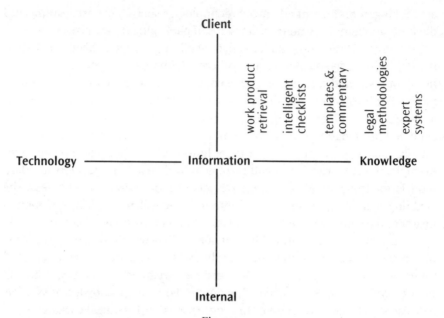

Fig. 1.11

- diagnostic and planning expert systems;
- knowledge embedded in business processes;
- document assembly systems;
- legal methodologies;
- intelligent front-ends;
- templates with commentary;
- procedure manuals;
- intelligent checklists;
- workflow systems;
- genuine know-how systems;
- indexes of collections;
- know-who and know-where systems; and
- work product retrieval systems.

It is not my purpose in this chapter to explain each of these categories in detail. Explanations of each are peppered throughout this book. And more detailed discussions of many types of knowledge system also appear in *The Future of Law*.

Online legal services (top right-quadrant)

One of the great revelations in the knowledge management literature is that there is a heavy information and knowledge component underlying almost all business processes. If good business analysts are let loose on any organization, they will tend to identify huge reliance on flows of knowledge and information, both internally and externally. Although particular tasks within some industries, such as the actual manufacturing of products, may seem, at first blush, to be quite devoid of information and knowledge content, further digging often suggests that many underlying processes are indeed themselves the product of the application of knowledge (manufacturing tools are derived directly from highly refined engineering knowledge, for example). At the same time, careful analysis often shows that the broader business process in which particular tasks sit may itself be heavily dependent on information and knowledge (about market trends, customer preferences, and efficient logistics, for example).[8] Thus, much of today's fascination with knowledge management has been generated on the strength of thinking about organizations that are, in some sense, *underpinned* by knowledge.

When it comes to law firms (and professional services firms generally) the relevance of knowledge is far greater and more profound: not only do information and knowledge flows underpin law firms as they do any commercial organization, but the very *product* of the law firm is a form of knowledge itself. Law firms do not merely rely on knowledge. They sell it as well. With this in mind, it is easy to see the strong linkage between internal knowledge management (the bottom-right quadrant) and online legal services (the top-right quadrant).

Some years ago, we saw an inkling of this relationship when savvy clients asked law firms who were proclaiming sophistication of their internal knowledge systems if they could themselves have direct access to these systems. These clients recognized the value of law firms' templates, precedents, practice notes, and know-how databases and they sought direct transfer of that knowledge to them. In the wired world, where clients and law firms connect to one another by the Internet, what was a vague possibility just a few years ago will shortly become a standard requirement. Just as clients want access to some of the information held in their law firms' accounting systems, so too they will come to expect access, both on a chargeable and non-chargeable basis, to the content of the firm's internal knowledge management systems as well.

---

[8] See Bill Gates, *Business @ the Speed of Thought* (London: Penguin, 1999); and Ross Dawson, *Developing Knowledge-Based Client Relationships* (Boston: Butterworth-Heinemann, 2000).

Not all online legal services will be derived from internal knowledge management systems, however. Others will be services that have been put together with clients specifically in mind and may enjoy no particular internal success. Either way, the theme is the same—that clients gain access to the experience and insight of lawyers through consultation with online systems. Two firms have led the way, internationally, in the development and delivery of online legal services: Linklaters and Clifford Chance, each of whom has launched a suite of services.[9]

Once again, as with internal systems, it should be stressed that there is a variety of techniques and technologies which will come to underlie the delivery of online legal services. There is not just one type of system. Each of the categories of knowledge system mapped onto The Legal Grid in Figure 1.11 might underlie an online legal service. In so far as I am aware, the major focus of law firms to date has been on the following eight types of legal services (ordered here from the most to the least 'knowledgeable'):

- legal advice systems;
- document assembly systems;
- legal methodologies;
- compliance audits;
- intelligent checklists;
- use of law firms' know-how systems;
- standard documentation; and
- online alerts and updating services.

Critics of my book, *The Future of Law*, have marshalled a variety of objections to online legal services, as conceived here. In Chapter 6 of this book, I deal with what I take to be the most serious of these objections. For now, I think it important explicitly, if briefly, to address three.

The first objection is that the revolution I predicted in *The Future of Law*, leading to the widespread use of online legal services, has not come to pass. There are critics (although not many, to be fair) who say that lawyers are still advising clients in the traditional way and so my theory is misconceived. As I say periodically throughout this book, however, I estimated originally that the revolution I predicted, a 'shift in paradigm' in legal service and legal process, would take some 20 years. We are but four years into that 20-year period and so it is far too early to reject my claims for reasons of timing and take-up. That said, the changes in the past four years have been greater than I would have anticipated and I, like others, believe that the pace of change in the Internet is actually accelerating rapidly. Of the top 30 UK law firms, for

---

[9] See www.linklaters.com and www.nextlaw.com by Linklaters and Clifford Chance, respectively.

instance, I understand that at least half are already offering, or are at advanced stages of developing, some type of legal electronic commerce service (above the line in The Legal Grid). I have little doubt that, by 2005, the overwhelming majority of major law firms will be operating above the line in The Grid.

However, the full revolution of which I speak will require that, by 2015, the *main* way in which legal service is delivered across the world will be through access to online legal service as opposed to consultation with human lawyers. I still stick to that prediction.

The second objection often directed at my views on online legal services is summarized in the assertion that 'a computer cannot be better than a lawyer'. Even if, for now, I concede that point for the sake of argument (which I need not see my discussion of the Latent Damage System, as described in Chapters 8 and 9, which clearly outperformed leading specialists), it does not matter for my purposes. In the first place, many of the applications of online legal services that I anticipate will not replace any existing lawyer, but will be available precisely when conventional legal service is not affordable, practicable, or accessible. This is the essence of what I call the 'latent legal market', as described more fully in Chapter 3. Thus, I believe online legal service can and will be invaluable not simply to supplant the work of existing lawyers, but to enable greater access to legal help (noting also that future generations of online legal services will exhibit more human features, including voice and video renditions of guidance). The test, often, is not whether online legal service is better than a human lawyer, but whether or not online legal service is better than nothing at all. (Again, this point is addressed in greater detail in Chapters 3 and 4.) In any event, it may well be that, in some areas of legal practice, lawyers today provide *too* good a service; that they over-engineer (not necessarily intentionally) their work product and provide a level of service beyond that which is needed by the client. If this is the case, and I raise it as no more than a possibility that I would like to investigate further (see Chapter 2 in the context of my discussion of 'disruptive technologies'), it may well be that online legal service is preferable to the service traditionally delivered by human lawyers precisely because it is not over-engineered and so does not over-deliver (assuming, of course, that it is also cheaper, quicker, or in some other way more convenient).

The final objection to online legal services that I would like to address is well captured as a series of propositions: information is not advice; a computer cannot offer advice; and lawyers are not publishers and so should avoid involvement in the provision of online legal services. My short responses are as follows: I agree that information is not advice but claim that well-packaged information (perhaps in the form of intelligent checklists or compliance audits) can nonetheless be of immense practical value; and I have had this view echoed by innumerable clients of law firms. I disagree that computers are unable to offer legal advice. Part III of this book, relating to expert systems in law, directly and demonstrably contradicts that assumption.

Finally, I think it is short-sighted for lawyers to reject out of hand the possibility of delivering information services. On the one hand, I know that clients are very keen to receive timely, punchy, practical news services and alerts, as well as more general audit tools. And if clients would indeed welcome such service, and its capability is comfortably within a law firm's capacity, then it seems to me to be missing a commercial opportunity to fail to provide such a service. Similarly, withholding a service on the grounds of a too restricted conception of the scope of legal services would be to offer the chance for competitors (and again I point to legal publishers and accountants for this purpose) to exploit the opportunity to provide information services and so establish a foothold in the legal marketplace.

4. Eight Strategies for the Future

The Legal Grid that I have introduced in this chapter can also be used as a tool to help law firms map out their IT, information, and knowledge strategies. In the same way that the shaded areas were placed on Figures 1.7–1.10 to show the extent of uptake of various systems during given time periods, then so too with individual firms. By shading areas within The Legal Grid, firms can plot their proposed areas of investment in respect of particular periods of time. A series of grids referring to different time periods can depict the evolution of systems over a number of years (again, as in Figures 1.7–1.10).

Where a firm is made up of a number of diverse practice areas, a grid (or series of grids) can be devoted to each. It is important to do this for precisely the reasons identified earlier—in particular, that the knowledge systems requirements of different practice areas can be quite divergent.

One of the major advantages of using The Legal Grid to model strategy, is that it is possible to reduce a statement of strategic direction to just one page, in sharp contrast to the multipage tomes that are often produced in the name of strategic planning. It should be stressed, however, that when I speak in this context of 'strategy', I am not referring to detailed plans complete with milestones, budgets, and time scales. I use the term 'strategic direction' advisedly—the process is one of setting the overall direction for an investment; choosing an approximate point on the horizon; but doing so in terms which are widely understood within a firm and not just by enthusiasts, specialists, and managers.

Using The Legal Grid, I have identified eight plausible strategies which may be favoured by firms or practice areas. In what follows, I discuss each in turn, plotting them onto grids.

Strategy 1—Consolidation

This approach, as depicted Figure 1.12, calls for an exclusive focus on back-office systems (the bottom-left quadrant). Many disillusioned partners in law firms will support this strategy, citing particular instances of failed technology (such as a broken printer or some e-mail delivery failure) as unassailable evidence that the infrastructure needs sustained attention before any attempts should be made at further 'frills'. I agree that the infrastructure is vital for any firm and that continuous improvement must be the order of the day. Indeed, I believe maintenance and investment in the bottom-left quadrant is vital for any plausible strategy. However, I do not regard systems

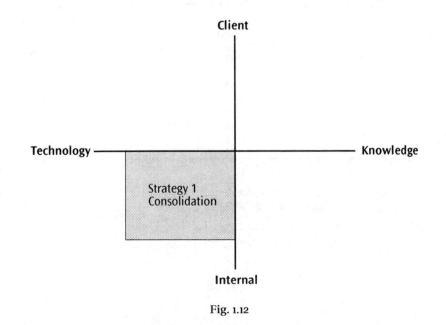

Fig. 1.12

belonging to the other three quadrants as 'frills'. Over the next five years, they will become central to legal service, in my view. Accordingly, unless focus on the bottom-left quadrant is a very short-term response to some catastrophic problems, I would urge every firm to look beyond Strategy 1.

Strategy 2—Putting the house in order

Figure 1.13 captures the thrust of the second strategy. The focus here is on back-office systems and internal knowledge systems; and so electronic commerce is thereby rejected. This strategy has much in common with the previous one in that it frequently betrays a lack of confidence in internal systems (in this case of both technology and knowledge systems). There is often, quite naturally, a nervousness amongst partners about extending systems into the hands of clients when there are lingering doubts about their efficacy internally. Again, if there are extreme and profound difficulties internally, then this internal focus may be a sustainable short-term approach. It may be helpful (or insulting) for me to note in passing, however, that I invariably find that most partners of law firms are ill-qualified to assess the robustness or stability of their internal systems and are rarely able to comment authoritatively on the scalability and extendibility of internal systems. Strong management requires the views of partners to be respected but not always followed when they are not based on genuine expertise.

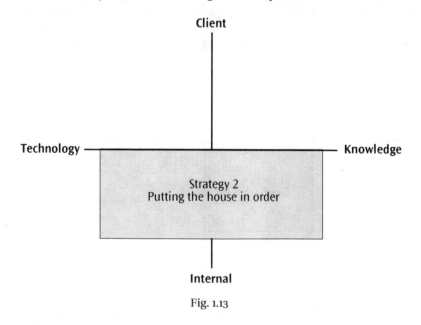

Fig. 1.13

In any event, systems and services that belong to the upper half of The Grid do not necessarily need to offer direct access to the internal systems over which there is doubt. It is not uncommon for entirely separate systems to be set up in the first instance—hosted, supported, and maintained by a group other than those who deliver internal services. This leads to a potentially sensitive point. If there is a genuine question-mark over the ability of internal staff and their systems, the appropriate management response is surely not to be constrained to working within their limitations, but to develop or extend teams and skills so as to meet the existing demands of the marketplace.

There is also a sense in which many partners may never feel that their internal systems are good enough; and they may always identify areas where further improvement or refinement may be possible. I am reminded here of a leading UK supermarket which was castigated in the computer press for its first foray into online shopping. The story ran that the web-based system into which users entered their shopping lists was incompatible with the stock control and merchandizing applications used within their stores, stockrooms, and warehouses. As a result, manual operators were actually rekeying the orders (as entered by web users) into the supermarket's back-office systems. The press criticized this incompatibility and lack of 'seamless integration'. But the press were wrong. From the point of view of the customer, so long as the web interface was pleasant and easy to use and the shopping arrived on the doorstep at the appointed hour, the online shopper will care little about the underlying operations and logistics that lead from online ordering to on-step delivery.

Consider the swan moving serenely across the lake with no apparent effort. Few of us would want to know about any frenetic flapping that there might be beneath the surface. The same goes for legal electronic commerce. Even if current means of delivering client relationship systems or online legal services are rather cumbersome and antiquated from the legal firm's own point of view, as long as client satisfaction is achieved, it seems to me to be misconceived to hold back for reasons of technical inelegance or impurity.

Strategy 3—Client relationship systems

This strategy concentrates on the delivery of client relationship systems, as discussed earlier in this chapter. As Figure 1.14 shows, the emphasis is on the top-left quadrant, but supported by improved back-office systems. There is perhaps frank resignation here—that a particular firm or practice area is incapable of sharing its knowledge (whether internally or with clients) and so that possibility is removed as an option. As a medium-term strategy for a small- or medium-sized law firm, this may be an acceptable tack, although I do not believe it will give rise to serious competitive advantage. Indeed, as I have said, within two years, I suspect it will be standard practice to provide client relationship systems. Accordingly, small- to medium-sized firms should be thinking beyond this two-year period and extending to the quadrants to the right of the vertical axis. At the same time, larger firms, or smaller ones with investment capability, should want, even within this two-year period, to be making a move into the realm of legal knowledge systems.

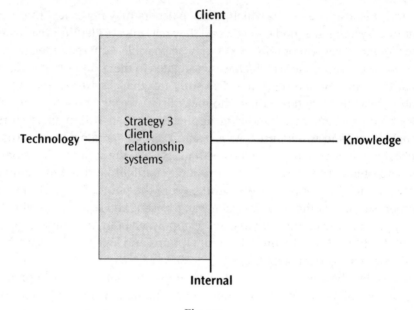

Fig. 1.14

Strategy 4—Knowledge management

Figure 1.15 depicts a strategy which emphasizes knowledge management (again built on improved back-office systems) but neglects client relationship systems. Accordingly, while it is laudably ambitious, I believe this one is commercially wrong-headed. If I am right and client relationship systems are due, within two years, to become the standard platform upon which the client–lawyer relationship is based, then it must be folly for any law firm that intends to continue providing traditional legal service to ignore the top-left quadrant.

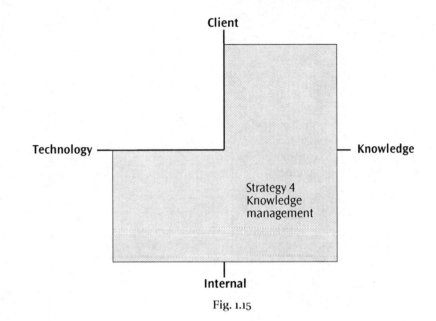

Fig. 1.15

It is conceivable, however, that a law firm could decide to phase out its traditional, consultative advisory work in anticipation of becoming, very largely, an online legal service provider. In that event, Strategy 4 would make sense. This could be the approach of a firm whose conventional market has shrunk; or of a highly innovative firm, fuelled by the 'dot.com' spirit.

Strategy 5—Legal electronic commerce

A firm, or practice area, that had little confidence in its ability to develop robust internal systems might adopt Strategy 5, as illustrated in Figure 1.16. The theme here is of legal electronic commerce, majoring on client relationship systems and online legal services (but, as ever, underpinned by further investment in the back office). The potential anomaly here is that many online legal services of today have evolved from existing internal knowledge systems and so have avoided the expense of developing knowledge repositories from scratch. In truth, this conversion from internal system to online legal service has often proven to be something of a false economy; and I have heard it said that it would indeed have been less costly to have started with a blank sheet of paper. In this context, Strategy 5 makes sense, although, on balance, I would recommend firms adopt a coherent knowledge

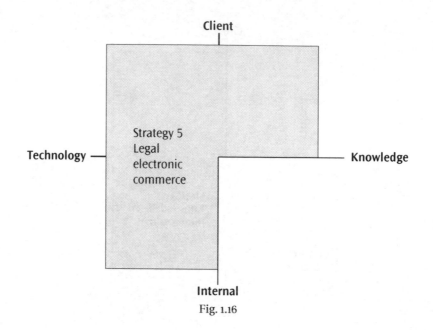

Fig. 1.16

management strategy which calls for the development of services to be made available within the firm as well as externally.

Strategy 6—Entrepreneurial

This sixth possible strategy, as plotted in Figure 1.17, is a variant of Strategy 4, in which connection I discussed the possibility of an innovative law firm scaling down its traditional operations and moving towards a predominantly online legal practice. Strategy 6 takes this strategy to one radical end position: the law firm whose *only* service is online. This could be the approach of the entrepreneurial firm that has chosen to reinvent itself completely. Alternatively, this might be the preferred strategy of a start-up whose owners wish to deliver online legal services from a business that is set up as a law firm regulated by its appropriate professional body. In either event, there are no conventional clients with whom to interrelate in the top-left quadrant. Nor is there any need to maintain an internal knowledge management capability, for it would have no conventional service to support and render more efficient.

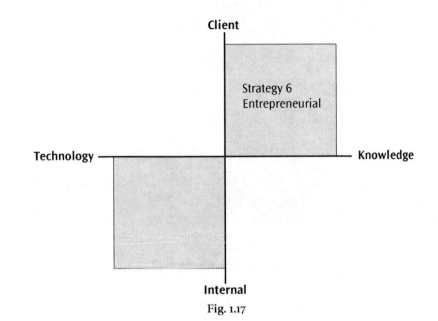

Fig. 1.17

Strategy 7—Progressive

Many senior lawyers approve of the seventh strategy (see Figure 1.18). I use the term 'progressive' with a little irony because in fact I feel that the strategy, certainly in so far as major firms are concerned, might better be termed 'conservative'. I can, however, see the appeal. On the one hand, it commits to some form of legal electronic commerce in the shape of client relationship systems. And, on the other hand, it embraces knowledge management, if only for internal purposes. Brushing with electronic commerce and knowledge management in this way may indeed give a strong sense to its owners that a firm is being progressive. Yet, on closer examination, if this is anything other than a short- to medium-term strategy (say, extending about two years hence) it is rather conservative. On analysis, it entails investment in 'sustaining technologies' (as discussed in Chapter 2), that is, technologies that support and enhance the existing way of doing business. But it denies the possibility of online legal service. I believe this to be a mistake as a five-year strategy, not just because I expect client demand for online legal services to increase rapidly, but also because it fails to make maximum use of the investment in internal knowledge systems which, as I have stressed, should have a dual purpose—of immense use internally and capable of external delivery.

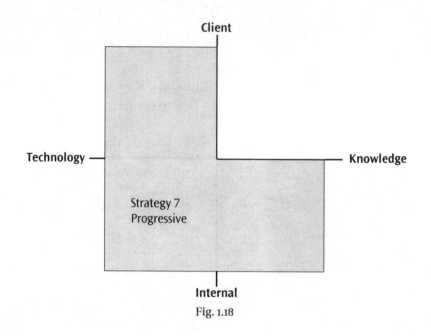

Fig. 1.18

An interesting case study in this context is the service known as *newchange documents*, developed by Allen & Overy, a leading London-based law firm.[10] Through the use of automated document assembly technology (see Chapter 7), Allen & Overy is able to produce and amend certain complex legal documents (loan documentation) far more quickly than before, and so more swiftly than its competitors as well. The most interesting aspect of this service is that, as part of the project, Allen & Overy re-engineered its standard loan documentation so that it now fits together in Lego-like modules, ideally suited to the imposition of IT. At the time of launch, Allen & Overy perceived this tool, in my terms, as falling clearly within the bottom-right quadrant— they conceived it as an innovative, internal knowledge management tool. Although they may to wish to keep it as such, I anticipate that clients in due course will make strong requests that *newchange documents*, or similar such systems, be directly available to them across the Internet. Consequently, even if a firm such as Allen & Overy is committed to my seventh strategy, it may be that market demands will be such that movement into the top-right quadrant becomes unavoidable.

[10] www.newchange.com

Strategy 8—Complete commitment

It should be apparent from the tone of my arguments so far that I regard this eighth option as the mandatory, overall, five-year strategy for any law firm that wishes to enjoy commercial success in the new economy. I take the view that presence in the two quadrants to the left of the vertical axis, that is, investment in back-office technology and client relationship systems, will be expected as a matter of course from any competent legal service provider. To compete effectively in the new legal marketplace, however, I believe that by 2005 firms will also need to have made serious moves (in some, but not necessarily all practice areas) into the internal knowledge management and online legal service quadrants. It is here that competitive advantage will be secured, that new business opportunities will arise, that legal brands will be strengthened, and, ultimately, it is here that profits will be made.

Given that law firms should be fully committed across all four quadrants by 2005, the far more difficult question is the path along which they should travel to reach that position. In other words, Figure 1.19 may represent the 2005 strategy but offers little insight into the investment priorities during the intervening years. How should firms evolve towards this position of complete commitment? Should they move, for example, from Strategy 3 to Strategy 7 and thence to Strategy 8? Or should they prefer a jump to Strategy 5 and from there to Strategy 8? And how many practice areas within a firm

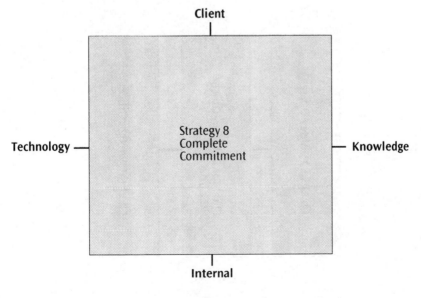

Fig. 1.19

need to participate in all four quadrants? I can offer no definitive, generic response to these questions. The choice between these competing strategic options should be dictated by a firm's overall business strategy, its vision, and its overriding values. Of one thing I am certain, however, and that is that firms must address these issues explicitly rather than jumping aimlessly from one relatively random IT project to another.

5. Who is Going to Make this Happen?

Before I leave The Grid behind, it is worth considering the human resource requirements of tomorrow's law firm. What kind of people are needed to pursue the various strategies? Again, The Legal Grid helps to provide an answer, for the three most important future roles can be mapped onto it. I have in mind here: the Chief Technology Officer, the Chief Information Officer, and the Chief Knowledge Officer. Figure 1.20 indicates the parts of The Legal Grid covered by their various areas of expertise. In seeking to identify what kind of people a firm needs, I suggest that a firm should: (a) articulate its strategy, using The Legal Grid; and then, using Figure 1.20, (b) identify which of the three main roles (and maybe more than one) most

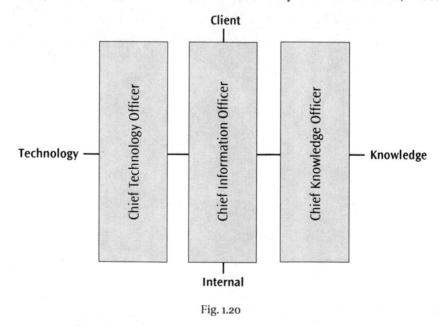

Fig. 1.20

clearly match the strategy. Thus, for example, a firm following Strategy 3 (Client Relationship Systems) will need a Chief Technology Officer, a job that requires much more than the role of a traditional IT Director, whose skills and experience tend to be suitable only for the bottom-left quadrant.

Firms that are keen to go for more ambitious strategies might need to recruit new, highly skilled individuals: for example, a new Chief Knowledge Officer to spearhead internal knowledge management and online legal services. Alternatively, it may be possible to offer exciting new opportunities for existing staff who are determined, through extensive training and development, to extend their current responsibilities.

Either way, the prosperity of the best law firms of the future will depend as much on attracting and retaining outstanding technology and knowledge specialists as on employing first-rate lawyers.

2

The Client Service Chain

In Chapter 1, I said I would introduce two models to help explain and clarify, in practical terms, the way in which the Internet is transforming legal practice. The first model, which was the focus of the previous chapter, was The Grid. The second model, to which I now turn, is what I term the 'Client Service Chain'. With these two models to hand, I hope lawyers will be able to think in a more structured and systematic way about the way in which the law, legal institutions, and legal services are being transformed by information technology.

I also seek to go further in this chapter, in two ways. First, I try to explain the way in which 'disruptive technologies' are shaping the new legal economy; with new players (especially the global accounting firms) poised to capture a considerable share of the legal marketplace. And, second, I close the chapter with a series of practical suggestions intended to help lawyers participate effectively in the transformation of legal service that is the central theme of this book.

1. The Client Service Chain

Figure 2.1 depicts a simple model of what I take to be the Client Service Chain of today. As with The Grid, I must stress at the outset that this model does not aspire to being a detailed, complete, and comprehensive description or analysis. It is a simplification of reality, a framework that I have found to be of help in explaining to practising lawyers the quite fundamental changes that are afoot in the commercial legal marketplace.

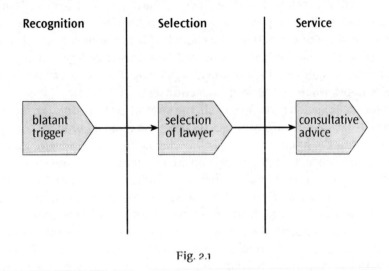

Fig. 2.1

From Figure 2.1, it will be seen that there are three basic, underlying elements that make up the legal Client Service Chain:

- *recognition*—the process by which non-lawyers and clients recognize, in respect of their particular circumstances, that they would benefit from legal service.
- *selection*—the process by which non-lawyers and clients select the particular source of legal guidance to help them in their particular circumstances.
- *service*—the process by which legal guidance is imparted.

Today's client service chain

Figure 2.1 suggests that the initiation of client service today—the process of recognition—is characterized by what I call the 'blatant trigger'. By this I mean that the non-lawyer or non-specialist is urged to take advice from a legal professional on the occurrence of some event, or in a set of circumstances, that quite unambiguously call for formal legal input. It is at the client's instigation, therefore, that the legal machinery rolls into action. It is in this context, in Chapter 3 of this book, that I identify traditional legal service as being 'reactive' in nature. The blatant trigger (perhaps the receipt of a claim, the commencement of negotiations on some major deal, or some similar such occurrence which clearly demands formal legal help) leads a client of today to instruct his or her lawyer. The lawyer, in other words, *reacts* to the client's call for help. All too often, and unhelpfully, the lawyer will note that it would have been better if the client had come along sooner. This is the basis of what I call the 'paradox of traditional reactive legal service'—you need to know quite a bit about the law to recognize not just that you need legal help but when best to seek such counsel.

As for the selection processes itself, the second element, this is a far-from-scientific exercise. A variety of factors have traditionally brought a lawyer's capability to the attention of potential clients, including advertising, local physical presence, professional recommendations, and reputation. Moreover, non-lawyers will often instruct a firm of lawyers, not with any knowledge that the firm has relevant skills but simply in the comfort that that same firm has undertaken legal work satisfactorily for them in the past. Even for the most sophisticated users of legal service, like the General Counsel in charge of a substantial in-house legal department, the full range of law firms in practice gives rise to a bewildering selection process, given the diversity, complexity, and sheer numbers of apparently qualified legal providers.

The third element in today's Client Service Chain—the service element—is the provision of traditional legal counsel, guidance, and transaction management. The dominant, current means of imparting legal guidance today is through the delivery of advice, invariably reduced at some stage to writing, usually after face-to-face consultation, and normally invoiced on an hourly billing basis. Moreover, the advice tendered is packaged for the direct consumption of one particular client; rarely is it intended that that guidance should be reused by others, even by clients themselves. (Further details of today's approach to the delivery of consultative advice is laid out in Chapter 3 of this book.)

Today's Client Service Chain, as just outlined, has evolved in a print-based society, in which legal practice has relied very largely on the creation and physical distribution of documents, face-to-face meetings, and extensive use of the telephone. These means of communication and interaction have, in effect, constrained the evolution or development of the Client Service Chain, so that legal service has remained substantially reactive, delivered as a consultative, advisory service by lawyers selected from a relatively narrow, available set.

In the new economy, characterized by pervasive, immediate, and global communications, along with the wider availability of online guidance and information services, I believe the traditional Client Service Chain will rapidly undergo a process of 'deconstruction'. I borrow this term from Philip Evans and Thomas Wurster who define deconstruction as 'the dismantling and reformulation of traditional business structures', resulting from 'the new economics of information'. More graphically, they suggest that traditional business structures will be 'blown to bits'. Thereafter, they anticipate 'the pieces will then recombine into new business structures'.[1]

This deconstruction and reconstruction in legal practice—undoubtedly a transformation—will, in my view, be characterized by two vital phenomena: disintermediation and re-intermediation.

Disintermediation and re-intermediation

The concept of disintermediation is discussed in Chapters 3 and 4 of this book. For now, the basic idea can be simply stated. In many walks of life, we find intermediaries (alternatively known as brokers, agents or middlemen). These intermediaries often represent the interests of consumers, invariably by simplifying some process or activity. Thus, travel agents act as intermediaries in pointing would-be holidaymakers towards appropriate resorts; insurance brokers seek to secure cover for their clients on favourable terms; and professional advisers (lawyers, doctors, and accountants, for example) guide those they advise by applying their specialist knowledge when their clients do not have sufficient understanding or experience to cope with their circumstances.

Over the last couple of years, however, as a direct result of the Internet, the work of intermediaries has come under threat. The key question that intermediaries have been asked to address is whether or not the human service that they have traditionally offered adds value or contributes benefit beyond that which can be delivered by an Internet-based service. As a general rule, if no such value can be added, then intermediaries will, sooner or later, become disintermediated, that is, removed from the information chain in which they work. Disintermediation of travel agents and insurance agents has already come about as a result of the existence of quite primitive web sites. Users who are both confident and patient are able to browse and find suppliers, products, and services for themselves. Online services that help with the selection of travel arrangements and insurance policies are becoming commonplace. One of the central themes of this book is that professional

[1] See Philip Evans and Thomas Wuster, *Blown to Bits: How the Economics of Information Transforms Strategy* (Boston: Harvard Business School Press, 2000), p. 39.

advisers generally, and lawyers in particular, are similarly threatened by dis-intermediation. If clients can obtain a cheaper, quicker, better, or more convenient service through the Internet, then lawyers may find their traditional work to be under threat.

The potential disintermediation of lawyers affects only the third element of the Client Service Chain, that relating to the delivery of service. The heart of my argument here, and this is developed in far greater detail in Chapters 3 and 4 of this book, is that some, but by no means all, additional consultative, advisory legal service will be displaced by the availability and provision of online legal guidance. I have no doubt, as I stress in Chapter 4, that a good deal of 'high-end' legal work, by which I mean high value, complex and socially significant service, as well as arcane, obscure or esoteric legal work, will still require the services of specialist legal advisers operating in the traditional fashion. The crucial point here, in the terms of the Client Service Chain, is that a wider range of options will replace human, consultative advisory service, which up until recently has remained the only realistic mechanism through which non-lawyers could secure legal guidance.

Even when high-end work continues to be delivered in the traditional one-to-one, consultative, advisory manner, this mode of working will no doubt also be streamlined and improved (although not changed by IT). For example, traditional service will come to be delivered through the use of client relationship systems and the knowledge created in delivering the advice will be captured and preserved for later use in internal knowledge systems (both of which types of system were discussed in Chapter 1).

To understand the additional and sometimes alternative options to consultative service, it is helpful to grasp another concept—that of 're-intermediation'. According to Don Tapscott: 'Re-intermediaries create new value between producers and consumers using the Net'.[2] In the context of legal service, the challenge of re-intermediation is to develop new systems and services, accessible on the Internet, which are of direct help and assistance to legal clients, often in situations where guidance may not otherwise have been available at all. I have identified four categories of re-intermediation that are applicable in the legal context. Together, these transform the traditional Client Service Chain.

---

[2] See Don Tapscott (ed.) *Creating Value in the Network Economy* (Boston: Harvard Business School Press, 1999), p. xi.

Transforming legal service

My first category of re-intermediation corresponds in many ways to the increasingly popular notion of 'unbundling'. Here, it is frankly recognized that the services delivered by a firm on any particular matter (whether it be a dispute, a deal, or a piece of advisory work) can often be decomposed, so that some of the constituent tasks may more cost effectively be delivered by providers other than law firms. Already it is not uncommon for tasks such as photocopying, scanning, and document assessment to be outsourced to external bureaux or teams of paralegals, thereby enabling considerable costs savings. I believe it is both possible and desirable to go further and, using the interconnectivity provided by the Internet, for document management (and even project management) to be undertaken, on individual matters, by specialists in these disciplines, working alongside law firms but not belonging to them. More challenging still, legal research itself, including traditional library work as well as online searching, can similarly be undertaken (often more quickly and cheaply) by specialists who do not belong to the firm that has been instructed to deliver the final product. Indeed, such a service already exists—The Legal Research Network.[3] The most radical form of unbundling perhaps is when the strategic work on a deal or dispute is taken out of the hands of a firm that is undertaking the bulk of the operational side and given over to legal strategy specialists.

The second category of re-intermediation in the law is the provision of online legal service itself, whereby some or all of the legal guidance required by a client is delivered through interaction with some online system rather than through direct consultation with human lawyers. As is more fully explained in Chapter 4, online legal service relates to current legal service in two ways. On the one hand, some online services will involve the commoditization of services that are today provided by human lawyers. This is a clear example of disintermediation. Where legal work is routine and repetitive, the possibility of packaging the work in question as an online service rears its head. This is quite different from the second type of online legal service whereby the guidance is imparted in circumstances in which the user in question would otherwise have no access to legal guidance at all. This is what I call, throughout Part II of this book, the 'latent legal market'. Online legal services, in this context, do not replace the work of human lawyer. Instead, they provide legal help where, in the past, none would have been available.

---

[3] www.lrn.com

These first two categories of legal re-intermediation are mapped onto the *service* element of the Client Service Chain in Figure 2.2. Rather than legal service being provided by one type of provider in one particular way, a far richer, Internet-enabled model emerges, comprising a blend of traditional advisory service, unbundled support services, and online legal service. An additional twist, discussed later in this chapter, is that online services will come to be multidisciplinary in content and not just focused exclusively on legal issues.

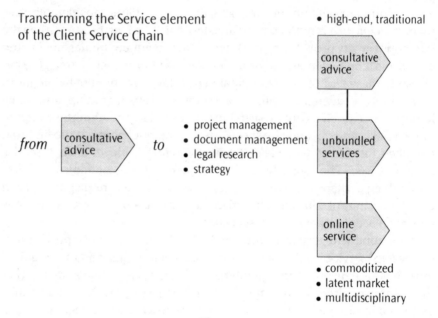

Fig. 2.2

For many lawyers, this model may seem anathema and contrary to the very nature of professional service. Some will argue, no doubt, that a truly professional service is an irreducibly human service. From a client's point of view, I have discerned two broad views of the legal professional. First, there is what might be called the 'trust model', according to which clients put trust in legal professionals largely because of who they are. Lawyers are experts with competence and state-of-the-art knowledge not possessed by lay people and, on this view, they are regarded as the benevolent custodians of the law and legal institutions, well qualified to guide non-lawyers in relevant legal intricacies. There is a second view, however, which might be called the 'George Bernard Shaw model', in accordance with which 'all professions are conspiracies against the laity'. This view regards legal professionals not as benevolent custodians, but as jealous guards, who have for too long hindered access to the law and legal processes.

On a personal note, I think it is dangerous to generalize across the profession. I have no doubt that, within the legal population, there are both benevolent custodians and jealous guards. I do feel strongly, however, as I stressed in *The Future of Law*, that the law and legal institutions are no more there to provide a livelihood for lawyers than ill-health exists to provide a living for doctors. If deployment of the Internet can result in a quicker, better, more widely available or cheaper service than that offered today, then I support legal disintermediation wholeheartedly even if its effect is commercially detrimental to some lawyers.

The deconstruction of legal service delivery, as depicted in Figure 2.2, should not be taken to assume that individual legal matters fall neatly into particular categories. In the real world, clients' problems will very rarely belong exclusively to one category alone; as purely high-end or entirely routine, for instance. In a complex deal in the future, for example, a vital task at the outset will be to assess which modes of service (whether human, unbundled, or online) are best suited for particular tasks required by the deal. The product to the client will be a blend of these different channels of service delivery. That said, in so far as the latent legal market is concerned, I do also expect that there will be innumerable legal problems, especially of a social or domestic nature, that will be solved through the use of online services alone.

Transforming the selection of legal services

Traditionally, the sophisticated buyer of legal services (an in-house lawyer, for example) has been familiar, for many areas of legal work, with a range of law firms who are sufficiently experienced to take on any particular job. Through analysis and distillation of rumour and reputation, relying on personal experience and that of colleagues, as well as on directories and word of mouth, the client has identified a manageable number of matches between his or her needs and what is available in the marketplace. Sometimes, the in-house lawyer has chosen a firm without any tendering process; while, on other occasions, competitive bidding might have been required, mainly through proposal writing and so-called 'beauty parades'.

There are two problems with this approach. First, given the search process is neither fully comprehensive nor highly systematic, it is possible, if not likely, that the traditional procurer of legal services might have missed other firms, or other individual lawyers, who would have been better suited (on grounds of experience, cost, or convenience, for example) than those advisers ultimately selected.

A second problem, which arises from the extended model of the *service* element of the Client Service Chain is that clients, in the future, will be seeking to identify not only a lawyer or a firm, but also appropriate providers of support services and online legal services as well.

Even in relation to the selection of lawyers to undertake traditional services, the Internet enables new configurations of legal teams; such as the 'dream team' model, whereby individual specialist lawyers from different firms can be brought together to collaborate on one matter alone; or 'virtual law firms' where a group of smaller practices, for instance, band together to provide a range of services as though they were one single practice.

In this connection, the process by which lawyers, systems, and services are identified and selected becomes far more complex and sophisticated. My prediction is that a new category of service provider—the 'legal infomediary'—will emerge precisely to help clients identify the optimum sources of advice and guidance for their particular circumstances. The advent of legal infomediaries represents my third category of re-intermediation. I borrow the term 'infomediary' from John Hagel III and Marc Singer, the authors of *Net Worth*, in which they argue that considerable power is shifting to the consumer and procurer of services in the information economy.[4] They predict the rise of the infomediary, a new kind of agent (human or technology-based) who acts on behalf of large numbers of consumers and is able, first, to ensure an optimum match between individual consumers' needs and available market offerings and, second, to secure favourable deals, on the strength of the combined buying power of the set of consumers whom they represent. Further, in using technology to deliver this service, they will manage to capture invaluable information about trends in marketplaces and, crucially, the likely future needs of their customers.

By analogy, I am suggesting that legal infomediaries will specialize in helping clients to understand the nature and scope of their legal problems, identifying a suitable blend of human and technology-based service for each particular matter, and securing favourable commercial arrangements on the strength of their bulk purchasing capability. More, they may even have sufficient understanding of their clients and the industry within which they operate to be able to anticipate clients' likely legal needs and so initiate the legal guidance process earlier than has been possible in the past because of the problems of traditional reactive legal service, as noted above. Advising

---

[4] *Net Worth: Shaping Markets When Customers Make the Rules* (Boston: Harvard Business School Press, 1999).

clients on what legal help they need, and from whom and when, these legal infomediaries will come to lie at the heart of the commercial legal world. They will help create a far more efficient marketplace, characterized by greater choice, better service, lower cost, and genuine proactivity.

Legal infomediaries are already in operation. Online services are already helping to match buyers with sellers of legal services.[5] At the same time, online auctioning for legal services has also begun, whereby clients lodge requests for proposals for legal services and registered law firms bid against one another, stating their qualifications, experience, ability, and pricing.[6]

Another service that will be delivered by legal infomediaries will be devoted to those clients who are looking for exclusively online legal solutions to their problems. It is easy to imagine an interactive, online service that helps its users to specify the nature of their legal requirements; and the system will identify the best suited online legal services given the stated circumstances. This is not simply a set of links to potentially relevant resources. Rather, this would be a form of diagnostic tool capable of matching the clients' circumstances with the capabilities of available services (and there will be thousands to choose from before too long).

Figure 2.3 depicts the increasing sophistication of the selection process as just described, reflecting the likely impact of legal infomediaries on the *selection* element of the Client Service Chain.

Transforming the process of recognizing the need for legal service

Earlier in the chapter, I identified current legal service as essentially reactive in nature. This is a theme to which I return in Chapter 3. For now, the key point to note is that non-lawyers are frequently ill-equipped to identify not only that they need legal guidance but when best to seek such guidance. As I mentioned above, too often when clients consult their lawyers today, they hear that it would have been better had they sought legal help earlier. This is a notoriously unhelpful observation by the lawyer, leaving the client with the impression that one needs to know quite a bit about the law to recognize when best to instruct a lawyer. Or it may even appear that you need to be a lawyer to be able to know if you need formal legal help! This is the essence of what I call the paradox of traditional reactive legal service.

What I am suggesting is that some blatant trigger—an event or set of circumstances of indubitable and unambiguous legal significance—is the main factor today to initiate the legal service process. The difficulty here is that the

[5] www.firstlaw.co.uk   [6] www.elawforum.com

Transforming the Selection element
of the Client Service Chain

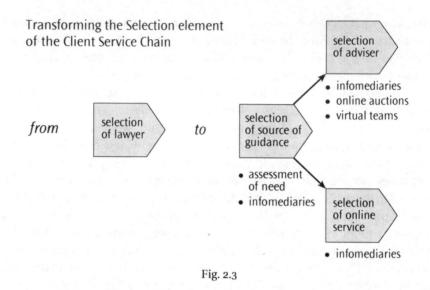

Fig. 2.3

blatant trigger often occurs too late in the life cycle of clients' affairs, so that a problem may, unnecessarily, have escalated dramatically before lawyers are even instructed.

In this connection, I frequently hear clients (from citizens with domestic problems through to in-house lawyers in multinational corporations) wishing they were in receipt of more proactive legal service. As explained in the following chapter, this would entail a focus on dispute pre-emption or dispute avoidance rather than dispute resolution; a shift towards the management of legal risk instead of the solving of legal problems. More graphically, clients would like a fence at the top of the cliff rather than an ambulance at the bottom. Much of today's focus on the application of IT is on improving the performance of the metaphorical ambulance—rendering it better equipped, quicker, and perhaps cheaper to run. The overwhelming majority of clients with whom I speak, however, would prefer not to engage the ambulance in the first place.

Accordingly, in terms of the Client Service Chain, an additional trigger is needed. It is here we find my fourth and final category of re-intermediation—the insertion of a proactive trigger into the Client Service Chain.

What kind of tools, then, can be used to create genuinely proactive facilities that would help clients to anticipate their legal problems and seek guidance at the optimum time? Earlier in this chapter, when considering my third category of re-intermediation (legal infomediaries involved in the selection of legal services), we saw one possible approach. I suggested there that, as legal infomediaries build up detailed profiles of the clients they represent and gather mountains of data about the nature, scope, and content of innumerable legal matters, it is entirely feasible that such experience could form the basis of an additional facility to forewarn or advise clients of possible legal issues or impending difficulties. Thus, a legal infomediary that had selected service providers (human or IT-based) for one of its clients, in a particular industry in respect of a specific type of deal, may then be able to recognize analogous situations where other clients, in similar industries and circumstances, would quite naturally require analogous services.

A range of other proactive facilities can also be conceived (further descriptions of which are given throughout Part II of this book) such as:

- Legal audits—whether undertaken by human analysts or conducted by consultation with systems,[7] this involves the appraisal of certain activities and operations within an organization to help identify legal weaknesses, compliance failures as well as opportunities that might be capitalized upon through legal techniques.
- The use of 'push' technologies—information services that obviate the need for users to search across, and then pull information from, online services; using a variety of techniques useful information is pushed automatically towards the user.
- Intelligent agents—software tools that act like research assistants, by roaming around a wide range of information systems and bringing information back to their users; information that is relevant, accurate, timely, and distilled.
- Embedded legal expertise—where legal help, prompts, triggers and documents are fully integrated into the business systems of clients or their project management methods, so that events in the ordinary course of business automatically trigger the provision of legal guidance or of tailored documentation.
- Intranet implants—the placement of online legal services on clients' Intranets, so that practical, punchy, jargon-free guidance is at the fingertips of all employees via corporate Intranets.

The last two examples are also illustrations of what I will introduce in the final section of this chapter as 'business episode-based' facilities.

Figure 2.4 illustrates the place of the proactive trigger in the recognition element of the Client Service Chain. Figure 2.5 integrates the transformations in each of the three elements and so presents my final model of

---

[7] See, e.g., the legal technology products at www.bdw.com.au

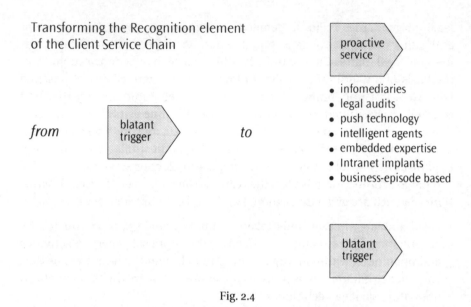

Transforming the Recognition element
of the Client Service Chain

proactive
service

• infomediaries
• legal audits
• push technology
• intelligent agents
• embedded expertise
• Intranet implants
• business-episode based

from   blatant
trigger   *to*

blatant
trigger

Fig. 2.4

tomorrow's Client Service Chain. This chain is very different from today's Client Service Chain (Figure 2.1). Above all else, it shows graphically that clients will have greater choice and flexibility in securing legal service. The challenge for law firms is to decide where they want to position themselves in the new chain.

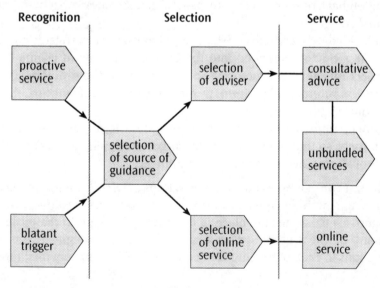

Recognition	Selection	Service

proactive
service

selection
of adviser

consultative
advice

selection
of source of
guidance

unbundled
services

blatant
trigger

selection
of online
service

online
service

Fig. 2.5

2. Disruptive Technologies in the New Legal Economy

Lawyers tend to be busy people. Increasingly, they set themselves ambitious targets, the direct result of which is that they will rarely have time for anything other than fee earning activities. Inviting lawyers to embrace and progress many of the ideas presented here is akin to asking for a wheel to be changed on a moving car.

From my consulting work and from feedback at seminars and conferences, I frequently encounter a strong reluctance, especially from senior lawyers in outstanding firms around the world, to consider moving away from the traditional, highly profitable lines of legal service. It is not easy, of course, to convince a roomful of millionaires that their business model is ultimately misconceived or that their practices face greater threats to prosperity than ever before. The challenge of persuading senior lawyers in great firms is further compounded by the fact that these businesses tend to be managed by partners who have but a few years left before retirement. In so many of the world's leading firms, the almost obsessive focus on short-term financial targets combines with the limited horizons of the top managers to produce firms of short-termist orientation, whose long-term strategic health, for reasons discussed, may suffer drastically. In summary, with a very few exceptions, my experience is that the top few hundred law firms in the world are committed to squeezing as much profit as possible out of traditional legal service. In other words, they will cling dearly to the old economy until there are overwhelming reasons to do otherwise.

In contrast, I am increasingly finding that small- and medium-sized firms (especially non-niche, generalist practices) are coming to recognize squarely the variety of threats that they face, not the least of which is the ability of larger firms to dominate much of the high-end work of the legal marketplace. Where the most successful firms are simply not hungry enough for change, many smaller and medium-sized practices acknowledge that they have no choice. While the larger firms have the investment capability to develop all manner of systems on their own, I anticipate all manner of joint ventures, collaborations,[8] and entrepreneurial exploits by the hungrier, smaller, and sometimes less profitable firms.

[8] See, e.g., www.sjberwin.com/media—collaboration between KPMG and S J Berwin & Co., a medium-sized City firm. Also see the multidisciplinary web site that guides US law firms considering opening a London office (www.lawinlondon.com). The site results from collaboration between the law firm, Fox Williams, The Royal Bank of Scotland, Smith & Williamson Chartered Accountants and Strutt & Parker, real estate consultants.

I predict that two enormously significant consequences will flow from the current state of affairs. The first is that some major firms, even some of the world's outstanding practices, may collapse over the next ten years unless they embrace various new technologies. Second, it is precisely by adopting and exploiting online legal service that the global accounting firms may come to dominate the international legal marketplace.

'Disruptive Techonologies' and the collapse of leading law firms

I have benefited greatly in my understanding of the likely impact of technology on leading law firms from reading Clayton Christensen's outstanding book, *The Innovator's Dilemma*.[9] In the introduction to his book, Christensen, a professor at Harvard Business School, sets out his stall in the following way:

This book is about the failure of companies to stay atop their industries when they confront certain types of market and technological change. It's not about the failure of simply any company, but of *good* companies—the kinds that many managers have admired and tried to emulate, the companies known for their abilities to innovate and execute. Companies stumble for many reasons, of course, among them bureaucracy, arrogance, tired executive blood, poor planning, short-term investment horizons, inadequate skills and resources, and just plain bad luck. This book is not about companies with such weaknesses: It is about well-managed companies that have their competitive antennae up, listen astutely to customers, invest aggressively in new technologies, and yet still lose market dominance.[10]

The reason these companies fail, according to Christensen, is that they are too late in recognizing the impact of what he terms 'disruptive technologies'. These are new, innovative technologies that periodically emerge and fundamentally transform companies, industries, and markets. However, in the early days of these disruptive technologies, they 'result in *worse* product performance'. Christensen goes on: 'Generally, disruptive technologies underperform established products in mainstream markets . . . are typically cheaper, simpler, smaller, and, frequently, more convenient to use.'[11] Accordingly, at the outset, many outstanding companies *and* their customers reject these new technologies.

Meanwhile, smaller entrepreneurial outfits embrace and exploit them; and by the time their impact is fully recognized by the incumbents, it is too

---

[9] Boston: Harvard Business School Press, 1997. I am grateful to Elizabeth Broderick for bringing this book to my attention.

[10] ibid., p. ix (emphasis in original).   [11] ibid., p. xv (emphasis in original).

late. Through case studies in a variety of industries, including retail, auto-mobiles, computers, pharmaceuticals, and steel, Christensen convincingly demonstrates the way in which disruptive technologies have frequently been ignored or rejected by leading companies (such as Sears, IBM, Digital, and Xerox). In so doing, he points to the huge commercial opportunities that were missed and, more significantly, to the ways that smaller, more entre-preneurial competitors have entered a marketplace and often displaced the apparently invincible leaders. In turn, he shows that these newcomers have come to dominate the next phase of development of an industry or market-place.

It is not that these great companies have failed to listen to their customers. The enduring irony to which Christensen also points us is that it is precisely because leading firms:

listened to their customers, invested aggressively in new technologies that would pro-vide their customers more and better products of the sort they wanted, and because they carefully studied market trends and systematically allocated investment capital to Innovations that promised the best returns, they lost their positions of leadership.[12]

Crucially, these companies did invest heavily in technology. However, Christensen argues compellingly that they invested in the *wrong* types of technology. In a vital distinction, he contrasts disruptive technologies with what he calls 'sustaining technologies'—those that 'improve the perfor-mance of established products, along the dimensions of performance that mainstream customers in major markets have historically valued'.[13] In other words, successful companies have tended to inject capital and effort into improving and optimizing their current successful offerings rather than into developing new business models.

In the context of the legal marketplace, my hypothesis is that Christensen's analysis of the failure of great companies will come to apply equally to leading professional services firms and so to legal practices as well. I have found considerable synergy between Christensen's thesis on the one hand and my arguments in *The Future of Law* and in this book on the other.[14] I would suggest that Christensen's distinction between sustaining and dis-ruptive technologies maps directly onto The Legal Grid that I introduced in the previous chapter (illustrated in Figure 2.6—this version of The Grid, it will be recalled, is configured with the law firm in mind). I believe that the bottom-left, top-left and bottom-right quadrants, those that represent

---

[12] ibid., p. xii.   [13] ibid., p. xv.
[14] I am grateful to Paul Greenwood for very helpful discussions on the applicability of Christensen's work to the legal marketplace.

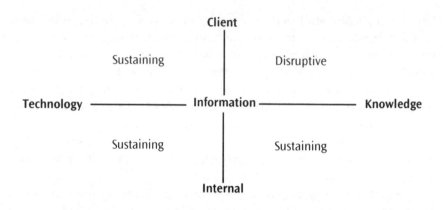

Fig. 2.6

back-office technology, client relationship systems and internal knowledge management systems respectively, all fall within the category of sustaining technologies. The systems in these quadrants do not radically change or challenge traditional legal service. Instead, they support it. Following another distinction that pervades this book and *The Future of Law*, these sustaining technologies tend to be about automation rather than innovation, in the sense that they computerize, systematize, improve, and streamline existing legal processes, tasks, and organizations; but they do not fundamentally change the traditional one-to-one consultative advisory service. (I say 'tend to' because there are instances of innovative, sustaining technologies, such as some categories of client relationship systems.)

Disruptive technologies are quite different and they seem to me to fall unambiguously into the top-right quadrant, representing online legal services. Here is an example of genuine innovation. The delivery of legal guidance through direct consultation with online legal services is not a refinement or tweak of the traditional model. It is a fundamentally new way of imparting legal help. The performance of the first wave of these online services corresponds fairly clearly to the characteristics that Christensen associates with disruptive technologies—they do not work as well as human lawyers, but they are less costly and often easier to use.

Where the under-performance of these systems constitutes a fatal flaw for many lawyers, this of itself would be a vital theme for Christensen. He says 'suppliers often "overshoot" their market: They give customers more than they need or ultimately are willing to pay for'. However, and this is absolutely crucial, he goes on to say that 'disruptive technologies that may underperform today, relative to what users in the market demand, may be fully performance-competitive in that same market tomorrow'.[15] In other words, lawyers who reject online legal services for their current level of perform- ance, or dismiss some of the application areas in which they operate (such as divorce) as indicative of their irrelevance, are missing a vital signal. Today's low-key online legal services will grow in strength and sophistication; and indeed are poised, I believe, to disrupt the entire legal marketplace.

What makes all of this particularly difficult for the top manager is, as Christensen suggests, that it may appear irrational, for three reasons, for suc- cessful organizations to invest in disruptive technology:

First, disruptive products are simpler and cheaper; they generally promise lower margins, not greater profits. Second, disruptive technologies typically are first com- mercialized in emerging or insignificant markets. Leading firms' most profitable cus- tomers generally don't want, and initially can't use, products based on disruptive technologies. By and large, a disruptive technology is initially embraced by the least profitable customers in a market.[16]

And yet, many great companies that have neglected to embrace disruptive technologies have failed for reason of that neglect alone. This is so because '(d)isruptive technologies, though they initially can only be used in small markets remote from the mainstream, are disruptive because they subse- quently can become fully performance-competitive within the mainstream market against established products'.[17]

The prime challenge for law firms in this context, therefore, is to assess whether or not online legal services are disruptive in the sense that Christensen identifies. I strongly believe that they are indeed disruptive and so may lead to the collapse of many firms who ignore their impact.

The response of many firms is to fall back on investment in sustaining technologies. Allen & Overy, a leading City firm, provides an interesting case study here. Their *newchange* products, one being a client relationship sys- tem (their virtual deal room) and the other an internal knowledge manage- ment system (a loan documentation assembly system) are powerful illustrations of sustaining technologies. My earlier observations about com- petitive advantage from IT are on all fours with Christensen when he sug- gests that 'In many instances, leadership in sustaining innovations—about which information is known and for which plans can be made—is not com- petitively important. In such cases, technology followers do about as well as technology leaders'.[18] Thus, I believe Allen & Overy will not achieve any great competitive advantage from being the first firm to provide virtual deal rooms, which is a sustaining technology. However, perhaps the biggest

---

[15] n. 9 above, p. xvi.   [16] ibid., p. xvii.   [17] ibid., p. xxii.   [18] ibid., p. xxi.

challenge for Allen & Overy is to decide whether or not their loan documentation system should be made available directly to clients as an online legal service, that is, it should move from being a sustaining technology in the bottom-right quadrant to being a disruptive, online legal service in the top-right quadrant. That move could yield, I believe, very considerable competitive advantage.

For Allen & Overy, who might consider this idea, but even more so for Linklaters and Clifford Chance who, to their considerable credit, have already invested in disruptive online legal services, there will arise the 'innovator's dilemma'. For, in Christensen's words:

It is in disruptive innovations, where we know least about the market, that there are such strong, first-mover advantages . . . Companies whose investment processes demand quantification of market sizes and financial turns before they can enter a market get paralyzed or make serious mistakes when faced with disruptive technologies. They demand market data when none exists and make judgments based upon financial projections when neither revenues or costs can, in fact, be known. Using planning and marketing techniques that were developed to manage sustaining technologies in the very different context of disruptive ones is an exercise in flapping wings.[19]

Christensen pinpoints here the grave difficulty I have always had in persuading lawyers of the potential of the 'latent legal market'. I have no doubt that online legal services will help create new demand for legal guidance (and through client work I have had this confirmed), but it is not possible to quantify any latent legal market for the very reasons Christensen notes. Accordingly, firms run by conservative characters will tend not to invest in disruptive technologies; while those managed by innovative, entrepreneurial types will be more likely to take the plunge.

To reiterate my main conclusion in bringing Christensen's work into my own—if online legal service does indeed transpire to be a disruptive technology (and I strongly believe that it will), then the strategic health of many of the world's finest law firms must be in doubt.

3. The Accountants' Time Has Come

Over the past year or so, the leading accountancy and consulting giants have made it clear that they intend to be leaders in the legal market within five

---

[19] n. 9 above, pp. xxi–xxii.

years. What has been less clear is precisely the types of legal work that they seek to dominate. Following the thoughts of this chapter, it might be asked whether the legal arms of the accounting firms will seek to capture the market for traditional, legal advisory service or whether they have aspirations to become the pre-eminent online legal service providers? Do they plan to become legal infomediaries? Or might their strategy be to develop the definitive proactive legal triggers?

From the public statements that I have read, it is not possible to respond confidently to any of these questions. If the arguments of this chapter are sound, however, it seems to me that the most fruitful way ahead for the accountants is to move into the online legal services market, into my top-right quadrant—the part of The Legal Grid that for law firms represents investment in disruptive technology. This raises an interesting point about disruptive technologies—a technology that may well be disruptive for one set of organizations in a given market may well be sustaining for others.

Looking back a little, when the accounting firms began to take the legal marketplace seriously in the 1990s, many had seemed to set their sights on competing directly with the pre-eminent law firms in London and New York. The market that seemed attractive, lucrative, and prestigious was the high-end work—the complex, high value, and often highly specialist work that I argue in this book will continue for many years to require the judgment, experience, and knowledge of skilled practitioners operating in the traditional, one-to-one, consultative advisory manner (although, as I have noted, this type of conventional service will be streamlined and improved throughout IT).

Looking at the cream of the high-end work, however, a huge proportion of the really plum jobs in the global market—the supertanker transactions, the big ticket projects, and the vast disputes—tend to be undertaken by a handful of law firms in London and New York. So far, the accountants have not managed to penetrate this market to any significant extent.

If I am right about this type of work still needing lawyers performing in the traditional way, it seems that the only way for the accountants to break into the market would be to acquire large teams of leading legal specialists. One route here would be mega-merger—a coming together of a major global accounting firm and a top legal law firm. In the medium term, however, and leaving any regulatory barriers to one side, the business case for this type of merger is not at all convincing for the law firms—they are, generally, much more profitable (on a profit per partner basis) than the accounting firms. Nor do they appear to be immediately anxious to adapt to the quite different cultures and working practices of the so-called Big 5. My own suspicion is that a merger on this scale will not happen until it needs to happen—by dint per-haps of some commercial disaster within a law firm.

Nor is acquisition of medium-sized law firms likely to help accountants make the leap, because the resultant multidisciplinary practice will become no more plausible a provider of high-end legal service by reason of such a development. There is little reason to think that a medium-sized law firm, once it becomes an appendage to a major accounting practice, will automat-ically win high-end clients and work that it could not attract prior to its takeover. I conclude that, for about a decade, the legal arms of the accounting firms will not emerge as leading players in the market for high-end legal work.

In contrast, I find it entirely foreseeable that the accountants could dom-inate the online legal services market, by which I mean both the commod-itization of appropriate existing legal work as well as the realization of the latent legal market. In other words, I see great scope for them to identify and commoditize the great swathes of routine and repetitive work that are cur-rently handled by lawyers in the traditional manner; and I see potential also for them to create new legal markets.

In their favour, the accountants are generally more sophisticated in their exploitation of IT and knowledge management. More than this, it is highly significant that online legal service technologies are disruptive for law firms but not for accountants. It is precisely because of their pre-eminence and success in the old economy—and with it their commitment, both cultural and structural, to traditional legal service models—that the move to online legal service, to a quite different paradigm, is so thoroughly disruptive for law firms. In contrast, for the accountants, who do not have legal practices as dominant, committed, or as established as the law firms, the move to online legal service provision is far from disruptive. Indeed, it is more akin to a start-up situation, where the entrepreneurial leap to online legal services is, ulti-mately, a far lower risk.

It may be that the accountants would begin their campaign for online legal service delivery in areas of work and with clients that are lower key than those preferred by the major law firms. But this mode of entry to the market would precisely match the trend that Christensen notes—that although dis-ruptive technology is, in the first instance, only deployed in smaller markets, they are disruptive exactly because they may later be 'directly performance-competitive'.[20]

Exploiting their existing and undeniable strong corporate connections, moving towards the provision of multidisciplinary online service (see later in this chapter), and blending their approach with existing consulting and

[20] n. 9 above, p. xxii.

information systems know-how, it is, then, the accountants who may embrace precisely the technologies that come to be the downfall of lawyers.

Emerging markets that might seem unattractive to law firms may become the platform on which the accountants could build world-class legal service capability. And, to change the metaphor, it may transpire that the real battleground between the accounting firms and law firms is not at the high end of the marketplace but in the market for online legal services.

As things stand, the accounting firms, through sheer grit and scale will surely have a massive impact over the next decade; but not in the high-end market as they had hoped. If they deploy IT as effectively in respect of online legal services as they have done in their auditing and consulting practices, however, they could take the legal marketplace by storm very quickly and only the genuinely, global, IT-committed law firms may stand a chance in the face of this opposition.

The gut reaction of many lawyers to the idea of accountancy firms establishing legal arms is one of abhorrence. For my own part, having spent years working in major law *and* accounting firms, I am less concerned with the nature of the business vehicle from which legal service is delivered than the quality, consistency, and value of the legal service itself. If accountancy firms manage to create a business from which first-rate legal guidance can be delivered at reasonable cost, then I would welcome this as much as I would welcome similar success from a major law firm.

4. Practical Suggestions

To conclude this chapter and indeed the first part of the book, I will now bring together a number of strands of thinking that I have presented thus far and summarize many of my major findings and predictions in the form of a series of six practical suggestions. It is my firm belief that legal businesses wishing to succeed in the new economy must pursue all of these suggestions with some considerable vigour.

1. establish an off-site new economy unit;
2. achieve a blend of 'clicks and mortar';
3. work under the same virtual roof as clients;
4. set up online resources for every matter;
5. identify clients' main business episodes; and
6. provide a wider range of services to clients.

In the remainder of this chapter, I will deal with each of these six suggestions in turn (leaving for another occasion detailed consideration of the huge
cultural challenges that my suggestions raise for firms that are trying to build
up teams of new economy lawyers).

1. Establish an off-site new economy unit

To keep apace with the market, it is clear that firms will need to be innovative
and imaginative in their thinking and planning. But how can innovation
actually be encouraged and achieved within a law firm? I believe the answer
to this question lies with the discipline of research and development (R&D).
For some sectors, such as consumer electronics and pharmaceuticals, R&D
has been their very lifeblood. Without innovation in laboratories, no future
products can come into being. Yet the very philosophy of R&D is anathema
to many organizations, especially those, such as law firms, that tend to 'eat
what they kill'.

IT, the Internet and e-commerce surely require *all* businesses to sustain
an R&D capability, because innovation (and so success) will increasingly
require new ways of delivering conventional services and products, as well as
new offerings altogether. These innovations will come from a combination
of imaginative thinking and a commitment to piloting, prototyping, and testing new ideas in the spirit of traditional R&D.

It is inconceivable, on this model, that every IT project will yield business
benefits for law firms that invest in R&D. Indeed, regular failure must be
expected. This will prove to be culturally difficult for law firms because most
are entirely intolerant of failure and are unable to recognize its potential as a
well-spring of radical, innovative, and ultimately successful, commercial
ideas.[21] Nonetheless, commercial winners should emerge from a balanced
portfolio of experimental activities. The justification for R&D will not be
found, therefore, at the level of each and every individual project. Rather,
the benefits will emerge from a collection of initiatives, some of which will
enjoy enormous success while others will wither and die. Medium- and
long-term business health will be sustained by a spread of research oriented
initiatives.

I am not optimistic that R&D can be conducted productively within the
buildings and confines of traditional law firms. In many firms, there is an overwhelming focus on fee earning activities so that all else is disparagingly

---

[21] See Charles Leadbeater, *Living on Thin Air* (Middlesex: Viking, 1999), pp. 77–8, where he discusses
the notion of 'creative failure'.

rejected and discouraged as 'fee spending'; the decision-making processes are cumbersome; conservatism is prevalent; and non-lawyers and often non-partners are regarded as second-class citizens. This is not a culture in which creativity will flourish. My suggestion is that every medium- to large-sized firm should set up a geographically distinct new economy unit, an off-site resource, whose very purpose is to engage in R&D and in entrepreneurial thinking on behalf of its parent law firm. In this way, it may be possible to avoid the 'super-tanker syndrome' that fetters progress in so many of today's successful law firms—their inability to change direction quickly and easily, often sustained by the related inability to make decisions swiftly. In the new economy, we hear regularly of the need to be able to think quickly, to choose decisively between options, and to avoid the risk of conservatism that is characterized by successful stable businesses. This does not imply a requirement for commercial recklessness but it does call for an open-mindedness and an excitement about new business models that is rarely fostered within a law firm.

I am reminded in this connection of a meeting with a client some years ago when I recommended the engagement of an entrepreneur to drive ahead an exciting and ambitious, proposed project. The managing partner to whom I was offering this advice welcomed the idea but cautioned he would only want 'a manageable entrepreneur'. This oxymoron is most revealing. Almost as a matter of definition, entrepreneurs are not manageable. It is their very freedom of spirit and frequently their idiosyncrasies that lead to commercial success, although they are doubtless less structured and methodical than most lawyers would prefer. One of the reasons for my proposing the establishment of a geographically distinct unit is precisely to remove the day-to-day shackles of conventional law office management. Accountability is vital but for entrepreneurs to flourish, I suspect some physical and organizational distance is imperative.

There is a further function for the off-site new economy unit that I recommend—relentlessly to assess and exploit Christensen's 'disruptive technologies'. Christensen's justifies this cogently: 'It is very difficult for a company whose cost structure is tailored to compete in high-end markets to be profitable in low-end markets as well. Creating an independent organization, with the cost structure honed to achieve profitability at the low margins characteristic of most disruptive technologies, is the only viable way for established firms to harness this principle'.[22] And so, I am proposing a new economy unit, in a different building, not just to undertake research and development and to promote the generation of innovate entrepreneurial

[22] n. 9 above, p. xx.

business models but also to identify, design, develop, and market online legal services, based on disruptive technology. (I accept that some firms might prefer to have two separate units—one for the thinking and the other for product development. With this I am equally comfortable, because my central proposition is that this work cannot most fruitfully be carried out within existing firms.)

I know of only two firms in the world that have taken a serious step in this direction: Linklaters, and Blake Dawson Waldron. Linklaters, a leading, London-based, international practice, recently announced their intention to launch a separate company to deliver their Internet-based services, including their Blue Flag products. The Australian firm, Blake Dawson Waldron, is a legal business that has been innovative in its use technology since the early 1990s. Although they have not established a unit of the scale and scope that I have advocated, they have taken the new economy sufficiently seriously to release three very senior individuals for five months to work offsite exclusively on the analysis of promising business models emerging from disruptive technologies. While many traditional lawyers will raise their eyebrows at the very thought of such an expense, major law firms can easily afford to do this; and in so doing invest in their future.

2. Achieve a blend of 'clicks and mortar'

It is almost impossible today to sit through a meeting on e-commerce without someone uttering the buzz phrase, 'clicks and mortar'. Before it joins the ranks of vacuous cliché, it is instructive to pay heed to a vital underlying message. I take the phrase to be drawing attention to the fact that most organizations will find success in the new economy not by devotion exclusively to the Internet but by creating a blend of online activity and physical presence. To jump uncritically to clicks and clicks alone may well be to miss significant business opportunities.

The challenge here is not simply for traditional law firms to divert more of their imaginative energies to thinking how best to exploit (or minimize losses from) their property legacies—their long leases or capital assets tied up in costly or now unnecessary geographical locations. Nor is it just that many new economy law firms will require considerable capacity in new types of buildings, better suited, for example, to technical staff, information engineers and sales and marketing forces (to support the emerging online businesses).

While all these factors are important, the bigger strategic point is that firms must work hard to identify those situations in which physical presence and buildings actually add some relevant value in the legal marketplace that Internet service cannot simulate or improve upon.

As ever in Web-based business thinking, the world of bookselling is enlightening, because here there are clearly strong market demands both for online and for store-based service. For quick, competitively priced, procurement of books, the online services are proving invaluable. And yet, it does seem that customers do still want to browse in the time-honoured fashion (and not just on the Web). This is causing some booksellers to reorientate their physical properties away from functional procurement towards creating an environment in which customers can happily roam around, touch, skim, and even smell the books. Coffee shops, lounge furniture, open spaces and more imaginative displays do create an atmosphere that encourages shoppers to stay longer and indeed to return and enjoy their shopping experience again. This physical experience still seems to constitute a big slice of the market that online bookselling cannot challenge. In the long run, the successful booksellers may well be those that sustain both online and high street stores.

My prediction is that the great legal businesses of the future will similarly maintain a blend of online service and traditional service supported by physical meetings with clients. Indeed, one very positive experience of the small number of firms who currently offer a sophisticated online service is that clients have often subscribed on the understanding that it will be bundled together with conventional human service as well (which has itself, in turn, entailed an increase in conventional fee income).

Where, in the past, a business justification had to be made for working or setting up an operation beyond a law firm's city presence, I believe the reverse will soon be the case—that lawyers will need to put forward business arguments for basing their operations in expensive city locations. More generally, the challenge for legal managers is to ensure that different and appropriate physical locations are made available to staff, in support of the two quite different service lines that this book points to—traditional legal service and online legal service. In this connection, legal businesses must also ask themselves when the congregation of their people in one place is necessary for internal management and operations. To what extent can virtual meetings remove the need for their people to meet face-to-face?

The importance of achieving the right blend between clicks and mortar is well illustrated by the success of Strathclyde University's online Masters Degree in information technology and telecommunications law, which has been running since 1995.[23] By mid-2000, 25 students had graduated, while

---

[23] www.law.strath.ac.uk

100 more from 18 different countries, were taking the course. Physical get-togethers are optional but well attended, perhaps because the study weekends take place at an idyllic spot beside Loch Lomond. Interestingly, graduates on the course are very reluctant to sign off for good. They are keen to remain part of the online community. Crucially, most of the students are full-time workers who would not otherwise have been able to embark on and sustain further studies. This blend of clicks and mortar has liberated a latent market of its own.

3. Work under the same virtual roof as clients

As physical location diminishes in significance for law firms, and face-to-face meetings with clients decline in number, it will be essential for the law firm to maintain a rich set of electronic relationships and connections with clients. Just as lawyers running firms with global aspirations are often heard to say that technology is enabling them to work under the one virtual roof, then the same metaphor should be extended to working alongside clients. Law firms must operate under the same virtual roof as their clients, sharing information and files and communicating as though part of the same organization.

Videoconferencing and online communities undoubtedly hold enormous potential here and, in the long run, are likely to revolutionize communications and collaborative working. Today, however, the enabling technologies are still in their infancy and it will be some years yet before all the information pulsating around a conventional meeting will be simulated or superseded by advanced systems. A slight inclination of head, or exhalation of breath, or movement of eyebrow, may speak volumes in a meeting but not be captured or conveyed through current technology. Interpersonal chemistry does not yet seem to travel well down the wire.

But this does not mean, as Luddites would argue, that there is no value in using today's technologies. By way of illustration, one of the UK's most active online communities, contrary to the preconceptions of most, is an e-mail conferencing and bulletin board system for the English judiciary. While the underlying system (known as Felix) is, frankly, in need of upgrade, the attraction of the system for judges is highly illuminating. This online community is not a replacement for, or a challenge to, conventional face-to-face meetings. Instead, Felix offers a form of community interaction where very often there would not be any interaction at all. Judges in England are spread around hundreds of court buildings and many, on a day-to-day basis, do not actually belong to a physical community of judges who meet together regularly. One of the main values of Felix is that it creates a community where otherwise it would simply not exist. It may not be as good as face-to-face interaction but it is immeasurably better than nothing at all.

Similarly with clients, videoconferencing and bulletin boards are in no way a substitute for physical meetings but they are a richer means of communication than conventional telephone calls and electronic mail.

A further and vital technique to bring a law firm together with its clients is for the firm to become an invaluable presence on clients' Intranets. At a modest level, this may simply involve the implanting of useful legal tools and services which in turn might be made widely available on clients' corporate Intranets—perhaps an intelligent checklist, or some standard form documentation or procedural guides. Far more ambitiously, law firms might take on the task of designing, developing, and maintaining clients' entire legal Intranets or at least significant parts of them. While it would seem eminently reasonable that such a service would be provided for a fee, it is not inconceivable that law firms may come to compete to offer such a service on a non-charging basis, in the hope of deepening their relationship with clients and better positioning themselves for more frequent future instructions, engagements, or subscriptions.

A variant of this last option would be the provision by a law firm of second-generation client relationship systems, as discussed in the previous chapter. These would help clients more effectively to manage the individual matters being handled for them by external law firms; as well as their collective workloads. Although these tools would be designed to enable clients to monitor, review, and control all the legal work being conducted for them, the particular firm that provided the tool itself would no doubt brand it in a way that its capability and excellence would be reinforced each time the system was used.

Whatever technique is preferred for positioning a firm under the same virtual roof as its clients, it is clear that this requires a major focus on ensuring that the full range of client systems (the two upper quadrants of The Legal Grid introduced in the previous chapter) are tightly managed. Although many partners might prefer much greater focus on internal systems in the first instance, it is my experience that a wonderful by-product of delivering systems to clients is the need at the same time to improve internal systems. And this imperative has proven to be stronger than a simple focus on internal improvement for its own sake.

4. Set up online resources for every matter

Before long, I believe that every legal matter (whether relating to a deal, dispute, or advice) will occupy its own spaces in the online world.

On instruction by a client (whether online or by conventional means), it will become common practice immediately, and often automatically when integrated with an advanced practice management system, to create at least four sites devoted to any particular matter.

The first will be an online area to which the client on any particular matter will have ready and private access. This may be by setting up a secure site on the World Wide Web; or perhaps by offering access to a firm's Extranet (part of its Intranet, as explained more fully in Chapter 4). And, of course, in the longer term, consistent with my earlier comments in the last chapter about second-generation client relationship systems, these 'matter sites' are likely to be located in, or very closely linked to, the client's own Intranet. In any event, the client version of the matter site will offer the various facilities that I outlined in my discussion of client relationship systems in Chapter 1. These will include, therefore, status reporting, online financial reporting and virtual deal room facilities for transaction-based work and virtual case room facilities where the matter in question is a dispute. It is likely, for any client, that this matter site will be the first port of call when seeking to assess progress or retrieve documentation.

At the same time, a matter site will also be established within the law firm, for purely internal purposes. It may be that this will embrace the client matter site in its entirety but supplement it with a variety of utilities for use by the law firm alone. Alternatively, and rather less efficiently, it may be that the two sites are maintained quite separately (although perhaps with common data feeds). In either scenario, the overriding purpose of the internal matter site is to support what I take to be one of the key business processes within any law firm—matter management. I have in mind here the application of traditional project management techniques in support of the progression of any particular matter from inception to final disposal, in a systematic, controlled, methodical and, where possible, standardized manner. By and large, lawyers are poor project managers. While some display some natural talent in this direction, very few are formally trained in the discipline. This is immensely regrettable. Many matters are highly complex, sophisticated, human resource intensive, and lengthy processes, which need tight control, not just to ensure the client receives a high quality of legal service but so that this happens in a cost-effective, timely and non-stressful way. Project management is precisely about bringing this discipline and control, using well-tested and highly refined techniques, to transform a complex mess into a coherent and manageable initiative.

One vital tool for the project manager, and in turn, for the lawyers being managed, would be an internal matter site. This would be the focal point, the first port of call, for everyone within a particular firm working on a particular matter. Over and above the tools and information that one would expect in a tightly managed project, such as a definition of the scope of the matter, an indication of relevant milestones and deadlines, an articulation of the various deliverables, alongside all manner of other status reports, the matter site would also be a definitive repository of all documents produced in a matter, including electronic mail messages, presentation graphics, spreadsheets, and other files over and above word-processed documents.

This environment would support what I argue to be the central business processes in any law firm (over and above project management):

- service delivery (lawyers would access their client relationship system, as discussed earlier in this chapter, from the internal matter sites);
- business development (up-to-date information about the overall relationship between the client and the firm would be directly accessible from this site);
- client care (access to intelligence about working relationships with particular clients on particular matters);
- knowledge maintenance (work product created would automatically be archived for consideration for the firm's internal knowledge systems; and, at the same time, knowledge relevant to the particular matter would be expressly linked into that site);
- financial management (from the site, accurate information about all relevant financial matters would also be accessible, such as an indication of work in progress and bills not yet paid).

The internal matter site will therefore become the nerve centre of any matter. The third type of matter site that is likely to become popular in the short to medium term is a resource, whether available on the World Wide Web or through Extranet technology, to which all parties with shared interests, in a deal or dispute, will have access. In a major piece of litigation, for example, this would be a site that might hold all the documentation relating to one claimant's case and would be accessible by all professional advisers, expert witnesses, and other authorized individuals and organizations acting on that side. Again, this would probably be a subset (logically or technically) of the internal matter site, because it is reasonable to expect that all materials that would be of interest to one side in a transaction or dispute are certain also to be of interest to the lawyers themselves.

The fourth and final category of matter site will be a common document repository, to which all parties on a deal or dispute would have access. This clearing house or exchange may well be run by an independent third party, offering a secure managed place to which documents can be posted and from which they can be retrieved.

I have no doubt that many other categories of matter web site will emerge; for example, a public web site, relating to a deal or dispute in which there is public interest, may well emerge as a common phenomenon. Further, there will unquestionably be many variations of each category that I have noted.

The key point for law firms to acknowledge and act upon is that a series of interrelated, online, shared spaces will be created for every new matter in the future.

5. Identify clients' main business episodes

One of the most interesting themes of the UK Government's modernization programme is the concerted effort to ensure that changes in government are made with citizens primarily in mind. Accordingly, when organizational or structural upheavals are being assessed, the major motivating force should not be the convenience of ministers and civil servants, but the effect on the quality and availability of services to the citizens on behalf of whom they govern.

In this context, one immensely instructive set of insights has arisen in the context of electronic government. In documents and public statements which can be traced back to a 1996 green paper, entitled 'government. direct',[24] great emphasis has been placed on the need to focus on the 'life episodes' or 'life events' of citizens. In Chapter 4 of this book, I have the same idea in mind when I speak, in the context of systems, of them being 'real life'. In government, the idea is that services and organizational structures should be organized with a primary focus on the actual, everyday situations in which citizens find themselves. Typical life episodes or life events might be: moving house, suffering an accident, or setting up a new business. The last example is one upon which the Central IT Unit within the Cabinet Office in the UK Government has done some considerable work. In the past, someone who was establishing a new business in the first instance had to identify the various organs of state with which he or she had to deal; and, thereafter, contact each separately, with all the duplication of effort that that involved.

---

[24] www.citu.gov.uk/greenpaper.htm

Thus, our would-be trader would need to contact, amongst others, department or agencies that are responsible for: income tax, Value Added Tax, employment, and social security.

The alternative vision of the Central IT Unit was that this business person could go online, indicate the life episode in which he found himself (that is, setting up a new business) and be guided through the process and led to the appropriate agencies, in one seamless interaction whose overriding aim is convenience of the citizen rather than that of the government agencies involved.

There is a salutary lesson here for all law firms. For at least two decades, it has been observed by innumerable commentators that law firms should be more 'market-facing'. Rather than structuring and organizing a firm around traditional legal boundaries (for example, tax, property, company and commercial, and finance), it has been proposed that legal practices should organize themselves into industry groups, serving the full range of legal requirements within particular sectors, such as retail, manufacturing, technology, and financial markets. To some extent, many leading firms have followed this advice, often implemented in some form of matrix structure, which enables, in principle, a legal and an industry focus to be maintained simultaneously. In the new economy, firms are recognizing just how important this issue is in relation to their e-commerce services. While, historically, computer and telecommunications law has tended to be conducted by small specialist units, the pervasive nature of electronic commerce (quite rapidly, all deals and disputes have some e-commerce dimension) is requiring firms to have an e-commerce capability that cuts across all their practice areas and all their industries too.

I am suggesting here, however, that firms go one step further, especially in relation to their online services. Just as the government is seeking to identify the life events or life episodes in which citizens most frequently find themselves, then I would strongly recommend that law firms seek to pinpoint the most common business episodes which their clients confront. These will, of course, vary enormously across different industries and in respect of particular clients, but the key challenge is to identify recurrent, important, often high value, situations in which clients require efficient service, business-like treatment and value for money. Accordingly, in developing online services, it is wise not to put together systems that offer guidance in respect of particular branches of law. Instead, the emphasis should be on providing legal help across the life cycle of standard business episodes.

Business episodes in which very many organizations find themselves will stand out as strong candidates for the development of generic, online legal services on the World Wide Web. For specific clients, however, more tailored applications should be put in place. Building on suggestions made earlier in the chapter, this might involve the implanting of guidance systems onto clients' Intranets; or even embedding legal knowledge into the processes, systems, and structures of clients.

Adopting a business episode approach leads, in my view, to an important consequence. When clients come to take legal guidance through online services, and this help is built around business episodes, it will be manifestly inefficient for such clients to have to consult a handful of different online services in respect of the other sources of professional guidance they might need. Thus, for a client to have to visit a legal site, then an investment banking site, and thereafter an accounting site would be frustrating at best. Instead, it is inevitable that a cluster of online professional services will be built around individual sites devoted to particular business episodes. In the first instance, these different professional services might simply be linked to one another but, gradually, it is likely that the knowledge from the respective disciplines will be integrated so as to provide one seamless body of professional guidance to help clients through their business episodes.

I fully expect, therefore, that online multidisciplinary services will be widely available before long.

6. Provide a wider range of services to clients

Although, in the past, many solicitors assumed the role of 'man of affairs' and in that capacity frequently advised private clients on many general business issues as well as legal matters, law firms have increasingly assumed a more restricted role and have tended not to stray from the purely legal. In contrast, accountants have greatly broadened their scope of services, such that auditing and accounting is now but one of a large number of business lines offered by these large professional firms.

For lawyers concerned to safeguard the future of their firms, I would suggest that serious consideration be given to providing a wider range of services, even if sometimes the legal component is relatively minor.

Although much of this book advocates the development of online legal services, so that clients can receive legal guidance without direct consultation with lawyers, in one sense this is not such a radical departure because it entails the repackaging of the traditional asset of a law firm—its knowledge and expertise. While I urge all law firms to take online legal services seriously, I am also suggesting here that law firms might widen the scope of their services still further.

To give a flavour of the kind of diversification I have in mind, I would propose the following lines of service be developed and taken to market by law firms:

- legal infomediary services (as discussed earlier in this chapter) whereby law firms can help clients assess their legal requirements, point them in the direction of systems or lawyers who may be able to help, even if the firm offering this service itself does not secure the resultant legal work.
- the design, development, implementation, and maintenance of legal Intranets for clients. Most in-house legal departments are building up their own legal Intranets but their resources are generally limited. These clients might welcome the opportunity of outsourcing the whole enterprise to law firms, who could in turn provide this as a service to many clients.
- training services—not as a non-chargeable add-on to conventional services, but as a serious business in its own right, exploiting the very best specialists within a practice.
- recruitment advice to in-house lawyers—particularly in relation to senior appointments, such as General Counsel, law firms could provide far more informed executive search services than many non-legal service organizations do today.
- management consultancy services—helping in-house legal departments with the full range of management challenges that they face, including issues of strategy, organizational structure, human resource management, information systems, and internal marketing.
- legal risk management services—these proactive services, as discussed earlier in this chapter, would include legal risk assessment projects and compliance audits.
- creation of online communities—an online, shared space for clients to come together in a non-competitive way (this might include the pooling of resources amongst clients working in the same industry; or clients from different industries learning from wider experience).

I find many lawyers are rather sceptical about the provision of such services. They tend to claim that their core business is that of traditional legal service and that their business development plans should focus exclusively on this traditional competence. I fear this is short-sighted. On the one hand, as traditional boundaries between service providers break down, there can be little doubt that accountancy firms and others will offer such services and, in so doing, will establish sound working relationships with major clients of law firms (even if, in early days, traditional legal services are not offered). As these relationships build, so too will the possibility of these competitors being invited to provide traditional service.

On the other hand, there are huge opportunities here for profitable new lines of business. Lawyers in the new economy have to think imaginatively and entrepreneurially about the development of their businesses. I believe successful firms will be those that embrace new services, with fervour and excitement, and are keen to exploit opportunities that might have been unimaginable in the past.

Ultimately, the marketplace itself will determine the future of law firms. I am less influenced in my thinking by the thoughts of lawyers and law firms than by the perceptions of clients themselves. Where a managing partner of a firm might express the view that some proposed new service does not fall within the scope of his or her business, I am always more interested to hear if clients would like the law firms they instruct to provide such a service. If indeed they would, then there is immediately, for me, a potentially compelling business case.

There is a lesson here for lawyers and it is one with which I will finish this chapter. The lesson is that lawyers must listen very carefully to what clients want. Most lawyers will protest and say that they do, but I know of very few firms that have systematically invited their clients to indicate what types of technology and systems they would like them to embrace; what investment direction they, as clients, would welcome of the firms they instruct. There is a marvellous opportunity, in the new economy, for lawyers and their clients to get together and to discuss the common challenges that they face. In that context, and preferably with the assistance of specialists who understand what is possible and likely in the future, lawyers and their clients can collaborate productively in transforming the law.

Part II

The Future of Law

3

The Future of Law Summarized[1]

Since early 1981, when I stumbled into the field as a legal undergraduate, I have been fascinated by the possibilities of using information technology in the law. I quickly became convinced that IT would radically transform modern legal systems; and well within my lifetime. Today, I am more certain than ever that a revolution in legal life is upon us. Indeed I believe that the practice of law and the administration of justice will be more radically affected in the coming 50 years by IT than by any other single factor of which we can be aware today.

My plan of action in this chapter is to substantiate these rather sweeping claims. First of all, I offer my summary of the state of the law today. Then, I seek to show that the advent of the so-called information society will transform our legal system. Thereafter, I present a vision of what the effects of this transformation will be in practice. And, finally, I hazard a guess or two at the future of law and lawyers.

This chapter is a summary of the central ideas underlying my book, *The Future of Law*.[2] Although several years of radical progress have passed since its original publication, I stand firmly by the main themes and arguments presented there. Accordingly, no substantive changes, deletions, or alterations have been made to this essay since its first appearance.

---

[1] This chapter was originally delivered as The Society for Computers and Law 1996 Lecture, at the Royal Society, London, on 12 June 1996; and was previously published in (1996) 7 *Computers and Law* 2: 23.

[2] Oxford: Oxford University Press, 1996. (A revised paperback version was published in 1998.)

I

I would like to begin by laying out what I call the 'legal paradigm' of today. I borrow the term 'paradigm' from the philosophy of science where it is used to refer, approximately, to the currently accepted view of the world and to the prevailing mindset and accepted background assumptions in a particular field. When there is a fundamental change in these assumptions and the discipline is then regarded in an entirely new light, there is said to be a 'shift in paradigm'. One of the clearest illustrations of such a shift in science was when Einsteinian theory superseded the Newtonian model in physics.

At the heart of my views on the future of law is the suggestion that we are on the brink of a shift in legal paradigm, a revolution in law, after which many of the current features of contemporary legal systems which we now take for granted will be displaced by a new set of underlying premises and presuppositions. Much of the law will be radically different.

I defer my projection of the details of this new legal paradigm until the fourth and final part of the chapter. For now, my priority is to identify and articulate twelve central features of today's legal paradigm and I do so under two broad categories—legal service and legal process, as illustrated in Figure 3.1.

Legal Service

advisory service
one-to-one
reactive service
time-based billing
restrictive
defensive
legal focus

Legal Process

legal problem solving
dispute resolution
publication of law
a dedicated legal profession
print-based

Figure 3.1 Today's Legal Paradigm

Legal Service

The delivery of legal service today can be characterized in many ways. For current purposes, I find it helpful to focus on the following seven features.

1. Advisory service

Legal service of today is predominantly advisory and consultative in nature. Generally, the lawyer is asked to provide advice in relation to the specific details of a client's case, problem, or circumstances. The relationship is advisory in that the lawyer's response takes the form of recommendations for action (or inaction), focusing only on these particular details; and so too with any implementation of the advice (for example, by drafting a contract or commencing an action in court). It is relatively rare for the lawyer to be invited to impart knowledge at a more generic level, in the form of reusable legal guidance or information. Rather, the advice tends to be more disposable in nature, geared to specific circumstances and to be relied upon only in the context of these specifics.

2. One-to-one

It follows that legal advice today is offered, in two senses, on a one-to-one basis. On the one hand, the advice is focused, as just mentioned, on the unique circumstances of one particular case; on the other hand, the basis of the lawyer–client contractual relationship is such that the advice should only be relied upon by that one individual client for whom it has been specifically tailored. Legal advice is generally not delivered with a view to its being recycled by clients for their own future use in other circumstances, nor for distribution or usage by others.

3. Reactive

Traditionally, clients come to their lawyers once they, the clients, have perceived that they have a legal problem. It is only then that the legal adviser is called upon to react. In this sense, I say that legal service is reactive. Solicitors in private practice, for example, rarely have much control over when their clients decide to seek help. If the client needs assistance in resolving a dispute or in completing a transaction, the timing of the lawyer's involvement tends to be in the hands of that client. The same is often also true of in-house lawyers (in industry or government) who regularly characterize themselves as 'firefighters', struggling always to respond to the demands of their colleagues in management.

There are two major problems here. First, it is unlikely that clients who are not themselves lawyers will be able to recognize all their potential legal problems and even those that they do perceive may in any event be noticed too late to allow the most effective precautionary steps. Second, clients may not themselves be able to prioritize amongst legal assignments and may direct work to be done in an order which does not reflect the relative legal risks involved.

There is, then, I suggest, a Paradox of Traditional Reactive Legal Service— the very decision as to whether and when to instruct lawyers itself requires legal insight and understanding. Thus you need to know quite a bit about the law if you want to be able to instruct lawyers at the optimum time and to balance, according to importance, competing claims for scarce legal resources. The Paradox seems to suggest you need to be a lawyer to know when best to seek legal guidance.

4. Time-based billing

In commercial practice, most lawyers of today still bill by the hour. Hourly billing rates vary according to many factors, including the geographical location of the office from which the adviser works and the nature and complexity of the advice on offer. The amount due from the client is generally calculated by multiplying the number of hours spent on a matter by the hourly rate. Critics of this system argue that it can and often does reward the inefficient lawyer who takes longer than necessary to complete tasks; and, conversely, may penalize the efficient practitioner who is able to complete assignments in shorter times than competitors.

The problem with hourly billing lies not in the value which lawyers can add through an hour's work. Rather, it is that there is insufficient incentive for lawyers to maximize value and, further, the system does not encourage lawyers and clients to think of the value of the service rendered as opposed to the costs incurred.

5. Restrictive

For most non-lawyers, the law seems to erects obstacles; it restricts courses of action, it obligates or inhibits; and to that extent is often a barrier to the achievement of domestic, social, or commercial goals. When executives refer to their in-house lawyers as their 'business obstruction unit', although this is not intended as a compliment, it does demonstrate a point. Lawyers are seen as obstructive rather than facilitative and are often regarded as erecting obstacles to otherwise impeccable commercial arrangements. In 1961, in his seminal book of legal theory, *The Concept of Law*,[3] the legal philosopher, Herbert Hart, made much of this theme. For Hart, most people regarded the law as 'duty imposing' and in so doing, he said, they disregarded or failed to take advantage of the law's 'power conferring' capabilities. These perceptions persist today. Few businessmen, for example, would describe the law as facilitative or empowering.

6. Defensive

Most legal advisers are defensive in the sense that they engage not in one but in two distinct tasks when providing legal advice. On the one hand, they are in advisory mode, conveying their conclusions to assist clients in their wider social or commercial decision making. On the other hand, lawyers tend to be trained to protect their own position and that of their firm in parallel—it is a rare lawyer, for instance, who writes an important letter of advice to a client without also reflecting on her own liability implications in doing so. Have reasonable steps been taken to ensure the currency of the advice? If loss, damage, or injury followed directly from reliance on this advice, could there be an action in negligence? These are the kinds of questions that spring quite naturally to the minds of lawyers. It is arguable, however, that this leads to a rather defensive species of lawyering, where the interests of the client are sometimes prejudiced by the risk aversion induced by the prospect of professional negligence litigation.

7. Legal focus

Coming hand in hand with reactive legal service is the tendency for lawyers to have little or no influence on the wider strategic or commercial context of a deal or dispute on which they are called upon to advise. Gone are the days, it seems, of the lawyer who is the 'man of affairs', the all-round business adviser who combined pragmatism and nous with legal insight. Today, although lawyers either deny or bemoan this, it is all too common for their activities to be restricted to legal analysis (or, at least, the client's perception

---

[3] 2nd edn., Oxford: Clarendon Press, 1994.

of this) without inviting their wider involvement in broader commercial and business issues.

In part, this is perpetuated by the legal profession itself, however, with many lawyers still spending their working lives operating in departmental structures which reflect the subject matters of textbooks or law lectures (property law or tax, for example) rather than the industries or markets which they serve. The way lawyers, especially in law firms, package their services is rather too introspective, focusing on legal disciplines rather than facing the market. Similarly, across the services market, the providers, quite naturally, cluster in organizations which match their initial specialist training (in law or accountancy or banking, for example) rather than the realities of commerce. In the real world, commercial problems do not come neatly packaged as, say, legal or accounting matters any more than legal problems arrive subdivided into textbook branches of the law. And yet the focus and point of departure of so many legal advisers remains legal rather than commercial.

Legal Process

Moving beyond legal practice to the administration of justice more generally, I would point to five factors which typify the legal process of today's legal paradigm.

1. Legal problem-solving

Given lawyers' essential reactivity, it is inevitable that their focus is on the solving of legal problems, once they have arisen or have been perceived to subsist. This contrasts with the more strategic management of legal risk which might come about through their earlier participation in the affairs of clients. Although some lawyers may argue that their advisory work extends well beyond that of solving legal problems, it is nonetheless the view of most clients that lawyers are generally there to remove problematic legal obstacles rather than, say, to facilitate and enable broader commercial objectives through a businesslike grasp of the underlying legal framework.

2. Dispute resolution

In the context of disputes, the legal advisers' main role, therefore, has evolved as one of assisting in their resolution. The principal presumptions here, of course, are that a dispute has actually arisen and only then do lawyers become relevant (as a necessary evil). There seems to be little appreciation of lawyers' potential role in advising on ways in which disputes can be pre-empted in the first place by their prescribing a more preventative form of legal medicine.

In common-law jurisdictions, the dominant mode of dispute resolution remains adversarial, whereby a judge, as an impartial arbiter, has to choose between two competing sets of argument (legal and factual) which are generally in diametric opposition to one another. And this adversarial ethos has extended into the (often excessively and unjustifiably) combative ways in which parties treat one another.

3. Publication of law

The formal name for the mechanism for letting the general public know when a new law is enacted is promulgation, a term which has an old-fashioned ring about it. In fact, it refers to a concept which is largely ignored today. Gone are the days in Scotland, for example, when Acts of the Scottish Parliament were promulgated in every country town or published at the market cross of Edinburgh; or in England, where sheriffs were once required to proclaim all new statutes throughout their bailiwicks. Instead, valid rules of law spring into life daily, very often attaching new significance to our working and social lives without most of us having any systematic means of learning of their impact.

In the middle of the nineteenth century, Jeremy Bentham, the influential legal and social thinker, in his book, *Of Laws In General*, wrote about promulgation that 'The notoriety of every law ought to be as extensive as its binding force. It ought indeed to be much more extensive . . . No axiom could be more self-evident: none more important: none more universally disregarded'.[4]

Things are no better today. In contemporary jurisdictions, the promulgation of the law is largely a publishing exercise with little further state involvement, commitment, or control. Legislation and regulation may well be published (conventionally or online) and marketed by a government agency

---

[4] See *Of Laws in General* H.L.A. Hart (ed.) (London: The Athlone Press, 1970), p. 71.

devoted to publishing but still the useful and usable versions of these materials are often sold or made available on a commercial basis. In relation to case law, not only is the publication process operated by private sector companies, but the materials selected for publication are themselves often chosen according to commercial criteria rather than through any constitutional commitment to the widespread dissemination of new, binding, legal developments.

4. A dedicated legal profession

The quantity and complexity of the law alone conspire to underline the need for a rich body of professional legal advisers to guide their clients and plan for the future. The lawyers remain the custodians of the formal legal sources and it is only they who have the confidence and insight to be able to convey their impact to non-lawyers.

Lawyers, in other words, hold the key to the vault containing the law, a stronghold which cynics argue the legal profession guards a little too jealousy. Slightly more pejoratively, it is sometimes suggested that the legal profession has a state-granted monopoly for the release of legal information. Certainly, the legal profession does today hold a key position in a democratic society, as a vital interface between individuals and the state.

5. Print-based

Finally, the legal process and the justice system of today continue to be dominated by print on paper, in legislating, in resolving disputes, and in advising clients and handling their affairs. Although IT has been playing a greater role in recent years, especially in photocopying, fax, electronic mail, and word-processing, these uses remain supportive of the generation and dissemination of print and paper rather than the electronic creation and transmission of digitally stored information.

One can summarize today's legal paradigm in another way. In the first place, we are governed by a body of law whose scope is so great that no one can pretend to have mastery over anything other than small subsets of a legal system. At the same time, we are, every one of us, under the law, expected to have knowledge of all legal provisions that affect us, even though the means by which the law is announced and published is haphazard. Not only that, it is conventional that non-lawyers have the responsibility of deciding when to seek professional guidance on the law, even though this itself requires legal insight and understanding. Once advice is sought, clients today become exposed to a legal marketplace very much in flux, one in which lawyers fight fiercely with their learned friends to win legal work and where the judges and administrators of the courts find themselves as much constrained by the need to establish financial justifications for all manner of facilities as by the requirements of justice.

Here we have mature legal systems that have in significant ways become alienated from citizens, from business, from lawyers, and from society itself. Such are the pressures, however, that I argue that we are on the brink of a fundamental shift in the way in which legal service is offered and justice is administered. For if the law is to remain the principal means of social control, it must be manageable, available, realistic, workable, and interwoven easily with all aspects of social life. If we look reality straight in the eye, currently the law is none of these.

II

After that rather downbeat message, I would like now, moving into the second part of this chapter, to be more constructive. My principal premise at this stage is that there is a significant connection between the law on the one hand and what I call the 'information substructure' in society, on the other. The information substructure is the dominant mechanism by which information is transmitted and conveyed in a society. The academic literature suggests a model for this substructure useful' for our analysis—the model proposes four phases of information substructure, where societies are dependent, respectively, on orality, script, print, and then on IT. The big question is how the substance of the law and the way it is administered differs across these four phases.

It is intuitively obvious that the nature of law and the way it is administered is conditioned by the information systems which are available for its storage and its dissemination. Thus, the information substructure, no doubt in complex and subtle ways, to some extent determines and constrains the quantity of law, the complexity of law, the regularity with which the law changes, and the people who are able to advise on the law. In fact, moving beyond our intuitions, it is also clear from research and writings on the history and development of communications as well as from legal anthropology and sociology, that the information substructure of society does impact considerably on each of these factors. And I believe that when we look at this impact across the four fundamental stages of the development of communications—through the stages dominated in turn by orality, script, print, and then IT—we can project, with some confidence, future developments in the administration of justice and the practice of law; and can begin to see how the shortcomings of today may be overcome tomorrow.

The Age of Orality

It is hard today to imagine what a society stripped of script, print, and IT might have been like. As Walter Ong puts it, in his splendid study, *Orality and Literacy*:

Fully literate persons can only with great difficulty imagine what a primary oral culture is like, that is, a culture with no knowledge whatsoever of writing or even of the possibility of writing. Try to imagine a culture where no-one has ever 'looked up' anything. In a primary oral culture, the expression 'to look up something' is an empty phrase: it would have no conceivable meaning. Without writing, words as such have no visual presence, even when the objects they represent are visual. They are sounds.[5]

Nonetheless, we can infer, from what might be regarded as the natural constraints inherent in a community only capable of oral communication, some likely features of the law during the phase of orality.

Although it is probable that the memories of human beings were better exercised and more retentive, it was surely not possible for there to have been huge quantities of detailed regulation covering all aspects of human life. No one could have remembered the equivalent even of tiny fractions of the quantity of law in force today. Rather, the general thrust of the rules of conduct were expressed in fairly general terms, as broad principles of which most people were generally aware.

Change in the law would have been fairly infrequent, in large part because there were no mechanisms for formally recording and promulgating such change.

Mastery of the law would have been given to only a few, senior elders of the community, of almost mystical status, who could recite the obligations and prohibitions in force and were called upon to apply them in situations of

---

[5] Walter Ong, *Orality and Literacy* (London: Routledge, 1982), p. 31.

doubt. They too were responsible for passing down the law from generation to generation.

The Era of Script

When we turn to reflect on the era of script as the information substructure, Ong is sobering in his findings: 'Writing . . . was a very late development in human history. Homo sapiens has been on earth perhaps some 50,000 years . . . The first script, or true writing, that we know, was developed among the Sumerians in Mesopotamia only around the year 3500 BC'.[6] And again: 'Indeed, language is so overwhelmingly oral that of all the many thousands of languages—possibly tens of thousands—spoken in the course of human history, only around 106 have ever been committed to writing to a degree sufficient to have produced literature, and most of them have never been written at all'.[7]

With the advent of script, in agrarian society, it became possible in writing (and other pictorial representations) to augment the capacity of human memories and so the quantity of law could and did increase. As it became articulated in a fixed form which was open to scrutiny (admittedly only by the relative few who could read), the law itself came to be expressed with greater precision and rigour. Legal jargon and shorthand evolved as mechanisms for expressing concepts which were frequently deployed, and so a new level of complexity was introduced.

Although the recording of change in the law was facilitated by script, the inability to reproduce material and disseminate it widely other than by manual transcription (which was, in any event, error prone) became a natural constraint on the frequency of change.

Again, however, it was necessary to have access to specialists—those who had a grasp of the evolving body of legal concepts and jargon (where the average citizen did not have). These individuals were both sources of advice on conduct and also called upon to settle disputes when the law, as articulated, was in doubt or disagreed upon. These individuals were lawyers.

---

[6] ibid., pp. 83–4.   [7] ibid., p. 7.

Print-based Society

With the advent of the printing press, in the middle of the fifteenth century, came a revolution in legal as well as social life. As Ethan Katsh says, in *The Electronic Media and the Transformation of Law*: 'Law as we know it would not be possible without the special properties of print . . . print structured the capabilities and functioning of law in various ways. It is not "fine print", as much of the public believes, that characterizes the law, but print itself. Print affected the organization, growth, and distribution of legal information'.[8]

With print, not only did it become easier to produce text, but, crucially, the capability to reproduce and disseminate printed material, exerted a radical influence. The quantity of legal materials was able to expand rapidly, extending into many more areas of social and commercial life. In a literate society, where the dominant means of expression became print on paper, exhaustive detail and so complexity seemed to evolve as objectives in themselves.

More significantly, with printing's capacity to reproduce and disseminate massive amounts of information came the facility for change in the law. Indeed, the mechanisms for change became more formalized, both in legislating and in the development of case law through the doctrine of precedent.

More than ever, then, there was, in what became a print-based industrial society, a pressing need for specialist help to handle the increase in quality, complexity as well as the volatility of the law. Advisory and judicial roles became more clearly distinguished and a dedicated legal profession and judiciary evolved. Gradually, only suitably trained individuals were permitted, by law, to offer legal advice in certain circumstances, while the dispute resolution process became increasingly formal.

IT—In a Transitional Phase

Our move into the age of IT has brought the capability for most people to become publishers in their own right. With powerful word processors available, legislators and draftsmen are not contained in their capacity to generate the printed word. The reproduction of printed material has also entered a new era: first with photocopying technology; later with transferable word-

[8] See Ethan Katsh, *The Electronic Media and the Transformation of Law* (Oxford: Oxford University Press, 1989), p. 12.

processing files and high-capacity laser printers; and, more recently, with telecommunications technology, text can be transmitted and disseminated electronically and at minimal cost.

IT cannot be blamed entirely for the huge quantity of legislation and case law which are now available (both in print and in electronic form in massive databases), but it has certainly not helped to check the verbosity of legislators around the world. Similarly, in the age of IT we have unparalleled complexity in our legal provisions. The specificity and detail of so much legal material today often renders the law impenetrable and too complex.

What is more, IT facilitates change in the law. In contrast with the eras of orality and script when change was a rarity, with IT available, the prevailing attitude towards documentation is that it is dynamic by nature, and subject to regular alteration, rather than static. At all stages in the life cycle in the generation and application of the law, IT supports rather than inhibits change.

With more legal source material than ever before and with the added challenge of some of this being available in legal databases that are themselves impenetrable, are specialist lawyers more or less in demand in the era of IT? In fact, it appears to have led to an increasingly lawyered society, with vast and growing quantities of legal material of unparalleled complexity, which, to cap it all, are subject to unprecedented frequency of change.

On this view, should we not conclude that IT is having a tragic effect on the law? I think not, for to do so is to make the mistaken assumption that we have completed the move from our industrial print-based society into what is called the IT-based information society. I believe instead that we are still in a transitional phase between these two eras and what you have just read are some of the rather unfortunate consequences or features of being in this transition.

My view is that it is both wrong and misleading to suggest that we have evolved into an information society. We are surely not there yet. The reality today is that our ability to use IT to capture, store, retrieve, and reproduce information wildly surpasses our ability to use technology to help analyse, refine, and manage the mass of information which conventional 'data processing' has itself created for us. We are great at getting information into systems and sending it around, but not so good at extracting all but only the information that we want. I call this disparity The Technology Lag. It is the all-important lag between what technologists call 'data processing' and 'knowledge processing'.

The point about The Technology Lag is not only that we are not yet getting computers to behave more intelligently. It is also that good old-fashioned data processing, through such technologies such as photocopiers and scanning machines, has actually created problems for us and these are problems which the latest, so-called 'knowledge-based systems' are not yet sophisticated enough to overcome. In law, for example, senior barristers and judges regularly reminisce about trials in the past when complete document sets could be held under the arm or in a briefcase. They curse the photocopier and attribute today's escalating costs and delays in the courtroom to the document analysis and management tasks which that technology seems to bring for us. Current litigation support systems, based on data processing, only go some small way to conquering the document mountains but it will be some years yet before advanced knowledge-based techniques (such as conceptual retrieval, expert systems, and hypertext) are refined and applied successfully to help manage the difficulties which earlier technology has left as its legacy.

So, until The Technology Lag is overcome, I believe we will remain in a confusing transitional position between the print-based industrial world and the IT-based information society; a position where IT might sometimes be thought to be doing more harm than good. But when the transition is complete (say, in 15 years' time), the legal world, in its turn, will have changed as radically as it did when society moved, first, from being one based on orality to one in which script was the principal means of communicating; and later from a script-based culture to one dominated by print. Because, I claim, the dominant way in which information is processed in society (whether orally, by script, by print, or through IT) directly influences the quantity of law, the complexity of law, the regularity with which the law changes, and the people who are able to advise on the law.

The IT-based Information Society

The shortcomings of the transitional phase to which I refer are all fine illustrations of the way in which our data processing capabilities have, so far, surpassed our knowledge processing capacity. But we are now refining our techniques in the field of knowledge processing and gradually developing systems which will help us to analyse and manage the vast bodies of information we have created for ourselves. And these systems will themselves help us pinpoint all but only the material relevant to our particular purposes as users.

Once these technologies are in place, quantity becomes a non-issue because users will be assisted with accuracy in the retrieval of manageable quantities of legal materials; complexity will largely be hidden from them, as systems will effortlessly guide hitherto perplexed users through the labyrinths of the law; and change will either be hidden from the user with updating a continuous phenomenon or, more proactively, be brought to the attention of users by systems which themselves have the ability to monitor all relevant developments for individuals.

Perhaps even more radically, knowledge processing will spawn a multitude of legal information products and services for direct consultation by non-lawyers and so, in the information society, there will be less rather than more reliance on specialist legal advice.

I must stress that this vision of a transformed legal service on the strength of knowledge processing is not one which is likely to be realized in the next few years. Researchers have battled for a quarter of a century in trying to develop knowledge-based systems for lawyers and the results so far have been modest. Elsewhere, however, the investment in using IT to harness the power of information is enormous. I have some considerable confidence (some might say faith) that advances in knowledge processing will be stunning in the coming 20 years, thus easing us from this transitional period into the fully fledged, IT-based information society.

Let me offer one illustration of an emerging technology which gives me cause for such optimism. One of the latest and most intriguing techniques for overcoming the problems of basic information retrieval is that of 'intelligent agents'. Although still the subject of more experimentation and speculation than actual live usage, the fundamental idea is eminently plausible and strikes me as having great potential. Intelligent agents (of one type) are programs which can be instructed to roam around specified bodies of new information in search of materials which are likely to be of interest to those who instruct them. Like tireless and ever-willing paralegals, these agents monitor the content of documents as they are loaded and draw attention to those that seem relevant.

On one model, intelligent agents could work like this. A user would build up a detailed profile of her social and business interests selecting these from a rich set of categories which have been articulated in advance. At the same time, the information services community would commit not just to loading the entire text of documents but also to providing further information which classifies all searchable materials. In so classifying, they would use the same category set as that employed for users' profiles. The intelligent agents can be instructed for a specified or indefinite period to monitor all new materials and to identify all matches, in effect, between the interests of the user and the subject matter of the new information. Thus, a user passionate about nineteenth-century French painting and paranoid about European environmental regulations relating to waste might log on to her machine in the morning to learn of an auction in her locality and a high-powered meeting of ministers in Brussels.

Alternatively, such information would be ready and waiting on the breakfast table, embodied in that same user's *Daily Me*. This is the fascinating notion, as described so well by Nicholas Negroponte in his excellent book, *Being Digital*,[9] of a personalized newspaper which is generated each day but is filled only with items which have been specified in advance as being of interest to the particular reader. (The prospect of never receiving a newspaper stuffed with reports of cricket or football is, for me, joyous beyond words. Instead, my *Daily Me* would have huge coverage of track athletics.)

For intelligent agents to work, user profiles and document classifications must be detailed, accurate, and precise. Even then, given the amount of information being generated in our world, users will be well advised to state further requirements. For example, a user might add refinements such as his preference for no academic articles, for pieces only in the English language, and for no items more than 2000 words in length. Additionally, most users might want, in the first instance, to be provided only with an index of relevant items (perhaps ordered according to superficial relevancy) indicating matters such as the title, author, length, level of technical detail, and source of each piece of information.

In any event, there is more than a glimmer here of a useful tool to help diminish the effects of The Technology Lag, with technology itself being used to seek to overcome information overload.

In relation to the law, intelligent agents are a promising technique to help encourage promulgation, in that new legal developments could be brought automatically to the attention of lawyers and non-lawyers. There is also the basis here for an innovative information service for clients—as lawyers add materials to their own in-house know-how systems, these could also be classified and then relevant materials could immediately be routed to clients with matching profiles. And where clients are operating on the same system as their lawyers—for example, through 'groupware' or 'Extranets' (see Chapter 4)—notification of the arrival of this information could pop up on their screens and the details could be accessed there and then. There would be no need to dial up periodically to see if anything new had arrived.

---

[9] *Being Digital* (London: Hodder & Stoughton, 1995), p. 153.

Intelligent agents should offer an especially proactive enhancement to basic information retrieval systems in that they might deliver information even when it has not been explicitly requested for a particular purpose. It is, then, the basis of a novel form of information service rather than a way of improving an existing advisory service.

More generally, fascinating work on a variety of enabling technologies (including workflow systems, groupware, hypertext, intelligent checklisting, and project management) is currently being conducted. Increasingly, the influence of these developments will be felt by lawyers and my bet is that from around the turn of the millennium onwards[10] (that is, within the time frame of most lawyers' current strategic planning), the world of practising lawyers will become a very different place—we will all (without exception) be using the global 'information highway', communicating with one another electronically, using all manner of information services (domestically and in business), and there will be no practical limitations on the amount of information we can store and distribute, while the systems themselves will become more and more useful.

What does all of this mean in practice? I turn now, in the third part of this chapter, to provide one view.

III

I envisage in the world to come that much of the lawyer's work will shift from being advisory in nature to becoming, in large part, a form of information service, a kind of legal service which might meet most of the needs of individual citizens and businesses and yet differ markedly from the traditional means of working as a lawyer.

Legal service will become a form of information service in two broad ways. First, as various technologies are refined, much of today's conventional legal work will be systematized, routinized, and proceduralized and then made available on the much-vaunted information highway as one amongst many consultative information services. The second dimension is potentially far more significant and this is the use of IT to help realize what I call the latent legal market—the myriad of circumstances, in domestic and business life, in which non-lawyers today are generally unable to benefit from the legal input

---

[10] This was written in 1996. I believe my expectations then were realistic and have come to be supported in practice.

they require because conventional legal service is too expensive or impractical in the circumstances. IT will help bring legal guidance to this latent legal market.

In both instances, there will be a major change in the underlying relationship between those who are involved in delivering legal service and those who receive it. On the traditional model, we have had lawyers and their clients, with the contractual commitment upon the legal adviser to offer some kind of advisory-based service, to their individual clients alone, on the basis of some more or less agreed charging structure (invariably, in the past, charging by the hour or day). When legal service becomes information service, there is a change, but not simply from the delivery of advice to the provision of information. Much more, a new set of relationships are established, under which those who are guided become users, the lawyers who analyse and organize the material become the legal information engineers and the organizations who develop and market the legal information products and services become the providers. The key relationship in this scenario is between the users and providers of the information service, with a secondary arrangement between the provider and the engineers.

Users of Legal Information

The users of legal information services of the future will consult, navigate about, and be empowered to apply legal information made more readily accessible and financially acceptable than in the past. Legal information will be but one of countless sorts of information available on the Internet, although the compartmentalization of information into legal and other such conventional categories will itself in time fade away. The information products and services available—and available, in due course, to all citizens—will be packaged and oriented towards providing practical and directly implementable guidance with little or no distinction between the disciplines from which the final information product has been derived. A user who has a problem which traditionally may have needed, say, accounting and banking expertise as well as legal advice, may consult a service which provides a synthesis of these three sources of guidance; but there will be no particular need or benefit in the overall guidance being broken down into units which reflect their original structure. This kind of compartmentalization may be a practical necessity of today but will have less place in the IT-based information society.

The basis for charging users for legal service will shift from being fixed in the number of hours expended by the lawyer towards a fee that is more likely to reflect the overall market value of the information to the user.

The number of such users will be vastly greater than the number of conventional clients of today; and the frequency with which these legal information services will be consulted will greatly outstrip the frequency of consultations with lawyers today. The difference will lie in the emergence and realization of the latent legal market, as innumerable situations in domestic and business life are enlightened by the law when this would or could not have happened in the past. For example, when a citizen crashes his car, purchases faulty goods, or considers taking out a loan, he will have at his fingertips practical, focused and applicable guidance which, it is likely, would not have been realistically available in the absence of some IT-based information service. Similarly, in the commercial world, in preliminary negotiations, in on-the-spot procurement or in business planning and legal risk management generally, a layer of legal counsel will be available when previously it may have been regarded as too cumbersome or costly to obtain any kind of legal input. Like guidance on medical matters, property, investments, and leisure, legal guidance will be available on the Internet.

Legal Information Engineers

At first glance, this may seem like tragic news for the average lawyer and be thought to be a harbinger of the end of the legal profession—asking the legal practitioner to buy into this model of the future may seem akin to inviting the proverbial turkey to vote for an early Christmas.

In fact, it will mean fundamental change and a very different market for legal knowledge and expertise will emerge. Those lawyers who fail to recognize and plan for this massive shift may well cease to trade profitably; whereas those of vision and entrepreneurial flare are already planning today for an exciting commercial future.

The systematization of work which is done manually today, in what I call the transitional phase of today, will be yet one more source of strain and reason for shrinkage in the pressurized legal marketplace. In contrast, the liberation and emergence of the hitherto latent legal market will create a range of opportunities for lawyers to package and sell their expertise in innovative ways.

What, then, might the lawyer's role be as an engineer of legal information? The main task, in the first instance, will be that of analyst—it will be for the lawyers, with their unparalleled knowledge of the legal system, to interpret and repackage the formal sources of law (legislation and case law) and articulate it in a structured format suitable for implementation as part of a legal information service. Trained lawyers will continue to possess a unique insight into the law and legal process. In the information society, they will repackage this insight and sell it not through one-to-one advisory work, but in the creation of legal information products and services.

There will be a natural opportunity here for collaboration between the academic and practising branches of the profession, although both will need to be adaptable and flexible in working together.

Who will be the Providers?

In print-based society, lawyers have enjoyed a dual role, combining that of being legal information engineers as well as providers. In fact, the two functions have become intertwined as one—those who gained expertise in law, in a world based on print and paper, were the only individuals who were in a practical position to apply it in particular circumstances in providing advice.

In the IT-based information society, in contrast, the process of analysis and formulation of information can and will be separated from that of the provision of legal information service. Knowing the law and being able to articulate legal information will no longer necessarily lead to domination in the sale of that information.

Lawyers will by no means be the only workers affected by this break from the past—many of the middlemen known as brokers or agents or intermediaries or the like who have also enjoyed their monopoly over various information services (estate agency, insurance broking, and travel agency, for example) will find they may no longer dominate their markets. Where the service being delivered is essentially information-based, other imaginative providers will enter the markets and strive to use IT to deliver greatly improved service on the information highway. 'Disintermediation' will be the order of the day and the middlemen will need to find new, imaginative ways of adding value.

In this, we see perhaps the greatest commercial challenge of all for lawyers, because with the shift in the nature of legal service comes their loss of a monopoly over the provision of legal services. While at first glance, today's lawyer may be most apprehensive about moving from an advisory role to that of an engineer and analyst, the far graver and fundamental challenge is actually that of retaining market share in the provision of legal information.

In the past, conventional legal publishers have delivered products (textbooks and journals, generally) which clarify formal legal sources and put them in their wider legal, business, and social contexts. The market for these products was confined mainly to lawyers themselves, as the nature of printing imposed a natural constraint on the range of individuals who could directly derive benefit from books and articles. In short, legal publishing was for lawyers because no one else could really understand law books.

However, as legal publishers have diversified into electronic legal publishing and are gradually exploiting crucial enabling techniques such as hypertext, document assembly, enhanced text retrieval, and groupware, then the products they produce demand less legal expertise on the part of the users and so appeal to a wider user base. As these techniques are refined, legal publishers will slowly come to vie with practising lawyers in the market for legal information.[11] It is entirely conceivable, for example, that a leading legal practitioner may be invited to collaborate, even on a permanent basis, with imaginative electronic legal publishers who may retain the services of this lawyer at rates which could match or exceed the fee income which would be generated by traditional work on an hourly billing basis. At the same time, innovative lawyers will package their conventional work product, such as a well-drafted document, in electronic form, using techniques such as hypertext to enhance and clarify contractual and other materials, and to provide ready access to relevant legal sources.

As the markets of publishers and lawyers converge, both must also look beyond their own rivalry if they are together to dominate the market for the provision of legal information systems. For they are likely to have to confront and avert threats in the commercial world far graver than one another. I have in mind the large accounting and consulting firms, whose vast information systems resource will prepare them far sooner for the delivery of professional services on the Internet. It is entirely conceivable that the recruitment of legal specialists to act as sources for information service providers is as likely to occur at the instance of these multinational players as from the legal publishers. With mastery of the information services market which will outstrip

---

[11] This has begun to happen. Compare the news alerts of leading legal publishers (e.g. Butterworths, at www.butterworths.co.uk) with those of law firms (e.g. Cameron McKenna's *LawNow* at www.cmck.com).

the most technically advanced of lawyers, it is entirely conceivable that an accounting and consulting giant could cultivate and then dominate the latent legal market. On this model, lawyers would be relegated to the role of back-room technician, while the other professionals enjoy the glamour and profit of delivering the information service to business and society generally.

Equally, the same latent legal market may be recognized by the increasingly powerful telecommunications providers whose great experience of the information infrastructure would stand them in splendid stead to exploit the legal market. While the telecommunications industry may be less attuned to the nature of professional services than the accounting and consulting firms, it may be that professional service, as we know it in the industrial print-based society, may be superseded by some other ethos and organizational infrastructure in the IT-based information society.

And as for Traditional Advisory Service . . .

All of that said, I accept that an important market for legal service delivered in the traditional, advisory manner will remain (although streamlined through IT), because there will be a variety of situations in which it will not be possible or appropriate for legal information systems to supplant or replace the conventional approach. In all the excitement (or horror) of anticipating a shift from advisory to information service, it is vital not to overlook these areas of legal life which will remain the province of lawyers—high value, socially significant, or complex legal work, for example.

For most law firms, however, one of the biggest long-term strategic questions is whether they can survive by advisory work alone; or perhaps by information service in isolation; or whether a mutually supportive mix of both will always be needed.

IV

Let me return now, in this fourth and final part of my chapter, to one of my earlier suggestions: that we are on the brink of a shift in legal paradigm; and, that after this fundamental change has come about, many features of legal service and legal process of today will be displaced by a new way of legal life underpinned by a fresh set of basic assumptions about the law and lawyers.

I have argued that this shift in legal paradigm can and will only happen when we emerge from the transitional confusion in which we find ourselves into the fully fledged IT-based information society. Only then will The Technology Lag be overcome and will our capacity to manage legal information be more than equal to our ability to create and disseminate it.

As to providing some detail of the shift to this new legal paradigm, I use as my starting point the twelve central features of today's legal paradigm which I introduced at the outset. And again, my analysis is divided into the two general categories of legal service and legal process. Figure 3.2. summarizes the shift in legal paradigm.

Today's Legal Paradigm	Tomorrow's Legal Paradigm
Legal Service	**Legal Service**
advisory service	information service
one-to-one	one-to-many
reactive service	proactive service
time-based billing	commodity pricing
restrictive	empowering
defensive	pragmatic
legal focus	business focus
Legal Process	**Legal Process**
legal problem solving	legal risk management
dispute resolution	dispute pre-emption
publication of law	promulgation of law
a dedicated legal profession	legal specialists and information engineers
print-based	IT-based legal systems

Figure 3.2 The Shift in Legal Paradigm

Legal Service

Earlier, I characterized legal service by describing its prevailing characteristics under seven headings. I follow these again in an attempt to capture the shift in paradigm which I anticipate.

1. From advisory to information service

If I have any single, unifying theme, it is that IT will eventually enable and encourage legal service to change from being a form of advisory service to a type of information service. While most of the work of the lawyer in today's paradigm is advisory and consultative in nature, the emphasis will shift radically in the information society as many lawyers assume the role of legal information engineer and devote much of their professional lives to the design and development of legal information services and products. With the exception of specialist lawyers and judges, the work of lawyers will gradually become forms of information service, both serving and liberating the latent legal market. The ultimate deliverable will be reusable legal guidance and information services pitched at a level of generality considerably higher than the focused advice which characterizes the legal advisory work of today.

2. From one-to-one to one-to-many

As legal service becomes a form of information service, and lawyers package their knowledge and experience as information services designed for direct consultation by non-lawyers, the work product of individual lawyers will no longer be devoted only to one case and to one client. Instead, the legal information will be reusable and for that purpose cast in a form well suited to repeated consultation. It will be applicable in many circumstances and for many different users. In this way, far more citizens will benefit from individual lawyer's intellectual efforts.

3. From reactive to proactive service

Once it becomes practicable and financially viable for non-lawyers quickly to obtain usable legal guidance, earlier legal input in the life cycles of transactions and disputes will become commonplace. For lawyers to be proactive, they will no longer need to be instructed and involve themselves at the start of all projects, for example. Instead, they will develop suites of legal information products, legal health checks, legal risk management tools—the embodiment of proactivity—all of which will expressly overcome the paradox of traditional reactive legal service. For these systems will help non-lawyers to identify those situations in which specialist advice is required and, crucially, will assist them in identifying when to instigate any specialist advisory process.

4. From time-based billing to commodity pricing

When the work product of lawyers becomes reusable and the time and effort expended cannot sensibly be allocated amongst those who are paying for the service, there can be no question of hourly billing. This regime, which I have said can penalize the efficient and reward the indolent, will have no place in tomorrow's legal paradigm. Many commentators assume hourly billing will be displaced by some form of value billing which entails charging for the value of some service to the client. Others go further and suggest lawyers will be able to charge for time saved rather than for time spent (although I have never heard a client accept this suggestion with relish). Value billing may, however, prevail during the transitional period between the print-based industrial society and the IT-based information society, but I doubt it will survive in its pure form in the new legal paradigm when it is more likely that legal information services will be akin to commodities, for sale in the latent legal market and subject to the more prosaic economic models of supply and demand which apply to physical goods today. Gradually, access to legal service packaged as information service will sell in high volumes for mass consumption at low prices.

5. From restrictive to empowering

With the demystification of the law and its far wider availability will come the perception that the law does far more than set up obstacles in the path of domestic, social, or commercial aspirations. Instead of regarding the law as restrictive, users of legal information services will gradually appreciate that the law can be a source of empowerment and a powerful weapon which can be marshalled in support of the exploitation of opportunities and the attainment of all manner of objectives. While the business person would characterize this future feature of the law as empowering and catalysing, the citizen should come to regard this as meaning the law has become more helpful and supportive.

6. From defensive to pragmatic

One of the great debates which awaits us is over the extent to which legal liability can be attached to those who develop and market legal information services. While the courts have not indicated where they will draw the line, in liability terms, on the continuum between the professional adviser and the published book, as a matter of public and social policy it is likely that the state will want (or want to be seen to want) to promote and encourage the development of legal information systems and the realization of the latent legal market. But uncertainty over liability could well inhibit the growth of legal information services.

In any event, by their very nature, legal information services are pitched at a higher level of generality than legal advice. And so, while it may be reasonable for users to rely on the guidance offered, we have to accept that on those (rare) occasions where the guidance is inappropriate and gives rise to problems, the pragmatic social compromise will be not to attach liability to the developers other than in exceptional circumstances. Otherwise, all services would be emblazoned with disclaimers warning that the guidance should not be relied upon without taking conventional, professional advice. The essence of liberating the latent legal market, however, is precisely that such additional professional guidance is not sought.

The availability of legal information services will give rise to improvement but not perfection in making the law more usable and available and the marketplace itself will establish mechanisms for drawing attention to unreliable or defective services (perhaps allowing users—both disgruntled and content—to leave accessible evaluations of the systems on the service for future users to peruse). Legal information engineers may not often be held liable in the future but they will find their market severely eroded if their systems fail to do the job.

7. From legal focus to business focus

The successful information services of the future will be those that provide legal guidance which is packaged and integrated with more general commercial assistance. While I would not go so far as to suggest that the 'man of affairs' will mutate into some 'information system of affairs', it will surely be both beneficial for users and commercially astute for legal information engineers, to embed some street wisdom and business acuity into the legal services they provide. On this model, legal advice will be bundled with and embedded in more general business advice; other than for the legal specialists in their advisory role, who will probably retain the mantle of ivory tower legal analysts.

Legal service as information service will also have far greater business focus in another sense. The products and packages which will be developed will not be devoted exclusively to the conventional areas of law, as taught in today's law schools, or practised within individual departments of law firms. Nor will the services correspond to the subject matter of today's legal textbooks. Rather, the business focus will require that the guidance transcends many of our conventional legal boundaries and, no doubt, into other disciplines as well. Even if multidisciplinary practices do not come to fruition, multidisciplinary information systems most certainly will.

Legal Process

Lastly, looking now at the administration of justice rather than legal practice, I have once more used a structure that corresponds with the model laid out in the first part of this chapter.

1. From legal problem-solving to legal risk management

While legal problem-solving will not be eliminated in tomorrow's legal paradigm, it will nonetheless diminish markedly in significance. The emphasis will shift towards legal risk management supported by the proactive facilities which will be available in the form of legal information services and products. As citizens learn to seek legal guidance more regularly and far earlier than in the past, many potential legal difficulties will dissolve before needing to be resolved. Where legal problems of today are often symptomatic of delayed legal input, earlier consultation should result in users understanding and identifying their risks and controlling them before any question of escalation. Those legal problems that do slip through the net will be handled either by dedicated legal information products or, where complex, of high value, or of social significance, will be the province of specialist advisers and then perhaps judges.

2. From dispute resolution to dispute pre-emption

A corollary of effective legal risk management is an overall reduction in the need for formal dispute resolution. The effective control of legal risks prior to their escalation and realization as problems will mean that disputes will be pre-empted and avoided and so will not progress to any formal or alternative resolution process.

Furthermore, in a society which sustains the social compromise of not attaching liability to defective legal information systems, users will tend, on the first time round, to follow and accept the guidance offered by the 'living law'. Here I borrow a term coined by the legal sociologist Eugen Ehrlich, earlier this century—when he referred to the 'living law' he was meaning the law which actually reflects and conditions behaviour in society.[12]

The broad, generic representations of the law as embodied in legal information systems could themselves create a culture in which there will be little incentive to pursue legal matters at the high level of specificity and in the strictly literal terms which are so characteristic of today's legal paradigm. For all practical purposes, the law in action will be the law as held in legal information systems: less rigorous, less formal, and less adversarial than contemporary, common-law jurisdictions. By a quite different route, and following entirely different principles of interpreting legal sources, common-law jurisdictions of tomorrow may come in line, at least in spirit, with civil-law jurisdictions of today.

3. From publication of law to promulgation of law

Despite the current reluctance to make legislation and case law freely available on the Internet, international trends, political pressures, and relentless lobbying from within and beyond the legal profession will, in due course, convince the government of the day in the UK to reverse its policy. Far from endorsing the commercially oriented publication of primary sources which is characteristic of today's legal paradigm, the state will then play a far more positive role, in supporting promulgation in the future.[13] All primary and secondary legislative sources, eventually as the final stage of the legislative process itself, will be placed, as a matter of course, on the Internet. As for case law, when it is commonplace for judges to prepare their judgments in electronic form, specific electronic communications facilities will be provided to them by the state to enable and encourage the establishment of far more extensive and current bodies of judicial decisions than are available today. And, eventually, it will not make sense to speak of 'unreported cases'.

To help guide lawyers and non-lawyers through this far larger, projected mass of legal sources, a major legal information services industry will spring up. These providers will develop systems, products, front-ends, filters and agents, using a wide range of enabling techniques, which will take the user to all but only the relevant sources relevant to the user's purpose. Expert commentary, analysis, and practical prompts will also be packaged alongside the

---

[12] *Fundamental Principles of the Sociology of Law* (Cambridge: Harvard University Press, 1936), ch. XXI.

[13] This has happened, best evidenced perhaps by the existence of the pilot site for BAILII (British and Irish Legal Information Institute) at www.bailii.org which offers free access to an integrated body of British and Irish legislation and case law. This is discussed further in Chapter 11.

primary sources of law, building up the legal guidance which is set to become the 'living law'.

4. From a dedicated legal profession to legal specialists and information engineers

The information society will always need access to legal knowledge and expertise. What will not be sustainable is any continuation from the position in today's legal paradigm whereby the legal profession enjoys an exclusive position as the interface between individuals and businesses on the one hand and access to the rule of law on the other.

In place of lawyers at this interface, will lie ever more flexible, powerful, and accessible IT-based information systems serving both the latent legal market of the past and other areas of law amenable to systematization. For problems of great complexity or high value, legal specialists will continue to operate in their traditional advisory role. But they will represent a relatively small fraction of the legal profession of tomorrow. A far larger number of lawyers will have reoriented their careers and will become the legal information engineers whose knowledge forms the basis of the legal information services. Thus, the legal profession of the future will be constituted of two tiers, not the solicitors and barristers of today, but the legal specialists and legal information engineers of the information society. Whether or not the profession has sufficient entrepreneurial talent and general foresight to be involved in the third discipline of marketing as providers of the legal information services and products is a great unanswered question of today.

5. From print-based to IT-based legal systems

Finally, and in summary, legal practice and the administration of justice will no longer be dominated by print and paper in tomorrow's legal paradigm. Instead, legal systems of the information society will evolve rapidly under the considerable influence of ever more powerful information technologies. We will no longer suffer from the excessive quantity and complexity of legal material. There will be mechanisms in place to give everyone fair warning of the existence of new law and changes in old. Legal risks will be managed in advance of problems occurring and so dispute pre-emption rather than dispute resolution will be the order of the day. Our law will thus become far more fully integrated with our domestic, social, and business lives.

In all, then, I am optimistic about the future of law.

4

The Future of Legal Practice[1]

Within a very few years, I predict that almost everyone in developed societies will enjoy easy access to a much enhanced Internet and World Wide Web (WWW). This will be the natural and definitive first port of call for all sorts of entertainment, information, guidance, and services—not just for a few but for all of us. It will be commonplace for us to conduct our supermarket shopping and personal banking online; we will choose and book holidays, take out insurance cover and go house-hunting using electronic services which will for most purposes replace ('disintermediate') the agents and brokers of today; we will chat, face-to-face via first-rate videoconferencing to friends and colleagues around the world as though they were sitting next to us; we will be able to participate more actively in the schooling of our children and have direct access to most government services and information from our homes; we will have guidance on any conceivable topic at our fingertips, presented in wonderfully illustrative multimedia form; and information and services that are of interest to us will be brought to our attention directly without our needing to go out and search for them. In our working lives too, communication, trading, advice, funds transfer, negotiation, collaboration, management, and marketing, to name but a few, will come to be dominated by ever more focused and usable technologies. Some of the systems to which we will turn will not be

[1] This chapter is a revised version of a paper reproduced in the proceedings of the American Bar Association 2000 Annual Meeting in London. It is an updated statement of my position as presented in the revised paperback edition of *The Future of Law* (Oxford: Oxford University Press, 1998).

publicly available to everyone on the Internet but will instead be reserved for restricted classes of user. Even then, of course, these will be online facilities.

The statistics and the economics speak for themselves in two commonly cited graphs: in Figure 4.1, it is shown, relative to other technologies, just how rapidly (in years) the Internet came to have 50 million users; while Figure 4.2, in respect of banking, demonstrates how much less are the transaction costs of using the Internet, as compared with more conventional channels.

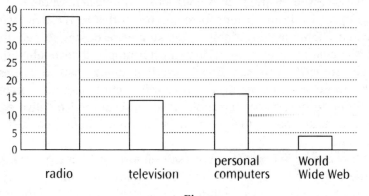

Fig. 4.1
Source: US Department of Commerce, The Emerging Digital Economy Report (1998),
at www.ecommerce.gov

More generally, according to recent research, about one-third of a billion people are now online. Almost one-half (147 million) are from North America, just over a quarter (92 million) are European, and roughly 6 per cent (19 million) are British.[2] Around the world, on average, the number of

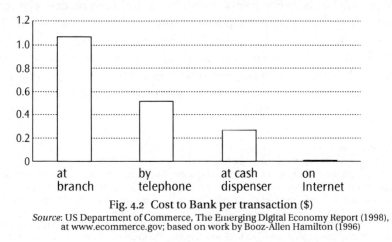

Fig. 4.2 Cost to Bank per transaction ($)
Source: US Department of Commerce, The Emerging Digital Economy Report (1998),
at www.ecommerce.gov; based on work by Booz-Allen Hamilton (1996)

[2] www.nua.ie/surveys/how_many_online/index.html

Internet users doubled in 1999. The official UK statistics site reports that 6.5 million UK households had Internet access in early 2000.[3] Although the statistics show that levels of access depend strongly on income, and so there are crucial social exclusion issues here, uptake in households in the lowest income groups also doubled in the past year. If the astounding growth patterns continue, and affordable Internet access is offered in libraries or other public buildings, then the UK Government's aspiration that all citizens should have access to the Internet by 2005 looks entirely achievable.[4]

Will legal practice in its current form survive in this increasingly wired world? When clients are invariably using online resources to run their businesses and all other professions are transforming and dovetailing their services accordingly (as we can already see happening), can we honestly believe that those who want legal assistance will be content to carry on with traditional one-to-one, across-the-desk, advisory legal service delivered in the time-honoured, consultative fashion on an hourly-billing basis? I am sure not.

Instead, as I argued in Chapter 3, alongside all sorts of other types of information, there will be legal guidance available online, offering non-lawyers access to practical help on legal matters. In fact, this is already happening today.[5] Across the World Wide Web, on internal 'Intranets' and on 'Extranets' (terms to be explained in this chapter), legal guidance is available now, providing help to clients and often a new source of revenue for providers. This is not speculation about what might be tomorrow. It is part of today's landscape and what is particularly ominous for lawyers is that the providers of these services are not all lawyers. As I have forewarned for some time, legal publishers, accountants, consultants, and entrepreneurs generally have already recognized the potential and snapped into action while most lawyers concoct complex rationalizations, explaining why none of this is desirable. There is little point in such denial. The genie, as they say, is out of the bottle; it is now time for lawyers to plan their future on the assumption that IT is here to stay and most will not be able to avoid its impact.[6]

---

[3] www.statistics.gov.uk

[4] www.citu.gov.uk/iagc/estrategy/foreword.htm

[5] See my regular column in the law pages of *The Times*, much of which is devoted to reporting on new online legal services (www.the-times.co.uk). For comprehensive coverage and news about legal web sites in the UK, see also www.venables.co.uk, www.legaltechnology.org, and Nick Holmes and Delia Venables, *Researching the Legal Web*, 2nd edn. (London: Butterworths, 1999).

[6] For other views on the impact of IT on legal practice, see Charles Christian, *Legal Practice in the Digital Age* (London: Bowerdean, 1998), and Andrew Terrett, *The Internet: Business Strategies for Law Firms* (London: Law Society Publishing, 1999).

Today's and tomorrow's systems do and will, of course, vary in complexity and sophistication, from electronic checklists through automated document assembly systems to diagnostic expert systems. But the theme in law, as elsewhere, will be that the natural, first port of call will be online facilities and services.

All of that said, I am categorically not suggesting that all of today's lawyers will be replaced by computers. My prediction instead is that legal work of today will divide into two quite distinct types of service, one enhanced and the other transformed by IT; and, at the same time, a whole new legal market will emerge, one which is only possible in the information age. And it is to these three categories of legal service that I now turn.

Three Types of Legal Service

Looking ahead to the medium and long term, I anticipate that legal service will be of three quite distinct kinds:

- traditional legal service;
- commoditized legal service; and
- legal service belonging to the latent legal market.

The first two will replace today's legal market, but the third dimension is new. I should say at the outset, because I have not made this clear enough before, that the three categories of service I am introducing here do not necessarily map directly onto the types of problems that clients often bring to their lawyers. Frequently, especially in major pieces of work, one deal or dispute may call for all three types of service; others may require a blend of two; although still others may indeed fall neatly into one category.

Traditional legal service

I have no doubt that complex, high value, and socially significant work (which can be called, for convenience if not elegance, or indeed accuracy, 'high-end' work) as well as obscure, arcane, or esoteric legal service, will continue to require the judgment, experience, and knowledge of skilled legal practitioners operating in the traditional, one-to-one, consultative manner. However, this conventional service will come to be streamlined and optimized through IT using, for example, ever more powerful communications and legal information systems. Pressure to introduce these systems will come in part from clients (who themselves are continually advancing in their own use of technology); partly from law reform (Lord Woolf's civil reforms in England, for instance, assume far greater uptake of IT amongst lawyers—see Chapter 11); and in large part also from the new legal marketplace in which competitors (including accounting firms) will be using IT extensively and where legal aid work will be viable only if conducted with the considerable efficiency that IT can bring.

I anticipate that the high-end work will also be affected by another significant trend, which will probably (but not necessarily) come to be implemented through technology. I have in mind here the development of legal methodologies, for want of a better term, analogous to the so-called methodologies used by auditors and management consultants in support of large-scale projects.

Like cradle-to-grave recipe books, these methodologies are highly detailed and documented procedure manuals which embody best practice and impose a standard approach on substantial audit or consulting assignments. With each phase, stage, task, and activity mapped out in advance, stipulating what should be done when, and glued together by strong project management, the idea is that the wheel need not be reinvented with every new client, duplication of effort is avoided, the service process is rendered far more efficient, and huge chunks of work can far more reliably be delegated to more junior staff than would otherwise be possible.

Many seasoned legal practitioners deny that legal work can be handled in this way. In support of this scepticism, they frequently argue that each matter they handle is unique and so ill-suited to prearticulated procedures. I have found this claim to be an exaggeration—of course all matters have features peculiar to them but there is nonetheless much in all legal work that would benefit from greater consistency of approach and improved project management at the very least. In any event, whether or not law firms are prepared to explore this angle, I am sure the accounting and consultancy giants will work in this direction.

In all, then, I expect that traditional legal service will continue to play a major role in society but it will come to be delivered more quickly, at lower cost, with greater consistency of approach and to a higher quality. IT will play its part here but in automating rather than innovating.

Commoditized legal service

While high value, socially significant and complex legal work will not, as I have just said, be fundamentally changed through IT, the same cannot be said of numerous other categories of legal practice of today. I have in mind much of the standard and repetitive work of our current lawyers. Non-lawyers have for long bemoaned the cost of apparently routine legal work and many have clamoured for precisely the proceduralization that IT can and will bring. Just as debt collection systems in operation today enable large volumes of cases to be processed efficiently and cost-effectively by paralegal staff with relatively little supervision and intervention by lawyers, then so too with countless other areas of legal work, especially where the case loads are large, the problem types are recurrent, and the tasks involved are highly procedural in nature.

Here, then, is what so many lawyers understandably dread: the disinter-mediation of legal advisers, whether in-house when firms recognize they need less legal staff for the delivery of service that can be systematized or, worse still, when entire legal tasks are prepackaged, productized and avail-able on the World Wide Web without the direct involvement of any lawyer or firm. In this connection, it will be the business of general legal practitioners that will be squeezed the most, if clients and consumers come to the view that the traditional advisory service is failing to add value.

There are only a limited number of responses open to lawyers in the face of this fundamental change. Those in denial might try to hang on to the old ways in the hope that the whole business of IT is a bad dream. I fear for their survival. Some may, rather drastically, choose to leave the law altogether, believing perhaps that the trends of which I speak are anathema to profes-sional service and simply not for them. Still others may try to diversify and take on the high-end work which I suggest will be affected far less. A few may seek to 're-intermediate' themselves by contributing their knowledge and experience, on a revenue generating basis, to the very systems and services which threaten their livelihoods. (On re-intermediation, see Chapter 2.)

The really entrepreneurial lawyers will take this last option a step further and seek to exploit the latent legal market.

The latent legal market

Perhaps the most important theme of my book, *The Future of Law*, is that there are innumerable situations, in the domestic and working lives of all non-lawyers, in which they need and would benefit from legal guidance (or earlier and more timely help) but obtaining that legal input today seems to be too costly, excessively time consuming, too cumbersome and convoluted, or just plain forbidding. This is the latent legal market, which I believe will be liberated by the availability of straightforward, no-nonsense, online legal guidance systems. They will not replace conventional legal services, but they will provide affordable, easy access to legal guidance where this may have been unaffordable or impractical in the past.

I have been asked on many occasions if my latent legal market is just a fancy term for the rather more earthy concept of 'unmet legal need'. In a sense it is, in that they are two sides of the same coin. The core phenomenon is that legal guidance is needed today far more extensively than it can be offered and taken. From the point of view of society generally, this is well characterized as unmet legal need; whereas from the lawyers' perspective, I regard this as a huge untapped market, happily not an opportunity for exploitation or monopoly but the chance to contribute, at a fair rate of return, to the grave problem of inaccess to justice.

Let me try to give a flavour of the kind of help that will be out there on the Web and elsewhere online. Several years ago, my wife was involved in a car accident. Fortunately, no one was injured but I was concerned that the circumstances could give rise to legal difficulties. It is my good fortune to have a brother, a solicitor in Scotland, who is familiar with road traffic law. I telephoned him and outlined the facts of the case. His response was instructive. He did not point me to a relevant piece of legislation; nor did he direct me to any case law; nor indeed did he say that he would write me a long letter by way of response. Instead, he told me that there were only four issues about which I should be concerned—the first concerned my insurance and insurers and he rattled off some thoughts on these and the remaining three matters.

In short—and I should immediately say that some lawyers squirm when I say this—he gave me the kind of guidance (I call them 'golden legal nuggets' or 'desert island legal points') that a lawyer will give his friends and his family but not his clients. I accept there are often perfectly proper professional reasons for not packaging legal guidance informally but I do feel strongly that legal guidance systems on the World Wide Web in the future will be far more useful and usable if they hold punchy, jargon-free, practical pointers rather than detailed legal analysis.

It is imperative that I am not interpreted as suggesting that informal legal guidance systems will deliver a better service than conventional advisers acting in traditional, one-to-one advisory fashion. Rather, my claim about the utility of legal guidance systems must be assessed in the context of the latent legal market, where the choice is not between human advisers and IT-based guidance systems. The choice there is between the system and nothing at all—and I for one would prefer to have at my fingertips the guidance that lawyers give to their friends and family than have nothing at all.

Lawyers who have read my work often say to me that they support my ideas about the future and can see how IT could indeed transform the work of many lawyers. However, they then go on to explain why their own area of practice will in some sense be immune from the changes. Matrimonial lawyers put a particularly powerful case, arguing that their clients rely on them not only for legal advice but as a shoulder to cry on, as a sympathetic counsellor who is removed from the trauma but always willing to listen. No computer can ever replace this human dimension, the argument concludes. And I agree.

However, I still maintain that there is a latent legal market even here, one that does not replace but supplements the counselling function. Consider the innumerable, tragic instances of women seeking divorce after long sustained periods of physical violence. Lawyers often ask these clients why they have waited so long to consult them, why they have tolerated this inhuman behaviour for so long. The response so frequently, it transpires, is that they were afraid as non-earners that they would have no entitlement to their house or money, and may indeed thereby have no chance of keeping custody of their children.

How much better it would be, surely, if clear, broad guidelines on basic legal issues were available through, say, the next generation of televisions, at low cost and in a non-forbidding style, accessible from the home. If such systems encouraged users to take conventional advice earlier, as in my divorce example, then that of itself would be desirable. There is a latent legal market not just for the provision of legal guidance where none would otherwise be available; there is also as significant a need for legal input earlier in the life cycle of clients' affairs. This is the essence of the proactive legal service that I claim is so lacking today. And in a world where most people's first port of call when they require information or guidance or service of any sort will be the World Wide Web, we can see immediately just how extensively usable legal guidance may eventually be consulted.

It is also important to note that these legal guidance systems are not conceived only as an informal source of legal input in people's domestic affairs. On the contrary, I have found my ideas on this matter to have been best received in fact by general counsel in the very largest of international corporations. These skilled commercial lawyers perceive an inevitable build-up in their legal workload and yet a freeze on legal resource in the future which can only be overcome by imaginative ways of packaging and distributing informal, practical legal experience for direct application by non-lawyers across their organizations. They too have a vast latent market for legal input and they are attracted to IT solutions more than ever before because so many of them find that an appropriate IT infrastructure (corporate Intranets) has recently been put in place and may serve as an ideal delivery mechanism for legal guidance.

In all, as these systems come to dominate access to the law, in business and in domestic and social life too, the conventional lawyer–client arrangement will be replaced by a new set of relationships, under which those who receive guidance are more users than clients; the lawyers who organize and analyse the material become 'legal information engineers'; and the organizations who develop and market the legal information products and services become the providers. Looking ahead, I predict that legal information engineering is destined to be a major new job for lawyers.

Lastly on the latent legal market, unlike for the high value and complex work, I expect that legal guidance systems will evolve quite rapidly to become multidisciplinary systems and services. For non-lawyers, as I said earlier, online legal guidance in isolation will come to be seen as rather peculiar. The social user will come to expect legal information to be integrated with other relevant guidance (for instance, with consumer or health information), while business users will prefer the guidance they receive to be oriented towards the realities and the flow of the ventures with which they are involved rather than with the underpinning legal disciplines. Thus, legal guidance systems will work alongside, or be fully embedded in, multidisciplinary systems, covering areas such as accounting, finance, and business and management consulting.

Can lawyers survive on high-end work alone?

In audiences to which I give presentations, I often see a visible and collective physical relaxation in the shoulders of the lawyers present when I suggest that high value, complex and socially significant work will not be radically changed by IT. It is clear that a great many legal practitioners regard this as what they do. It is as though their first thought is that this means they may just be able to hold out until retirement before this IT business engulfs them. The big question for those lawyers who genuinely do such work is whether they can live by high-end work alone.

My current view is that it would be foolhardy for any lawyers, no matter how pre-eminent in their fields or impressive in their client base, to feel confident that their business is immune from the impact of commoditization or the latent legal market. Quite apart from the massive commercial opportunities which they may be overlooking (and there is some irony in the fact that the high-end specialists and their organizations are probably the best equipped to develop legal guidance systems) there is a competitive issue here as well. I am convinced that the relatively small number of dominant high-end law firms will find growing competition not for their most highly specialized services but for other legal requirements of the very clients who do indeed pass them the high-end assignments. I have in mind general everyday legal guidance or, looking ahead, legal risk assessment and management services and indeed the development for clients of internal legal information systems and services. If firms are content to concentrate only at the tip of iceberg, then this may be a profitable strategy for the short to medium term. But I would suggest that they should be nervous about other firms, especially accounting firms, touting interdisciplinary services beneath the surface, so to speak. As confidence in these other firms grows and the relationships strengthen, those at the tip will be ever more precariously perched, always in danger of being knocked off by competitors who have managed to establish deeper relationships with their clients.

In any event, as I stressed earlier, there is not a simple stark choice for lawyers between high-end work and the rest, because the work involved in very few deals or disputes, especially large matters, is wholly high-end. Clients now recognize that much of what is done, even in major matters, can and should be systematized; and they will come to demand that appropriate methods and techniques are used for different parts of any matter.

The Role of the World Wide Web

I am often asked where the World Wide Web fits into my vision of online legal guidance systems. The short answer is that the Web is likely to play a crucial role. Before I give the longer answer it is important to have a common understanding of the basic terminology, or at least to know what I mean by three basic terms: 'World Wide Web', 'Intranet' and 'Extranet' (it is interesting to note that these last two terms came of age in 1996—they were barely part of our vocabulary when I finished the original manuscript of *The Future of Law* in late 1995).

Basic terminology and imminent developments

The World Wide Web is the publicly accessible, global information system to which Internet users around the world have access. An organization's web site (that is, its home on the Web) can be viewed, using a tool known as a 'browser', by anyone in the world who is on the Internet. Today, as I explain shortly, the Web is regarded by many lawyers as a vehicle for marketing, as a form of global electronic publishing; and many practitioners are coming to recognize that it will in large part (but not entirely) replace print on paper as the principal way of delivering promotional material. But the Web is also the mechanism that governments tend to favour in providing direct access to public information. The Web is the natural home, therefore, for public access to the law (see Chapter 12).

The idea of an Intranet is to use browser technology specifically and Internet technology generally as the access and delivery mechanism for the management of internal information within organizations, so that users can roam around this information as easily as they can the external Web. As such, Intranet is one enabling technology that helps lawyers capture and store their know-how and then make it available across their firms. In other commercial organizations, corporate Intranets are now commonly found. These are general repositories of information that are of wide internal interest. It is here, accordingly, that in-house lawyers are now putting useful legal guidance and information; but they are doing so for internal consumption only. Intranets also have two further, related dimensions: they can be set up as a shared resource to bring individuals from different organizations under the one virtual roof; and they are often regarded in so doing as a medium to support private electronic mail amongst a given user group (for example, a Judicial Intranet would provide a common e-mail system as well as a central repository of useful information).

My third and final basic term is 'Extranet'. Here, access to selected parts of an Intranet, to particular portions of an organization's internal information is provided, on a restricted basis, to a limited number of external organizations. Once again, this access is based on browser and Internet technology. Law firms are thus developing Extranets for access by their clients and favoured contacts only, sometimes as part of the value they wish to be seen to be adding to conventional services, while on other occasions on a charging basis. Indeed, Extranet is currently perceived as a principal means by which lawyers' online services might be delivered on a revenue generating basis. An alternative to using an Extranet for online services is to set up a secure site on the Web to which restricted access is offered, only to permitted users, enforced through password protection or the like. Such a site is not part of a law firm's Intranet but is a site in its own right.

As just described, these three approaches—the Web, Intranet and Extranet—seem to be relatively distinct in emphasis even though they deploy common enabling technologies. However, they are each developing rapidly and frenetically; and this is going to blur the boundaries.

Let me give a flavour of the confusion which will arise from the imminent changes. Solicitors in law firms will not be content just to have access to their own Intranets—they will also want access both to their own firms' web sites and to all the online services offered to their clients (which may or may not be Extranet-based and will tend to be different for different clients). And they will want to search across all these simultaneously. From the lawyers' point of view, they will want their Intranet, web site, and various Extranets to appear as one seamless system. At the same time, as law firms make ever more extravagant claims for the sophistication of their in-house know-how systems, clients will quite naturally ask for direct access to these Intranets. This will doubtless lead to the provision of more Extranet services. And, in due course, clients will unquestionably want to access the (competing) Extranets of many of their professional service providers. But they too will prefer to do so through one single point of access—this in turn is likely to be the Web itself. And, to cap it all, many clients will want their advisers' Extranets to appear to sit on their own Intranets!

If this all sounds rather complicated, I am afraid it is irreducibly so during what is a rather unstructured transitional period. Looking ahead, however, it seems to me that when the whole field has bedded down, lawyers and non-lawyers alike will want to be able to consult a wide variety of online sources. Some will be publicly available; others will be external but restricted; while still others will be internal. No matter what the source, however, no sane user will want to jump in and out of different systems in deference to the nature of the material. Instead, they will want the systems to appear integrated (as one 'virtual information source') and be confident that appropriate house-keeping issues (for example, security) have been handled. In my view, the common point of access will be the World Wide Web. This does not mean that all the information will be stored on the public Web itself. Much will not but will instead be held on secure machines whose only connection to the outside world will be the Web-based entrance. Security at this point will be vital as the World Wide Web becomes the one-stop shop both for public access to law and for the electronic legal marketplace.

Generations of web sites

Current users will be forgiven for complaining that the set-up just outlined is a far cry from today's World Wide Web. But bearing in mind how quickly the Web has progressed over the past few years, it is not fanciful to suppose that there will be innumerable further advances even in the short to medium term.

I believe the Web for lawyers will move through three generations, each adding to the developments of its predecessors. The first generation remains the most popular today—the Web being used by lawyers as a new medium for marketing activity. It is now commonplace for law firms to place their brochures and other such promotional materials on the Web; and many are finding this is a powerful and cost-effective way of setting out their proverbial stalls.

The second generation go further than the provision of marketing materials to offering useful, up-to-date information on legal issues. In some ways, this generation can be likened to conventional legal libraries and information services. Visitors to second generation sites, of which there are many already, browse and navigate around collections of publications, held substantially in their conventional form (for example, as articles, promotional brochures, and books). In many second generation legal sites, legal updates, brochures and articles are held together, so that users can see the full range of topics covered in each type of publication. In other sites, materials are organized according to their subject matter (for example, by legal specialities in law firms and by the subjects of courses in universities). The emphasis here is on allowing users to be exposed to all materials that relate to particular areas of law (no matter what the form of their publication).

The third and final generation is for me the most significant and useful. These are sites that offer services. In the language of Chapter 1 of this book, these may be client relationship systems or online legal services. In either event, the common theme is that they go much further than simply providing bodies of relatively unanalysed information. Instead, they provide more distilled and tailored services, suited to particular users' particular needs.

The most developed form of third generation sites I call 'real life' sites and these will eventually dominate the Web, Intranet and Extranet in the future. I discuss these in some detail in Chapter 2, where I speak of life episodes, life events, and business episodes. The common theme here is that systems and services will be set up to provide information and guidance which relates directly to problems, activities, tasks, and processes which arise in daily life as opposed to information that has been stored under some library or legal classification.

Non-lawyers do not care much about the nature and form of legal publications. Nor are they keen on ploughing through complex information systems to retrieve basic data about work being undertaken for them. Neither are they fussed about the particular branches of law which apply to their circumstances. Instead they generally want punchy reports of progress being made with their work (see further my discussion of client relationship systems in Chapter 1) and substantive guidance on how the law bears on their actual 'real life' position.

Looking at real-life online legal services, if a user needs guidance on, say, floating a company, trading in a particular country, or claiming under a car insurance policy, he will be presented, by advanced third generation systems, only with legal materials which are relevant to his particular situation. The materials themselves may be linked to formal legal sources (such as legislation and case law) or to articles or other secondary sources but the service is more likely to be packaged as practical guidance—in the form of guidance, as I like to say, that a lawyer gives to his friends and his family but not to his clients.

Of course, second and third generation techniques will underlie not just the Web but Intranets and Extranets as well. But the Web and Extranets will be further supplemented by facilities whereby users will be able to make contact and instruct lawyers directly from the sites themselves. It is also entirely conceivable that when more formal one-to-one legal advice is needed, video links may immediately be established putting users in immediate contact with conventional advisory service.

At the same time, even the first generation is requiring lawyers to rethink aspects of their businesses. I often point out to senior managers within law firms that while their individual publications on their own have tended not to be of great commercial value, when many of these are brought together, the whole becomes way greater than the sum of its parts. The upshot is that some firms are revisiting their approach to free publications, recognizing that their proper place may well be as, say, a chargeable Extranet service rather than being freely available on the Web.

The facilities on offer

I should say a little, finally, about the various types of facilities that will be on offer in due course. I believe at least four facilities will come to dominate legal web sites. The first will be search and retrieval systems which can operate across web sites, Intranets and Extranets. Initially, these will provide basic text searching but they will gradually involve more advanced identification of materials based on concepts and meaning as well. To improve upon the rather hit-and-miss performance of current search facilities on the Internet, the use of 'metadata' standards will be increasingly important. Crudely, the idea is to categorize legal sources on relevant web sites using a standard classification system. Each categorization is a piece of metadata—it is information about the document that it describes. When users search for sources, they are then able to search across this metadata as well as within the documents themselves. The result should be far greater success in identifying relevant documents, especially secondary sources.

Second, there will be legal guidance systems about which I have said a good deal in this chapter; and indeed they constitute a running theme of my work. These will present practical, step-by-step assistance on legal matters, helping visitors not by presenting extensive narrative but by delivering 'golden legal nuggets' or 'desert island points' to help them in all sorts of real-life situations. The technique of 'intelligent checklisting' will be deployed here, whereby complex areas of guidance will be distilled into key points, beneath each of which will be succeeding layers of greater detail and guidance, together with standard form documents.

A third and more advanced facility will be diagnostic applications—using expert systems techniques, users will engage in online interactive dialogues. These systems will elicit the details of visitors' circumstances and will draw conclusions, make recommendations and offer advice. The same technology will also be used in automatically assembling and drafting documents for users, based on their responses to a variety of questions asked of them. This approach is the focus of Part III of this book.

Finally, there will be genuinely proactive services and facilities, whereby relevant legal information and guidance will automatically be sent out to interested parties who have not made express requests for these but will nonetheless come to expect and welcome such updates. 'Intelligent agents' and similar technologies will be used here, so that the information held on web sites, Intranets, Extranets, and on linked resources, will automatically be distributed in accordance with pre-articulated profiles of the interests of the recipients.

Bringing a number of strands of thought together, it may seem rather science fictional to speak of 'real life' online services that can offer legal guidance, solve problems of law, and even send on useful and timely information to delighted recipients without having been asked to do so. It is categorically not fictional because we do already have the technologies in place today which can make this a reality. But it does represent a fundamental change in the administration of law in society. That is why I speak in Chapter 3 of the impending shift of paradigm in legal service and in legal process. In this book, generally, I try to show the many influences (commercial, technical, sociological, and ethical) that are inclining us towards this new world.

I do appreciate that it is a world that is threatening to lawyers, although some are already embracing the opportunities that the radical change will bring. More fundamentally, however, it will be a world in which non-lawyers will have immeasurably greater access to legal guidance and, in turn, to justice.

5

The Likely and the Possible[1]

Although it is always sensible to consult users when planning future applications of IT and to ask them what they want, a genuine difficulty encountered when the users in question are lawyers or judges is that they are often not fully conversant with what is commercially available or technically possible. Accordingly, the first phase in such a consultation process should be to immerse the users in likely technical developments and possible applications within the time frame of the planning process. Thus informed, the users are then better placed to draw up their shopping lists.

With that in mind, my purpose in this chapter is to take out my crystal ball. My aim is to try to predict what are likely to be the most significant developments in IT over the next ten years or so; and thereafter to point to a wide range of possibilities to which these developments could give rise. I hope that these projections into the future will help lawyers and judges specify their IT requirements more easily.

1. Can we Predict the Future?

It might immediately be wondered whether or not it is actually possible to make reliable long-term predictions about IT. Indeed, it is often argued that

[1] This chapter is an updated statement of my position as presented in the revised paperback version of *The Future of Law* (Oxford: Oxford University Press, 1998).

long-term planning for IT is futile because no one can confidently predict what technological advances might be made many years hence. In support of this, it might be said that if a long-term forecasting exercise analogous to the one in this chapter had been conducted in 1979 it might have neglected the advent and impact of the personal computer (which came to the market in 1981) while a similar initiative in 1989 would have had no insight into the World Wide Web (developed in 1990). Both of these developments fundamentally changed the world of IT (and the world generally) but neither could have been predicted in detail. Should we not therefore wait and see what new technologies emerge and focus instead today on making IT work for us in the short term?

On reflection, the position today (in 1999), is significantly different from 10 and 20 years ago. In particular, it is striking to note that even if there were to be no new advances in IT over the next decade as radical or fundamental as the PC and the World Wide Web have been, nonetheless the impact of the entirely foreseeable consequences of today's proven technologies is of itself extremely profound both for the administration of justice and for the practice of law. This was not so 10 or 20 years ago, when what was foreseeable did not promise such pervasive and penetrating change. Thus the predictions of this chapter assume no 'major step' changes and yet begin to offer a vision of a justice system and of legal practice which would be quite different from today's. (At the same time, the possibility of some far-reaching, new technical innovations emerging over the next 10 years cannot be discounted and this highlights the need constantly to monitor research activities across the world.)

In any event, pragmatic managers often harbour doubts about long-term strategy, fearing that it can result in unrealistic and impractical proposals which might distract IT specialists as well as users from the basic requirements of keeping existing systems running today and in the short term. There is a danger here; but so long as long-term strategy and day-to-day operational work are managed separately (even if closely linked), a strategic approach should actually support ongoing systems administration. It is surely crucial to think ahead, to choose from future possibilities and, in turn, to offer support to others who will benefit from direction when they come, for example, to be faced with a variety of options in implementation.

Finally, by way of introduction to this discussion of IT over the next ten years, the suggestion that the developments are likely within that particular period requires qualification in two respects. First, it is more responsible to claim that these developments might come to fruition some time between 5 and 15 years from now, which is to say that some will be realized more quickly than within a decade while others may be more challenging than currently appears and so make take longer than the 10 years. Second, and building on an earlier point, the predictions are restricted to developments which are clearly foreseeable and, of course, can take no account of radical new technologies into which we have no insight today.

2. Likely Developments in Technology

As for the developments themselves, I am now able to identify ten.

1. Ongoing expansion of global telecommunications capability
2. Burgeoning of the information industries
3. Emergence of virtual private networks
4. Relentless increase in computing power
5. Convergence of computers, television, games consoles, handheld machines, and other information appliances
6. The coming of ever smarter technologies
7. The rise of multimedia
8. Greater usability
9. More interpersonal and interorganizational computing
10. The Web emerging as the 'first port of call'

Each is discussed separately below.

1. Ongoing expansion of global telecommunications capability

With massive and ongoing improvements in a variety of telecommunications technologies (including advances in optical fibre and compression techniques and—vitally—in satellite technology as well), there will be broadband (roughly, very high capacity), interactive networks, across most of the world and in practically all of England, connecting all buildings and all computers to one another. If a crude analogy is drawn with the flow of water, this broadband network will be akin to a mains pipe through which water is pumped where most of today's links can be likened to encouraging water to dribble from a drinking straw.

This will mean, in due course, that there will be no practical limits to the quantities of information which can be transmitted around the world almost instantaneously. The information itself will not only be text but also sound, image, animation, and video as well, so that high-quality desktop to desktop videoconferencing will come of age. There will be a huge increase in digital traffic across this global telecommunications capability which will enable transmission costs to fall rapidly, eventually to a negligible level for individual transactions. A variety of techniques will be developed to ensure that transmissions can be secure, confidential, and capable of authentication; and to enable and encourage reliable payment and transfer of funds as well.

In summary, there will be a global telecommunications capability which, for practical purposes, will enable the instantaneous transmission of seemingly limitless amounts of digital information at negligible cost. Crucially, with the advent of a variety of wireless broadband technologies, this transmission will be available to users of mobile devices (for example, hand-held machines), as well as conventional desktop computers.

2. Burgeoning of the information industries

The global telecommunications capability will provide the basis for a rapidly growing range of information industries, early examples of which can be seen today in the form of Internet e-mail and the World Wide Web. Already there are said to be at least 300 million users of Internet e-mail; and most commentators believe this figure will rise to around 1 billion by 2005. Soon electronic mail will be more widely used than the telephone but its use will be extended to embrace the transfer not just of text but also of voice messages, photographs, images, and video as well (videoconferencing to and from computers and televisions will soon be commonplace).

As for the World Wide Web, today's position offers some insight into emerging methods of providing information and entertainment across the global telecommunications infrastructure. Even now, massive amounts of conventional published materials can be accessed through the Web. However, more sophisticated forms of information service are emerging rapidly. Systems which offer guidance and advice and not just raw data or information are already available; and the more advanced applications are interactive, whereby users can be tracked through complex issues on a question and answer basis. Domestically, for example, the online booking of restaurants and cinema tickets or the purchase and sale of cars are already commonplace; while in the business world, many of the middlemen now referred to as brokers or agents or intermediaries (estate agents, insurance brokers, and travel agents, for example) are finding an equivalent of their service being delivered by other information providers on the information highway. This 'disintermediation' (a dreadful word for a vital concept) will come to pervade the service industries. Middlemen will manage to survive only if they can add value that no system can replicate.

As stressed later, the natural first port of call for guidance on almost any issue will soon be electronic information services. More than this, trading, transacting, and business processes generally, will increasingly be conducted and mediated over the Internet. Here entirely new forms of business are emerging.

3. Emergence of virtual private networks

Although innumerable services and facilities will remain directly accessible to all users across the world, the same global telecommunications infrastructure will also support the establishment of restricted and sometimes even private networks. These will enable communities of users with shared interests to communicate easily with one another (by conventional electronic mail, voice messaging and video, for example), perhaps with enhanced security or confidentiality features as appropriate for the information and services involved. Identifying the addresses of individuals with such common interests will be straightforward and there will be common areas to visit to hold public and private, online and off-line, discussions and forums.

As a practical matter, participation within these private networks (sometimes referred to, somewhat inaccurately, as 'Intranets'—see Chapter 4) will make it far easier for users to identify information services suitable for their particular purposes. Today's World Wide Web is already rather unmanageable. Tomorrow's restricted networks will help steer users towards what they need. These private networks will support specific industry groups and professions for their members' internal purposes but will have an external face too, offering non-member users of their services limited access to parts of these networks and providing certification of the provenance and authenticity of the services on offer.

All these networks will not actually be separate systems, each with their own plumbing. They will be 'virtual' private networks—in the world of IT, the word 'virtual' has come to be used where technology is electronically creating some effect in the physical world. Thus, the networks will function as though they were discrete and separate.

Users will no doubt communicate across innumerable different private networks. I find it helpful to think of every user having a *portfolio of affiliations* to a range of networks, some devoted to particular projects, others to organizations to which they belong and still others to bodies of individuals with shared interests. A busy person might be affiliated to 50 or more such virtual private networks.

4. Relentless increase in computing power

Although advances in telecommunications may appear to be more dramatic, the power of computers will continue to burgeon. Until recently, it was widely held that for the foreseeable future, the performance of microprocessors is expected to continue doubling every 18 months and yet become 30 per cent cheaper per annum. It is now thought that performance will come to double in less than 18 months, so that within 15 years one personal computer will be as powerful as the sum total of all of today's machines in California's Silicon Valley. Even today, there is more processing power in a modern, luxury car than was on board the average Apollo spacecraft.

The storage capacity of computer disks is also set to increase astoundingly (although it is arguable that the relevance of computer storage will decline with the availability of cheap, online systems across the new telecommunications capability). Where a single compact disk (CD) of today can store a large set of encyclopaedias, more recently established technologies such as Digital Versatile Disk (DVD) can offer more than 30 times that capacity. Looking further ahead, holographic memory holds the promise of storing the entire contents of the British Library in a unit no bigger than a regular paperback book.

All the while, machines themselves will go on shrinking in size, such that credit-card sized machines more powerful than any PC of today with detachable, slimline screens (or even foldable displays) are entirely conceivable within the next ten years or so. Over the last few years, a whole array of hand-held machines have arrived, some the size of a pack of cards and many with power and capacity greater than state-of-the-art personal computers of a just a few years ago. Screen display technology continues to improve steadily, to the extent that the quality and resolution of today's most polished conventional colour publications (glossy magazines, for instance) will soon be rendered on digital display units.

5. Convergence of computers, television, games consoles, handheld machines, and other information appliances

Well over one-third of households in the UK already have home computers. The overwhelming majority also have television. Huge numbers of homes have electronic games (consoles and portables). Powerful hand-held units (personal digital assistants) are also becoming increasingly common. And mobile phones are becoming pervasive, for teenagers upwards. Together, these various display units are coming to play a major role in life in the UK and other developed countries.

Until recently, it would have been accurate enough to suggest that television and games machines are generally used for entertainment while computers, hand-helds, and mobile phones are deployed for the purposes of gaining access to, or transferring, information. One notable exception has been the text facilities available through television (said to be accessed by more than 18 million people in the UK every week) which have, for some years in the UK, demonstrated a willingness on the part of viewers to access information through their televisions.

Two rather different, future trends are now likely. First, within but a few years, along with the much vaunted convergence of information and entertainment will come a convergence of the television and the personal computer. For many purposes, users will have one window on the world and not two. The emerging generation of televisions are offering access to the Internet and to the World Wide Web, so that the majority of people in the UK, for example, will be online via PC/TVs within about three years. What with the greatly enhanced telecommunications capability, the systems will be far quicker today, bringing multimedia information onto wall screens in many homes and transforming their lives. Perhaps the most significant aspect of this convergence is a cultural dimension: it can comfortably be predicted, as I stress shortly, that users will come quite naturally to turn to the Internet as their first port of call in any quest for information and guidance; just as naturally as they might turn to their televisions for a variety of forms of entertainment. At the same time, the interactivity which characterizes the personal computer use today is likely to diminish the purely passive nature of television watching and the latter will develop as a more participative pastime.

The second trend relates to electronic games, hand-held machines and mobile phones. Internet access is already being provided through games consoles, so that what was a unit devoted exclusively to play is now emerging as yet another window on the information sources and wide range of services on the Internet. At the same time, hand-helds are swiftly evolving from digital diaries of low functionality to full-powered mobile computers, with Internet access (in the medium term to be made vastly superior through mobile broadband technology), games and entertainment facilities and, gradually, the capability to serve as electronic books. So too with mobile phones—with WAP (wireless application protocol) emerging rapidly and set to rocket in popularity, text-based Internet access will thereby be provided to mobile telephone users.

These are the information appliances of today and the next few years—personal computers, televisions, electronic games, hand-held machines, and mobile phones. I have no doubt that innumerable new points of entry into the Internet will also emerge. For current purposes, it is not necessary to try to guess what might come through as the dominant channel for delivery. What is pivotal is that everyone will be on the Internet before very long.

6. The coming of ever smarter technologies

It is a central theme of my work that our current capability to use IT to capture, store, retrieve, and reproduce data, easily surpasses our ability to use technology to help extract *all but only* the information we might need at any one time. Across industry, commerce, and government, managers and workers bemoan the quantity of information they are expected to digest. So far, IT is often said to have given rise to less rather than more control over information—we suffer from technologies which allow more documentation to be produced and disseminated but with no commensurate facilities to help sift through and identify relevant information. IT has given us 'information overload' but precious few tools as yet to help us cope with this surfeit.

Gradually, however, a variety of emerging techniques (such as intelligent agents, 'push' technologies, expert systems, and artificial intelligence) are actually helping users to analyse and manage the vast bodies of information out there. Smarter systems are emerging which themselves bring to users *all but only* the material relevant for their particular purposes. These smarter technologies represent a shift in IT towards systems that can provide help, offer guidance, solve problems, undertake research, eliminate irrelevant information, and pinpoint pertinent material. In due course, these technologies will, invariably and as a matter of course, deliver useful, distilled, relevant, accurate, timely, and focused information to all human beings who are online, doing so on the basis of an understanding of the interests and concerns of individuals.

Illuminating here is the observation of futurists that, within a few years, home refrigerators will be able to recognize when milk is running low and then automatically to order more. Like a small-scale stock control system, the fridge will be capable of monitoring its contents, and products will be packaged using IT that supports this ongoing assessment. Users will be able to set their refrigerators to initiate the ordering process when contents deplete to certain levels. A simple Internet link to some online supplier requiring the delivery of some standard quantity will complete the chain.

Underlying this domestic example of IT are three vital themes which will come to characterize smarter technologies. The first is that the kind of system just envisaged achieves a considerable level of *proactivity*. It does not wait for the consumer to recognize that more milk is needed. Instead, it anticipates need and can do so because it holds profiles of its users' preferences. Secondly, the facility is tailored and *personalized*. The technology will enable the precise needs of all consumers to be met on an individual basis. No more will one size need to fit all. Finally, the IT-based service is *integrated* which is to say that the recognition of need and the requisition process are bound together in one seamless process, with no need for manual intervention or transfer of information from one appliance to another. No longer will the consumer need to switch on the home PC and dial up the online supermarket.

7. The rise of multimedia

The traditional way of conveying information during the past few centuries has been through script or by print on paper. In the print-based society, there have been at least two assumptions. First, it is generally assumed that printed materials (for example, books and articles) will be tackled by their readers in more or less linear fashion. Although readers may skim or speed read, there is usually a sense of progression from one end (the beginning) to the other (the finish). Although indexes and other techniques may support the reading process and enable readers to initiate their reading in the middle of a publication, once entry has been made the procedure is usually linear thereafter. The second assumption is that the body of printed material being consulted is usually dominated by text, self-contained, with clear boundaries and with a strong indication, from the face of it, of the extent of the publication.

Print-based publication, however, is quite quickly being replaced by electronic multimedia publication. In the world of multimedia, text is but one means of conveying information because it is invariably supplemented by other media such as sound, animation, video, and image. Electronic publications frequently contain all these media together so that multimedia encyclopaedias of today, for example, provide text on screen with associated sound (perhaps music) or video (maybe a clip from a film) or images (for example, photographs), each instantaneously accessible at the click of a mouse.

Electronic multimedia publication challenges the two assumptions about printed materials as identified above. On the one hand, the principal means of progressing through this new media is rarely linear. Instead, the dominant technique is to 'browse', jumping within and between the media as the user prefers (this is the essence of 'hypertext' and 'hypermedia'). Users can thus take major detours from text into the world of video and then perhaps to sound, all in an exploratory spirit. On the other hand, multimedia challenges the second assumption about isolated, clearly bounded publications. Those which in the past were stand-alone come now, in the world of multimedia and most strikingly on the World Wide Web, to form one massive, seemingly infinite, single body of information. Where the conventional consultation of an encyclopaedia, for example, used to involve reading text-based entries from what was a clear beginning to an obvious end, electronic consultation today is not solely text-based and, for practical purposes, the amount of information to hand seems to be limitless.

8. Greater usability

The user-friendliness of systems is also set to change radically; and it is here, for instance, that the IT giant Microsoft is directing enormous research investment. On the one hand, there will be continual progress in the field of voice recognition, such that speaker-independent, large vocabulary, continuous speech systems will be widely available within five years, if not less. In practice, this means to enter text and instruct their computers, users will be able to talk to their machines in the same way as they would do to one another or as they would when using a dictating machine—with few practical limitations on the scope and richness of the vocabulary, no pauses between words and independently of the accents or idiosyncrasies of the speech patterns of particular speakers. Gradually, systems will also be able not only to recognize the spoken word of individuals but also to cope with conversations in which several people are engaged.

Furthermore, the user interfaces of systems will become ever more adaptable, such that, in operation, systems will be geared to the needs, habits, quirks, and preferences of particular users. No doubt through complex psychological tests, optimum interfaces will be identified for each and every user, extending from the colours of screen display through to the balance between graphical and textual information, for example.

Personalized and customizable systems to which human beings will be able to talk or which they will wear (on armbands or woven into clothing[2])

[2] www.media.mit.edu/affect/AC_research/wearables.html

will gradually remove fear of computer use and all generations within entire communities will come to be comfortable with IT as part of their daily lives. (Looking towards 10 years from now, and beyond, as advanced screen technology moves beyond the head-mounted displays characteristic of today's virtual reality games towards active contact lenses which will fill our fields of vision entirely with computer output, we will become attached, both figuratively and actually, to our information technology.)

9. More interpersonal and interorganizational computing

With improved telecommunications linking most computers to one another, it is becoming increasingly natural and worthwhile for individuals and organizations to take advantage of this interconnectivity and of the ability to share information, so that they can work more closely together than was ever possible in the past.

When I wrote the *The Future of Law* in 1996, the dominant enabling technique in this context was referred to as 'groupware'—a category of system and software specifically designed to encourage and enable collaborative, interpersonal, and interorganizational activity. Groupware stood out then as the best way to allow existing and newly created information to become a shared resource which all authorized users could contribute to and draw from. Today, however, the Internet and Intranets now provide a competing method of supporting and encouraging team working.

Whatever technique is preferred, however, IT generally can now be said genuinely to enable co-operative team working when the team members are not located together; as well as common access to work product. And this can happen today in an uninhibiting and non-threatening manner.

Online 'virtual meetings' are destined to dominate our lives, some conducted through the relatively flat medium of text; while others will be considerably enlivened by videoconferencing.

Looking a little further ahead, again towards a decade from now and beyond, by exploiting still more advanced techniques such as 'shared spaces' (being pioneered in the UK by British Telecom), users will commonly take on some electronic personae and actually venture into cyberspace and interact with others through these digital personae known as 'atavars'. Fantastic though this may sound, the 'virtual World Wide Web' has shown that it will not be too long before we can 'meet' and work with one another in a distant virtual land.

10. The Web emerging as the 'first port of call'

My tenth and final development derives from the impact of the previous nine. With all the advances to which I have drawn attention, usage of the Internet and IT is rapidly pervading society—for example, in homes, in education, in Government, in finance and commerce, in health, and in entertainment. As has been said, Internet access from the home is becoming increasingly popular. And the great majority of businesses today, of all sizes, deploy some form of IT, at least for their own internal purposes. As prices fall, and more uses are made available, the Internet will become as commonplace as the telephone and the television.

Before long, as was also suggested earlier, the natural first port of call for information, guidance, and for innumerable services as well, in both a social and business context, will be the World Wide Web. Human beings will come to expect to have information technology (and, in turn, information and information services) at their fingertips and, equally, will expect all others around them similarly to be using IT.

Think then of a society, one that is carpeted in fibre and supported also by mobile broadband facilities, where everyone is connected to everyone, and each has immediate access from the home to guidance on most topics and this guidance is presented in wonderfully graphic and easy-to-use form. Indeed, most users will, essentially, be speaking to their televisions or mobile machines when they want some information. Consider that this resource might indeed become the natural first port of call for the majority of people. In that context, can we honestly expect legal service will continue to be delivered in the time honoured fashion—through one-to-one, face-to-face, consultative, advisory service for which people are charged by the hour? I think not, but before I offer some rather specific predictions and recommendations, I believe it is helpful to take a step back and consider what, in theory and principle, is possible in law in the coming decade in the light of the advances in IT just outlined.

3. What will be Possible in Law

In the previous section, a variety of *likely* developments and trends in IT were laid out. One of the most pressing challenges for anyone interested in the justice system, or particular branches of it, is to identify the possibilities and opportunities that these developments might bring for the practice of law and for the administration of justice. Accordingly, the purpose of this section, in an exercise of what I call 'possibility analysis', is to suggest what, in turn, is *possible* in the justice system in the next decade.

When seeking to identify possibilities for the future, it is crucial to bear in mind—and this is an absolutely vital theme of my work—that IT can have an impact in two quite different ways:

- IT can be used to *automate*, streamline, and improve existing practices, activities, and organizations; or
- IT can be used to *innovate*, and so to bring about change and introduce new ways of working and carrying out tasks.

Beyond law, as I often say, the distinction is seen clearly when one thinks of IT-based cash dispensers. That technology did not automate pre-existing domestic banking practices. Instead it provided the basis for an entirely new way of conducting banking business. In the justice system too, it should be expected that IT may be used not only to streamline current practices and institutions and render them more efficient but also to change many aspects of the way in which the law is practised and justice is administered.

This section presents more than thirty possibilities for four categories of user and can be summarized as follows:

justice workers generally
- a national legal network
- virtual hearings and meetings
- multimedia and hypertext-based legal bundles
- legislation on the Internet
- searching for legal sources
- multimedia transcripts
- ongoing research and development

non-lawyers
- a legal 'portal'
- legal guidance systems
- a more participative legislative process
- promulgation
- case tracking
- enhanced voluntary services
- public administration systems
- multidisciplinary systems and services
- the law embedded in systems generally

lawyers and judges specifically
- online shared spaces for all matters
- widespread institutional memories
- sentencing systems
- a new international dimension
- virtual legal teams
- automated document assembly
- legal diagnostic systems
- virtual legal libraries
- judicial decisions on the Internet
- new roles for lawyers
- other providers of legal services
- distance legal learning
- online legal discussions

the court system specifically
- unified case management
- electronic transcription
- virtual hearings
- standards for litigation support systems
- various applications of IT in the courtroom

This categorization into four major groups is a pragmatic one. There can be no doubt that the categories overlap and that some possibilities could be put under two or more headings. Nonetheless, the general thrust should be clear. Note too that for many jurisdictions these are not future possibilities but current realities. A brief outline of each possibility is sketched below.

Justice workers generally

For those who work in the justice system generally, a wide range of far-reaching changes are possible.

A national legal network

With many hundreds of thousands of users, a secure, confidential, reliable, private (virtual) legal network may be developed, linking together everyone who works in the English justice system. This would be a communications infrastructure not just for conveying conventional messages and documents but also to carry videoconferencing, databases, bundles of document images, video recordings, and voice messaging as well. The network would link all users to one another, whether in court, chambers, law offices, at home, travelling and so forth. Much of the business of the courts and of legal practitioners would be carried on this network and it would be accessible both by physical connections and by wireless technology too.

Virtual hearings and meetings

Videoconferencing and telecommunications (across the Internet within a few years) might enable the conduct of certain court hearings and other legally oriented meetings without all the parties needing to assemble in the one physical location. (A virtual meeting or hearing is one where people do actually not meet face to face but IT reproduces many of the features of such physical meetings.) As legal standards and procedures emerge, virtual hearings and meetings could come to play a major role in the justice system, not only displacing some forums of today but also enabling more frequent and greatly improved communication where hitherto face-to-face meetings have not been feasible. In turn, this may enable a reduction in the number of court buildings across the country.

Multimedia and hypertext-based legal bundles

In due course, the preferred and perhaps required format for the lodging of documents in the courts or the exchange of documents amongst parties to a dispute or agreement could be in electronic form in accordance with some pre-specified formats or standards. Electronic document bundles would thus be created and supplemented as they pass through each stage in a commercial or judicial process. Whereas document bundles of today come in the form of discrete and invariably printed documents, with occasional internal cross-references which readers themselves have to pursue while reading, document bundles in the future will be electronically linked to one another (using technology such as hypertext), so that users will navigate around electronic bundles as though they were single sets of information. And the information itself will no longer simply be text based but will be presented using other media as well, including video, images, sound, and animation. Thus, an electronic bundle of legal documents will be more usable and more expressive than their paper counterparts of today.

Legislation on the Internet

The electronic publication of all primary and subordinate legislation could easily be required to coincide with the conventional publication of these materials in print and paper. Whether and how these materials are consolidated, cross-referenced to one another (in the manner of hypertext), linked to commentaries and indeed charged for will clearly be a matter for further debate.

Searching for legal sources

Advanced searching techniques and 'intelligent agents' would help to overcome the problems arising now from an ever-burgeoning body of legal source material. Where today those who are looking for legal information or guidance must actively search through materials, technologies of the future (the 'smarter' systems discussed earlier) will greatly assist in this process, guiding users to all but only information that is relevant for their purposes. And in due course, new legal developments which bear on an individual's or an organization's activities will automatically be brought to their attention, even in advance of the users being aware of the need for such input.

Multimedia transcripts

With technologies available to capture and later provide information in multimedia format, multimedia transcripts—of meetings and hearings—could be available, thus providing a record not just in textual form, but with accompanying sound and video as well, for example.

Ongoing research and development

Just as has always been the case in many hi-tech industries, research and development initiatives will become far more important in the legal world, not just for commercial organizations seeking to achieve competitive advantage and good practice in their sectors but also in government and in the court system as well, where it will be increasingly important for IT to be (and be seen to be) used efficiently, productively, and competitively too (in international terms).

Non-lawyers

More radically still, existing and emerging technologies could transform the ways in which non-lawyers are guided by the law and interact with the legal system.

A legal 'portal'

This could be a master web site or gateway for all legal services in the country—the definitive, first port of call for anyone who has a legal problem or worry. From this portal, there would be links to all appropriate legal sites which would be authorized, authenticated and regulated. For example, users might find directories of voluntary legal services and law firms, guidance on using the courts as well as links to professional bodies and to primary source materials. Ideally, the links and guidance would not be listed under conventional legal classifications but be oriented towards real-life events (for example, wanting to move house, recover a debt, or complain about a lawyer).

Legal guidance systems

Alongside all sorts of other types of information, legal guidance, legal knowledge, legal expertise, and legal experience can be available on Internet, offering non-lawyers (individuals and organizations, for social and business purposes) access to structured, practical guidance on legal affairs. These systems, a central theme of this book and of *The Future of Law*, can vary in complexity, from electronic checklists through automated document assembly systems to diagnostic expert systems (see Part III). While they may not replace conventional legal services, such systems would provide affordable, easy access to legal guidance where this may have been unaffordable or impractical in the past. These systems can offer guidance both on substantive legal matters, as well on legal processes (for example how to pursue a claim).

A more participative legislative process

Possibilities for far wider participation in the legislative process may also be enabled through general access to the electronic information infrastructure. Actual or exploratory voting will be possible as will improved opportunities for citizens to participate (perhaps through bulletin boards or online discussions) in discussions about issues before Parliament or even on draft bills. Today's form of representative parliamentary democracy is a function of a print-based society dominated by face-to-face interaction. In an information society, dominated by online interpersonal communication, expression of opinion and the exercise of voting rights may come to be mediated through IT.

Promulgation

It is entirely foreseeable that emerging technologies could enable the majority of citizens to be notified of relevant new laws (and changes in old law, too). In non-technical terms, this would involve users articulating profiles of their social and business interests. At the same time, legal information service providers would ensure that developments in the law would also be pro-filed and categorized and there would be mechanisms for automatic notifi-cation to these users where there were matches or partial matches between their profiles and the categorizations of the new legal developments. For businesses, such an information service would be invaluable and the rev-enue which could be secured from such a business service could perhaps give a low- or no-cost service of a similar sort for individual citizens.

Case tracking

Where case tracking and case management systems in the past have been the exclusive province of court administrators, and more recent proposals for reform suggest their extension to judges and lawyers as well, access to information about the status of particular cases (both civil and criminal) may be extended still further, beyond the court system and legal profession to pri-vate individuals and organizations who have legitimate interests in the progress of their own cases. This could even be achieved across the Internet directly from the homes of users.

Enhanced voluntary services

With a full-scale national legal network in place, voluntary legal organiza-tions may have easier and more extensive access to the experience and skills of legal practitioners across the country. Where in the past the input of lawyers on a *pro bono* basis has often depended on their physical presence at some location beyond their offices, some guidance may, in the future, be deliverable—directly or indirectly—through technology (for example, video-conferencing, legal guidance systems, electronic mail and bulletin boards). At the same time, the voluntary advice workers would be able to identify potential advisers in a more structured and coherent way, using the director-ies that will be available on the restricted, national legal network. Equally, advice workers can be provided with e-mail links to lawyers who have vol-unteered their help.

Public administration systems

Routine public administration and related form filling may also be enabled and undertaken electronically. The submission of tax returns and the grant-ing of licences, for example, will be possible online, as will the payment of social security and benefit claims and the provision of grants. With all such services, there could be focused guidance available for users with immediate assessment, explanation, and payment, where appropriate. Such public administration systems will extend to areas as diverse as obtaining pass-ports, driving and television licences (all probably in the form of smart cards) as well as numerous business-oriented pieces of administration, including the many formal requirements of disclosure and management imposed on those running companies.

The much vaunted 'one-stop shop' for the delivery of electronic government services will in due course extend to legal services and the justice system generally, although most thinking so far about one-stop shops has been focused rather restrictedly on physical locations. Within a few years, with near universal access to the Internet, it will be more appropriate to think of 'single points of access', most of which could be electronic and in the home.

Multidisciplinary systems and services

For non-lawyers, the availability of legal guidance and information in isolation will come to be seen as rather anomalous. The domestic user, while online, will gradually expect legal information to be bundled with other relevant information (integrated, say, with consumer or leisure or health information), while business users will expect and require the guidance they receive to be oriented towards the problems or projects with which they are involved rather than the underlying, individual, legal disciplines. Thus, legal guidance systems will either operate alongside or be fully integrated, as multi-disciplinary systems, with other guidance systems, extending into areas such as accountancy, banking, and business and management consultancy.

The law embedded in systems generally

Using expert systems techniques, it may be possible to develop diagnostic systems which will function alongside project management, document management, and even with process control systems, such that these expert systems will be able constantly to monitor the activities to which the other systems refer and will in turn be able to recognize combinations of circum-stances which raise legal questions or which require legal precautions. Thus computer systems will in due course themselves be able to identify the legal implications of the tasks they themselves are performing and even to recom-mend or take remedial action.

Lawyers and judges specifically

Turning now to lawyers and judges more specifically, once more a vast array of possible developments can be anticipated.

Online shared spaces for all matters

Every legal matter (dispute, deal, or other advisory work) can have its own online presence, so that documents and other relevant information are gathered in one easily accessible location for lawyers, clients, and other interested parties. In practice, there will no doubt be numerous shared spaces for each matter—for example, some for private use for client and lawyer only, others perhaps for public access.

Widespread institutional memories

Within organizations and bodies across the justice system, a number of enabling techniques (for example, Intranet technologies) might encourage and enable the establishment of substantial internal know-how systems, which could capture the internal experience of those who work within organizations and make that information more widely available internally and more easily accessible too. Thus, the know-how that is often locked in the heads of specialists or hidden in filing cabinets will become a widely used internal information resource. For users (who may be judges or legal practitioners), this resource would also be integrated with other external information services, so that, in searching for information, systems will help users simultaneously to look within and beyond their organizations for relevant material. Users may thus come to search a combination of their institutional memories and external virtual legal libraries (another possible development for lawyers and judges specifically, discussed later in this section).

Sentencing systems

In the criminal arena, considerable research and development work has already been undertaken around the world in the field of sentencing information systems. Some systems are able simply to provide judges with a convenient body of legal, factual, and statistical information, while others can go much further and are able to make specific suggestions as to sentences, based on the knowledge and data built within them.[3]

A new international dimension

With a global information infrastructure in place, it will be far easier than ever before for lawyers to collaborate and maintain contact on a genuinely international basis. Judges, legal practitioners, and academics as well, will be

---

[3] A special issue of the *International Journal of Law and Information Technology* (Vol. 6, No. 2, Summer 1998) is devoted entirely to judicial sentencing support systems.

able to establish and maintain regular dialogue with counterparts around the world as easily as communicating with colleagues in the same building. International collaboration will also be possible, through groupware, intranet technologies and videoconferencing.

At the same time, the international 'law of cyberspace', it is widely expected, will gradually bring a common (but not exhaustive) body of legal scholarship and legal practice to all jurisdictions. There are already strong (but not overwhelming) arguments for treating the law of cyberspace as a jurisdiction in its own right. From this might follow far greater collaboration and overlap between and amongst lawyers across the globe.

Virtual legal teams

With the availability of groupware, intranet techniques, videoconferencing and telecommunications generally, it will no longer be necessary for lawyers and judges to be physically co-located at all times in order for them to work together on the same case. Instead, these technologies may bring practitioners (and judges as well, especially in relation to case management) under the one virtual roof, enabling effective, practical collaboration amongst individuals who may even be thousands of miles apart.

Large law firms, in turn, may find that they have new competition in the shape of virtual law firms—these might be collaborative entities, established on a project basis, where smaller firms will be able to work together effectively, combining their talents and attaining a size of workforce which was simply not possible in the past. (Again the use of 'virtual' is intended to convey the idea that IT is bringing people together to work as though they were on one team in one physical location.)

Automated document assembly

A great deal of legal work is devoted to the drafting of legal documents. To some extent, and certainly for routine documents, this task can now be supported or even undertaken by what are known as automated document assembly or document generation systems. In operation, such systems ask their users questions, the responses to which insert or delete templates or parts of templates which have previously been set up by legal specialists. The templates are fixed portions of text together with precise instructions as to when given extracts should be used. In reliance on the users' input, the system will automatically generate a customized and polished document based on its knowledge of how its standard text should be used. Document assembly systems could be used not only to help lawyers and judges create their own documentation but also directly by consumers in supporting the drafting of far more legally reliable material than was possible in the past.

Legal diagnostic systems

This type of system, often based on rule-based expert systems technology, can provide specific answers to given problems. After an interactive consultation which helps clarify and classify the facts of a particular cases, these systems may be able to analyse the details and then draw conclusions or make recommendations. In many ways, these systems are analogous to the medical diagnostic systems which offer diagnoses on the strength of symptoms presented to them. Legal diagnostic systems have already been developed which can make recommendations on sentencing, bail decisions, quantum, and many other areas of common law, legislation and regulation. While they are often thought to be of greatest use to non-lawyers, in fact they may be invaluable for legally qualified individuals when faced with problems beyond their areas of expertise. In such circumstances, they can prompt the lawyers to focus on the key issues and help ensure uniformity of approach.

Virtual legal libraries

For use across the legal profession (and even beyond), it will be possible to bring together massive amounts of primary and secondary legal source materials (in conventional and multimedia format) into widely accessible virtual legal libraries. These collections would not only be vast in scope but would have sophisticated front-ends, filters, search facilities and other tools to guide users quickly and easily to all but only the materials they would need at any point in time. These facilities could be available to the academic and practising branches of the profession as well as to judges.

Judicial decisions on the Internet

As judges increasingly prepare their own judgments using word processors (perhaps through voice recognition technology) and so in machine readable form, it should be but a short final step to make these decisions widely available on the Internet. Indeed, all House of Lords' judgments in the UK and decisions from various other courts now appear on the Internet very soon after the judge has disposed of the case. This process of downloading judicial decisions could easily be automated, thereby making case reports immediately available across the legal profession and far more effectively within the judiciary as well. The judges themselves may choose in due course to supplement judgments downloaded in this way with their own commentary, indicating the significance of their cases and perhaps keywords which characterize each and every decision. This additional information and ever more sophisticated searching techniques will meet the concern that this automated downloading might lead to an unmanageable number of reported decisions.

New roles for lawyers

As legal guidance and other forms of legal information come to be widely available and easily accessible on the Internet and the World Wide Web, at least two new roles emerge for lawyers. On the one hand, there will be the new discipline of what I call 'legal information engineering': this is the job of reorganizing and presenting legal information in a form that can be of direct, practical use to non-lawyers; and this is a job which requires a blend of substantive legal knowledge together with an ability to break down complex legal topics and concepts into lay terms.

At the same time, and secondly, there will be a need for some kind of system of certification of the information and services which become available—non-lawyers will want some comfort and assurance that the systems upon which they are relying (and clearly there are profound liability issues here) have indeed been developed by appropriately qualified lawyers and some process of certification will probably be desirable. Once standards for the evaluation of services have been developed, there will be considerable work involved in reviewing new offerings as they are brought onto the Intranet. It may be that the professional bodies will have a major role to play here as well.

Other providers of legal services

As legal information and guidance becomes available on the global information infrastructure, many individuals and organizations beyond the legal profession are likely to want to compete in this marketplace and provide legal and quasi-legal services themselves. Accountancy firms, telecommunications providers, legal publishers, and electronic publishers are likely to be the main competitors, either working in isolation or perhaps in conjunction with lawyers.

Distance legal learning

Legal education will be transformed through the availability of online, interactive, multimedia systems, which will enable judges, lawyers, and students to learn and be trained remotely; and at times that suit their diaries. Today's techniques of electronic law tutorials, computer-based law 'courseware', computer-assisted learning and computer-assisted instruction will combine with telecommunications technology to provide distance legal learning. Already, Strathclyde University offers an Ll M in information technology and telecommunications law to students all over the world, who are given remote access to huge quantities of teaching material and are invited to participate in online group tutorials. While this is text-based today, future systems will be multimedia, so that, for instance, video recordings of trials or the sound of oral advocacy will be available online.

Online legal discussions

With all participants in the justice system able to communicate with one another electronically, this may support not just the formal conduct of business but could also greatly improve informal discussion and interaction. With bulletin board facilities, and the availability of online discussion services, interest groups and small communities may be established, attracting and bringing together, nationally and internationally, lawyers with shared interests in particular topics. Problems, new developments, interesting, and even obscure points of law and procedure will become the focus of IT-mediated discussion, offering users a far wider community within which to communicate; and there might well be a welcome immediacy and greater stimulation and enjoyment thorough this communication medium as well.

The court system specifically

As for the court system, the range of possible developments are similarly wide and radical.

Unified case management

With the introduction of an agreed standard specification for case management systems, the individual systems in operation across the country could interface and operate alongside one another and function as though they were one, single system. Judges, legal advisers, administrators, and parties themselves would be able to track the progress of any case (with appropriate security precautions) through one single system and one point of access. The documentation relating to each case would also be attached to the electronic record and so also accessible for appropriate users. And as cases progress from one court to another, they would be transferred as instantaneously and effortlessly as electronic case records.

Electronic transcription

With the advent of speaker-independent, continuous speech, large vocabu-lary, voice recognition systems (see my earlier discussion in this chapter of 'greater usability'), today's techniques for recording and transcribing—including shorthand writing, tape-recording and even computer-assisted real time transcription—may no longer be needed. Thus, proceedings in court may instantaneously, and in real time, be captured in electronic form, thereby revolutionizing court reporting. So too with meetings and, for exam-ple, the taking of witness statements. Voice recognition technology could immediately deliver polished transcripts, in printed or electronic form.

Virtual hearings

Using the Internet, parties may be able to conduct a variety of dispute reso-lution processes on an online basis. These can vary from the use of video-conferencing to replicate current practice through to entirely new processes such as submitting written pleadings for resolution by means of e-mail reply by some agreed neutral; through online negotiation of financial settlements by secret bidding; through to more structured, traditional adjudication mediated by IT without the need for parties to congregate together in one physical space.

Standards for litigation support systems

As ever more powerful document management systems and electronic com-munication systems operate together, the document loads for litigation will increasingly be stored, managed and distributed around the justice system in electronic form. Whereas there are currently many different approaches and formats used in litigation support, it would be possible to establish and even require that these systems correspond to a set of standards and for-mats, which could be articulated in a number of protocols appropriate for different classes of case or court (following the example of the ORSA (now the TeCSA) Protocol, the standards originally set by the Official Referees' Solicitors' Association in England—see Chapter 11).

Various applications of IT in the courtroom

On those occasions in the future where dedicated courtrooms are used for the hearing of cases, as distinct from virtual courts as discussed elsewhere, IT will come to play an ever more dominant role. With voice recognition technology capturing the proceedings, judges will no longer need to write notes by hand or type on their own machines; but instead may annotate and comment upon the text as it appears before them (in the manner of real time transcription of today).

There could be immediate access from the courtroom to all primary and secondary source material, entire document sets may be made easily accessible in the court with individual pages capable of presentation on all participants' screens, some evidence may be taken remotely by video-linking, and computer and video simulations, or even virtual reality, could be deployed in the presentation of evidence. Oral evidence might be supplemented by multimedia techniques which could take the court graphically through the evidence and legal arguments, while case management systems may be immediately to hand enabling decisions or directions to be implemented on the spot, with relevant documentation directed electronically to all relevant parties and bodies across the justice system.

In the courts, as elsewhere, the possibilities are limited more by the creativity and entrepreneurial flair of decision-makers than by the capabilities of emerging technologies.

6

A Response to Critics[1]

To my ongoing surprise, my book, *The Future of Law*,[2] has generated considerable interest and commentary since its original publication in 1996. Until recently, I am pleased to say that I managed to hold fast against the almost irresistible temptation to switch on my machine and dash off a quick retort to each and every commentary that appeared.

However, when I read a draft of Professor Ed Greenebaum's review article,[3] I regarded it as rather different from others that I had seen, because it gathered together in one place the most common criticisms of my book, added a few more, and did so in much more detail and with greater rigour than most others before him had attempted. Accordingly, I broke with my self-imposed tradition and put together this brief defence of my position not only as a reply to Professor Greenebaum but as a more generic retort to critics at large.

For the purposes of this exercise, I did not seek to address all the objections that Professor Greenebaum raised. Instead, I selected but two issues, each of which, it still seems to me, is central to *The Future of Law* and indeed fundamental for society more generally. The first is whether or not the changes

---

[1] This chapter is a revised version of an article first published in (1999) 6 *International Journal of the Legal Profession* 2: 208. It explores some of the same themes discussed in Chapter 3.

[2] Oxford: Oxford University Press, 1996. (References in this chapter are to the revised paperback edition published in 1998.)

[3] Edwin H. Greenebaum, 'Is the Medium the Message? A Discussion of Susskind's *The Future of Law*' (1999) 6 *International Journal of the Legal Profession* 2: 197.

that I predict IT will bring to the law will result in a shift in paradigm. The second issue is the viability and utility of online legal guidance systems.

A Shift in Legal Paradigm?

Turning first of all to the question of paradigm shift, Professor Greenebaum rightly notes in this connection that I predict massive change. Here is what I say (I hope I will be forgiven for quoting myself so liberally in this chapter):

I borrow the term 'paradigm' from the philosophy of science where it is used to refer, approximately, to the currently accepted view of the world and to the prevailing mind-set and accepted background assumptions in a particular field. When there is a fundamental change in these assumptions and a discipline is then regarded in an entirely new light, there is said to be a 'shift in paradigm'. One of the clearest illustrations of such a shift in science was when Einsteinian theory superseded the Newtonian model in physics.

At the heart of this book is the suggestion that we are on the brink of a shift in legal paradigm, a revolution in law, after which many of the current features of contemporary legal systems which we now take for granted will be displaced by a new set of underlying premises and presuppositions. Much of the law will be radically different.[4]

Professor Greenebaum disagrees, claiming that 'I have seen little evidence that the conception of law practice that informs work in my firms has changed in any fundamental way'[5] and summarizing his position in the following terms: 'changes in legal practice *occurring as a function of IT development* are not paradigmatic.'[6]

I have read his paper carefully and believe we are adrift in this context in two main dimensions: on timescales and on the scope of the projected changes.

Looking, first of all, at the question of timescales, Professor Greenebaum seems throughout his article to focus on changes that have already occurred or are poised to take place. When he says, for example, in the quotation above, that he has seen little evidence of fundamental change then that comes as no surprise to me whatsoever. It is early days in the huge shift that I project. We are at the very beginning of a transition, so that I would not expect the major upheaval to have occurred. I was at pains in writing *The Future of Law* to stress this very point. In the introduction, for example, I say

---

[4] *The Future of Law*, n. 2 above, p. 41.   [5] Greenebaum, n. 3 above, p. 198.
[6] ibid., p. 199 (emphasis in original).

that 'My general feel is that the major shift in a paradigm which I project will come about over the next 20 years or so; with innumerable advances and changes along the way.'[7]

A little later, in Chapter Three, I go on to say: 'I must stress that this vision of a transformed legal service on the strength of knowledge processing is not one which is likely to be realized in the next few years.'[8] I make this claim plainly because, as Professor Greenebaum notes, I believe that IT has some way to travel yet before it can deliver the 'knowledge processing' capabilities that are needed. This is the essence of what I term 'The Technology Lag':

Despite the burgeoning performance of IT, the shift in paradigm cannot be complete until *The Technology Lag* is no more. Much of what is said here, therefore, is premised on great advances in knowledge processing as a counterbalance to the great strides already made in data processing.[9]

So as to leave readers in no doubt that the paradigm shift is some way off, in the final chapter of the book I say once more:

I have argued again and again that this shift in legal paradigm can and will only happen when we emerge from the transitional confusion in which we find ourselves into the fully fledged IT-based information society. Only then will *The Technology Lag* be overcome and will our capacity to manage legal information be more than equal to our ability to create and disseminate it.[10]

Accordingly, I feel strongly that my hypothesis about a paradigm shift is surely not falsified by the fact that the changes I predict have not yet come about. It is simply far too soon to be able to tell. I would, of course, be happy to return to these pages in the future to review progress but it might be best to wait for about 15 years or so!

Turning now to the scope of the changes that I anticipate, this is the second issue concerning legal paradigms over which Professor Greenebaum and I seem to disagree. Where Professor Greenebaum focuses very largely on 'legal practice' (he uses the phrase again and again), my book goes much, *much* wider than that and looks to changes in legal process, in the administration of justice, and in the very way in which the law operates, and is regarded, in society.

Professor Greenebaum suggests that 'It is the new relations between lawyers and clients resulting from this shift that will constitute the new paradigm of legal practice'.[11] I cannot emphasize strongly enough that this does

---

[7] *The Future of Law*, n. 2 above, p. 7. Given that this passage was written about five years ago, I would now (in mid-2000) change the 20 years to 15 years.

[8] ibid., p. 96.   [9] ibid., p. 97.   [10] ibid., p. 285.

[11] Greenebaum, n. 3 above, p. 199.

not capture my position sufficiently. It is much too limited. Of course, I discuss and expect considerable changes in the working practices of lawyers and much of my book is devoted to that subject. But that of itself will not bring about any shift in paradigm. My position is stated as follows:

My fundamental claim is that IT will enable and help bring about a shift in paradigm of legal service, a fundamental change from a service that is substantially advisory in nature today to one which will become one of many information services in the IT-based information society of the future. In turn, basic aspects of the legal process and the administration of justice will also alter radically.[12]

We live in a fascinating time, as we move from our print-based industrial society into an IT-based information age. Our communication systems and patterns of communication are changing radically, as are our information systems and methods of packaging and delivering information. In this context, and in the context of the Internet coming to play such a prevalent part in all of our lives, I simply cannot believe that legal service and legal process will remain unchanged.

And so, in the final chapter of the book, I summarize the shift in legal paradigm that I expect. I do so in tabular form, reproduced here as Figure 6.1.[13]

This is not the place to explain each element of the table[14] but I hope it gives readers a flavour of the scope of my claims and the boundaries of the new paradigm. It may help further by revisiting the final page of *The Future of Law*, where I concluded by saying:

legal practice and the administration of justice will no longer be dominated by print and paper in tomorrow's legal paradigm. Instead, legal systems of the information society will evolve rapidly under the considerable influence of ever more powerful information technologies. We will no longer suffer from the excessive quantity and complexity of legal material. There will be mechanisms in place to give everyone fair warning of the existence of new law and changes in old. Legal risks will be managed in advance of problems occurring and so dispute pre-emption rather than dispute resolution will be the order of the day. Our law will thus become far more fully integrated with our domestic, social, and business lives.[15]

Professor Greenebaum does not do justice to the scope of these claims and to the detailed underlying jurisprudential argument. He focuses on what lawyers do today and he talks also of 'DIY law' (see later), but he does not lay out and deal with all the elements of the shift that is my concern. I agree that improving legal practice by the judicious use of IT and enabling a bit more 'DIY law' of the kind we have today does not constitute a shift in paradigm.

---

[12] *The Future of Law*, n. 2 above, p. 97.
[14] For a more detailed discussion, see Chapter 3.
[13] ibid., p. 286 (Figure 8.1).
[15] *The Future of Law*, n. 2 above, p. 292.

Today's Legal Paradigm	Tomorrow's Legal Paradigm
Legal Service	**Legal Service**
advisory service	information service
one-to-one	one-to-many
reactive service	proactive service
time-based billing	commodity pricing
restrictive	empowering
defensive	pragmatic
legal focus	business focus
Legal Process	**Legal Process**
legal problem solving	legal risk management
dispute resolution	dispute pre-emption
publication of law	promulgation of law
a dedicated legal profession	legal specialists and information engineers
print-based	IT-based legal systems

Figure 6.1 The Shift in Legal Paradigm

But I am saying far more. I am saying that online legal guidance systems and other Internet-based facilities (immeasurably more sophisticated than today's 'DIY law') will come to be the dominant means by which legal help is imparted. Lawyers will no longer occupy centre stage in dispensing legal assistance; and legal information systems will help in the avoidance of disputes in the first place. I am also suggesting huge changes in our legislative and judicial processes, not just some streamlining of the work of lawyers.

I hint here at just a few of the really substantial changes that my book discusses. Leaving aside the issue of timescales as discussed above, I believe Professor Greenebaum would only have succeeded in refuting my claim about a likely shift in legal paradigm if he had systematically assessed each element of my table together with the extended arguments supporting each; and then justified in that far broader context his assertion that 'Susskind's paradigm is not new'.[16] My feeling was and is that if the changes I project do indeed come to pass then our legal world will be so fundamentally different,

---

[16] Greenebaum, n. 3 above, p. 205.

and the way in which non-lawyers regard the law and legal process will be so radically unlike their views today, that we can then meaningfully say, in the sense in which the originator of the term, Thomas Kuhn, conceived the notion, that there will indeed have been a shift in legal paradigm.[17]

Online Legal Guidance Systems

The second major issue raised by Professor Greenebaum to which I would like to respond is the viability and utility of online legal guidance systems— broadly Internet-based services that provide legal help to non-lawyers without the direct involvement of legal practitioners.

At one stage, Professor Greenebaum comments that 'As I was reading *The Future of Law*, I repeatedly said to myself, "This is about do-it-yourself law" '.[18] In large part, I agree, in that what I have in mind is that non-lawyers themselves will frequently be able to find out, via online guidance systems, about their legal entitlements and obligations and they will be able to pursue legal remedies without needing to instruct lawyers. But the emerging and future systems that I discuss are of a different order of sophistication and utility as compared with, say, the legal manuals and information packs of today. For example, expert diagnostic systems, intelligent checklists, state-of-the-art document assembly systems and intelligent agents (as explained in *The Future of Law*) have no real analogies in the world of print and paper. When such facilities become commonplace for non-lawyers in the wired world, then DIY law will no longer be the useful but essentially peripheral resource that it is today. Instead, it will, I argue, be at the heart of the administration of law in society.

Building on the DIY law theme, Professor Greenebaum later claims that 'Basically, Susskind's paradigm is not new. DIY and unlicensed legal support has always competed with authorized practice'.[19] I have already addressed the point about whether or not the paradigm is new. What concerns me now is the suggestion that DIY law *competes* with 'authorized' practice. This is important for Professor Greenebaum because he argues that conventional legal service is better in a number of ways than online legal guidance systems can be. For example, he spends some considerable time showing how

---

[17] See *The Structure of Scientific Revolutions* (Chicago: University of Chicago Press, 1970).
[18] Greenebaum, n. 3 above, p. 199.   [19] ibid., p. 205.

lawyers add value to transactions in ways he doubts that online systems can.[20]

On another occasion, I might challenge Professor Greenebaum's analysis and his implicit views on the limitations of computer systems, but for current purposes such debate, and much of Professor Greenebaum's article, miss one of the main points about my book and that is my notion of there being a 'latent legal market'. In the preface to the revised paperback edition of my book, I explain this concept as follows:

Latent legal markets will be liberated by IT. These are the vast markets populated by those many millions of people who require legal help today but are deterred from obtaining it because it is too costly, complex or inconvenient. And these latent legal markets are as needy in large corporations as they are in society generally—citizens and business concerns everywhere face substantial legal risks today which they have no realistic hope of recognizing and controlling.[21]

Legal guidance will therefore become one of countless sorts of information available on the Internet. The law will no longer be the exclusive province of lawyers. It is important to be clear, however, about the nature of the help that I suggest will be online:

The guidance made available on the information highway will more closely resemble the kind of practical pointers that a lawyer might currently pass along to a friend: a short list of key points and reminders; maybe a few pieces of standard text; and perhaps an indication of some relevant, common pitfalls. From orienting a consumer dissatisfied with some purchase to briefing a chief executive on the basics of some deal, the help on offer will tend to be punchy, practical and free of legal jargon.[22]

I am suggesting, therefore, that online legal guidance will be different from conventional one-to-one consultative legal service in tone, scope and level of generality. I make it absolutely clear that I do not always see this as a rival or competitor to conventional service. Instead, and this is pivotal, I see this guidance as being a marvellous additional resource for use on these numerous occasions when formal legal help is not available. Thus, I say:

Such desert island guidelines may be no substitute for the formal advice of legal specialists provided in the time-honoured, consultative fashion, but they will be an immeasurable improvement over having no access to legal help whatsoever, which is the regrettable state in which so many now find themselves.[23]

---

[20] In passing, I should say that his analysis of transaction-based work does little to clarify the ways in which lawyers add value in contentious or advisory work, which are the other two main types of conventional legal service.

[21] *The Future of Law*, n. 2 above, pp. x–xi.   [22] ibid., p. x.   [23] ibid., p. x.

And, I go on:

It is imperative that I am not interpreted as suggesting that informal legal guidance systems will deliver a better service than conventional advisers acting in traditional, one-to-one advisory fashion. Rather, my claim about the utility of legal guidance systems must be assessed in the context of the latent legal market, where the choice is not between human advisers and IT-based guidance systems. The choice there is between the system and nothing at all—and I for one would prefer to have at my fingertips the guidance that lawyers give to their friends and family than have nothing at all.[24]

Accordingly, a significant portion of Professor Greenebaum's critique is simply not in point. In crude summary, he believes that online legal guidance systems fail to encapsulate and make available much of the value that lawyers can add; whereas I am suggesting, for the most part, that online legal guidance is way better than nothing when lawyers are not able to offer help and counsel.

I would have been inclined to suggest that our views in this connection are potentially compatible, but in one place Professor Greenebaum seems to be doubting the generic applicability and appropriateness of DIY law, in which context he cites comments of his 'informants' on its lack of suitability for CAB (Citizens' Advice Bureaux) clients.[25] I remain of the view, however, that the potential social benefits of online legal guidance systems comfortably outweighs the problems that might result from their shortcomings. Significantly, and contrary to the intimations of Professor Greenebaum's informants, my view seems to be shared by a whole body of advice workers (including many involved with the CAB), as is amply demonstrated by their own presence on and commitment to the World Wide Web.[26] Further, my position is also fortified by the recent government White Paper, entitled 'Modernising Government', in which ambitious targets are set for the electronic delivery of government services—by 2008, it is intended that *all* government service is deliverable electronically (unless there are policy or operational reasons for not doing so).[27]

[24] ibid., p. xlix.

[25] See footnote 24 of Professor Greenebaum's article, n. 3 above, pp. 215–16.

[26] See, e.g., www.nacab.org.uk and www.lawcentres.org.uk and www.lasa.org.uk

[27] *Modernising Government* (Cm 4310, March 1999). This target date has since been brought forward: in the UK government's published strategy for information age government, *e-government* (London: Central IT Unit, April 2000), it is said in the foreword: 'electronic access to government services will become increasingly important to citizens and by 2005 we plan to have all of our services available in this way.' www.citu.gov.uk/iagc/estrategy/foreword.htm.

Conclusion

To bring my response to a close, I would like to focus on what, for me, is the most important social issue of all. I could quote again from *The Future of Law* and my analysis of the 'alienation' of the law and my claims about the 'pressurized legal marketplace' but I prefer to keep it simpler and take it beyond the realms of academic debate.

One reality of modern societies is that there are not enough lawyers and public legal services (including courts) to go round. It is simply not possible (affordable or practicable) for each and every citizen and business to have conventional, legal advice on tap. Despite political protestations to the contrary across the globe, the rich and the (state-supported) poor still enjoy greater access to justice than the overwhelming majority. Legal needs go unmet all the time. I take the view that this is scandalous and one of the aims of my work over the last 20 years or so is to find other methods of providing legal help and ensuring justice.

I think that fundamentally different techniques are needed and they are needed urgently because the old system (traditional lawyers, textbooks, courts, voluntary legal services, and so forth) is strained to its limits and cannot provide the answer. I believe that the Internet can. It may deliver a rougher and readier legal service but, as I have said, that should be far better than no access to justice at all. I do not share Professor Greenebaum's rather unsupported assertion that my approach 'is likely to widen rather than narrow the gap between legal haves and have nots'.[28] Indeed, I would bet that more people (of all social classes) will have access to the Internet (and so to the law, on my theory) in five years' time than have access to justice today.

---

[28] Greenebaum, n. 3 above, p. 207.

Part III

Expert Systems in Law

7

An Introduction to Expert Systems in Law[1]

In the 1980s, there was great excitement in the academic community about the potential of expert systems technology for the law. Today, I sometimes hear critics of the field argue that the work conducted during that period was misconceived and yielded no findings of relevance. In support of this conclusion, it is often suggested that there have been very few commercial successes in the field.

I take a different view, as outlined in the Preface to this book. I believe that the early work—the failures and the successes—can guide us today in our work on legal knowledge management and online legal services. I accept that many of the enabling technologies that were investigated and prototyped in the 1980s have not directly borne fruit although there have been several major successes in document assembly and regulatory diagnostics.[2] I also accept that we were naïve about the business models that might best underlie the exploitation of these systems—we saw expert systems as internal efficiency tools and neglected their potential for packaging legal knowledge in new ways (in the terms of Chapter 1, we regarded expert systems as belonging to the bottom-right quadrant only and failed to see how they might fit

[1] This chapter was originally published as 'Artificial Intelligence, Expert Systems and Law' (1990) *Denning Law Journal* 105, an article based on an earlier report submitted to the Council of Europe in January 1990, entitled *Systems Based on Artificial Intelligence in the Legal Field*.

[2] See, e.g., the Blue Flag products of Linklaters, at www.blueflag.com, some of which rely on rule-based document assembly techniques; and www.softlaw.com.au for impressive regulatory applications.

into the top-right). And I further concede that building these systems was, frankly, more difficult than many of us thought.

However, notwithstanding these concessions, I strongly believe that a wider view of that early work must be taken—if it is accepted, as I always argued, that the main purpose of expert systems was to make scarce expertise and knowledge more widely available and more easily accessible, then this spirit is surely more alive today (in mid-2000) than ever before. Spreading knowledge is what the World Wide Web generally, and online legal services more particularly, is all about.

I believe a great deal of the *thinking* that went on in the 1980s is of the utmost relevance today. It may be that the systems developed then are themselves no longer relevant, but the underlying conceptual challenges have barely changed. I can point to innumerable, contemporary document assembly projects, legal diagnostic initiatives, online consultation services and many others which are confronting the same issues as researchers tackled in the 1980s.

With that in mind, in this and the following three chapters, I have reproduced, with very little alteration, past publications that I am convinced are relevant for the growing number of individuals and organizations that are working today on legal knowledge management and online legal services. The key issues are the same, even if the underlying, enabling technologies have changed.

This chapter introduces and explains the various branches of the field of 'artificial intelligence and law', with particular focus on expert systems in law. It offers a brief history of the early years of work in the field, within both Europe and the rest of the world; and, on a practical level, considers the feasibility and the benefits of these systems as well as the problems to which they give rise. Finally, the chapter points to the keys to successful development.

1. Artificial Intelligence and the Law

Artificial Intelligence (AI) is concerned with the design, development, and implementation of computer systems that can perform tasks and solve problems of a sort for which human intelligence is normally thought to be required. For example, AI programs have been written to understand the spoken word, to translate from one language into another, and to recognize images and objects in the physical world.

Artificial intelligence as applied in the legal field can be subdivided into two categories: expert systems and knowledge-based systems on the one hand; and enhancements to legal information retrieval systems on the other.

Expert Systems and knowledge-based systems

The broadly agreed goal of workers in the fields of expert systems and knowledge-based systems is to use computer technology to make scarce expertise and knowledge more widely available and easily accessible. Expert and knowledge-based systems are therefore computer applications that contain knowledge and expertise which they can apply—much as a human expert does—in solving problems, offering advice, and undertaking a variety of other tasks. In law, these systems should be able to apply their legal knowledge in guiding users through complex legal issues; in identifying solutions to problems; in planning tasks; compiling documents and managing the flow of cases; and in offering advice and making specific recommendations.

If there is any distinction at all between expert systems and knowledge-based systems, it is that the former are more powerful than (and are a subset of) the latter in that the former hold expertise and not just knowledge. There is a more fundamental set of distinctions, however, and that is between types of expert systems (the term hereafter used to refer both to expert systems and knowledge-based systems). There are currently six identifiable classes of expert systems as applied in law.

1. Diagnostic systems

These systems offer specific solutions to problems presented to them. From the facts of any particular case, as elicited by such a system, it will analyse the details and draw conclusions, usually after some kind of interactive consultation. These systems are analogous to the medical diagnostic systems which make diagnoses on the basis of symptoms presented to them. An example of a diagnostic system in law would be a taxation system that could pinpoint the extent to which and why a person is liable to pay tax, doing so on the basis of a mass of details provided to it.

2. Planning systems

In a sense, planning systems reason in reverse. For these systems are instructed as to a desired solution or outcome and their purpose is to identify *scenarios*, involving both factual and legal premises, that justify the preferred conclusion. In tax law, a planning system could recommend how best a taxpayer should arrange his affairs so as to minimize his exposure to liability. The knowledge held within planning systems can be very similar to that held within diagnostic systems; what is quite different is the way that that knowledge is applied.

3. Procedural guides

Many complex tasks facing legal professionals require extensive expertise and knowledge that is in fact procedural in nature. Expert systems as procedural guides take their users through such complex and extended procedures, ensuring that all matters are attended to and done within any prescribed time periods. An example of such a system would be one that managed the flow of a complex tax evasion case, providing detailed guidance and support from inception through to final disposal.[3]

4. The intelligent checklist

This category of system has most often been used to assist in auditing or reviewing compliance with legal regulations. Compliance reviews must be undertaken with relentless attention to detail and extensive reference to large bodies of regulations. Intelligent checklists provide a technique for performing such reviews. They formalize the process. In taxation, an intelligent checklist approach could be used to assist in the review of a company's compliance with corporation tax.

5. Document modelling systems

These systems—also referred to as document assembly systems—store templates set up by legal experts. These templates contain fixed portions of text together with precise indications as to the conditions under which given extracts should be used. In operation, such a system will elicit from its user all the details relevant to a proposed document. This is done by the user answering questions, responding to prompts and providing information. On the basis of the user's input, the system will automatically generate a customized and polished document on the basis of its knowledge of how its text should be used.

---

[3] This overlaps with contemporary work on the application of project management to legal processes and on legal methodologies. See Chapter 4.

6. Argument generation systems[4]

It is envisaged that these systems are able generate sets of competing legal arguments, in situations when legal sources do not provide definitive guidance. Rather than seeking to provide legal solutions (as diagnostic systems strive to do), argument generation systems will present sound lines of reasoning, backed both by legal authority and by propositions of principle and policy. These lines of reasoning will lead to a range of legal conclusions. Such systems would help users identify promising lines of reasoning in support of desired outcomes while, at the same time, advancing other arguments which may need to be refuted.

Enhancements to legal information retrieval systems

Although legal information retrieval systems such as *Lexis* (and now online retrieval systems) have dominated the field of computers in law, these systems nevertheless have serious shortcomings. Often they retrieve an excess of irrelevant documents, or alternatively not all pertinent documents within given databases are located during every consultation. There is much more to legal problem-solving than searching for the occurrence of words within documents and, in recognition of this, researchers have sought to improve the performance of legal information retrieval systems by using AI techniques. Two approaches can be adopted here: the introduction of a 'front-end'; and the deployment of conceptual retrieval techniques.

1. Front-ends

The idea here is that guidance on the use of an interactive system is offered to users before searching within the database commences. Such a front-end system will help the user actually formulate his search request. It will ask the user questions, help to pinpoint relevant terms and concepts, and help ensure that all but only the relevant documents are retrieved. Front-ends can be built using classical 'knowledge engineering'/AI techniques—they can embody the knowledge of experts in the use of legal information retrieval systems and make that expertise available to others.

2. Conceptual retrieval

Those who argue that there is more to legal problem-solving than searching for keywords will often suggest that legal reasoning and research involves

---

[4] This category of expert system in law was not mentioned in the original article. It came to my attention through James Palmer's excellent doctoral thesis, 'Artificial Intelligence and Legal Merit Arguments' (D.Phil. dissertation, Oxford University, 1997).

familiarity and manipulation of legal concepts. Accordingly, researchers have developed methods of augmenting the traditional approach with conceptual retrieval techniques which will allow users to search through massive bodies of legal data, not just on the basis of the occurrence of keywords but in terms of the fundamental concepts relating to any problem at hand. This could mean, for example, that systems will search not only for words expressly articulated by the user, but also for terms conceptually implicit in such requests.

The above analysis focuses on the functions of AI systems in law but says little of the enabling technologies. In developing expert systems or enhanced legal information retrieval systems, researchers have drawn and will continue to draw on a wide range of AI techniques. Over and above the techniques and methods normally associated with expert systems, workers in artificial intelligence and law increasingly make use, in particular, of natural language processing and neural computing.

2. Historical Analysis

The purpose of this section of the chapter is to put the field of AI and law in historical context. It proposes a four-stage model in terms of which activities in the field can be analysed and classified.

The four stages of evolution in the field of AI and law

Activities in the field of law and AI tend to progress through four key stages: negligible activity; preliminary research; extensive research and development; and commercial exploitation. Although these stages overlap, each has characteristics unique to it.

Stage 1—negligible activity

During this stage, there are no sustained attempts to carry out serious scientific investigations into the topic. Nevertheless, and even in the days prior to the coming of the computer, in this first stage there may still be considerable speculation about what might be called the mechanization of the legal problem-solving process. Some contributions in this connection may be no more than fictional, but others show remarkable foresight of the potential and the dangers of computerizing legal reasoning.

Stage 2—preliminary research

Eventually, speculation and fiction give way to the desire to inquire into the field more thoroughly and rigorously. In this second stage, the preliminary research will lay the foundations for later and larger initiatives, but at this stage work is confined largely to exploring AI and law from a theoretical perspective. Researchers may be from law as well as from the world of computing. Perhaps surprisingly, Stage 2 is often dominated by the latter tradition—it is computer scientists' basic research that will establish the technical feasibility of building AI systems in law and will stimulate lawyers into further inquiry.

Stage 3—extensive research and development

The potential of the field having been established during Stage 2, there will follow a period of great activity, involving many research projects, largely devoted to the development of prototype systems and demonstrators. At the same time, fundamental, theoretical research will continue and will have direct impact on the research and development projects. In this stage, as in the previous two, work will largely be confined to academic establishments. The findings of Stage 3 will progress AI in law from the research laboratory into the marketplace.

Stage 4—commercial exploitation

In this final stage, commercial organizations explore the technology with a view to profitable development. These organizations will draw heavily from Stage 3 activities, not simply in borrowing ideas but also in recruiting staff. The stage of commercial exploitation itself can be subdivided into several phases, each representing varying degrees of success and financial gain. The key feature of Stage 4 activities is their commercial orientation—there is little concern for theory, although it must be stressed that Stage 3 research and development will still continue (at increasingly advanced levels) in parallel with Stage 4 activity.

A brief history of artificial intelligence and law

The four-stage model set out above can be used in analysing the worldwide history of the field.[5]

---

[5] Further details and references are provided in the following chapter.

Stage 1 would correspond to the time period before 1970. During that period, visionaries, science fiction writers, and technologically oriented lawyers wrote on the topic of computers engaging in legal reasoning and even replacing judges. Interesting though these contributions were, they were often detached from the technical realities and from the nature of the legal process.

It was not until 1970 that work began in earnest. This was the beginning of about five years' preliminary research—Stage 2 activity. Buchanan and Headrick, a computer scientist and a lawyer from Stanford University, published the first detailed analysis of the field in 1970. Shortly afterwards, a man who is now considered to be the father of the field, Thorne McCarty, began his TAXMAN project, which was to run well into the 1980s. Other key projects during that period were carried out by Meldman in the United States, Popp and Schlink in Germany, Sprowl in the United States, and Stamper in England. Collectively, these workers and a few others, undertook the preliminary research that served as the foundation for later, more ambitious work.

During the decade between the mid-1970s and the mid-1980s there emerged about 30 sustained research and development projects throughout the world. These projects built upon the Stage 2 work, lending further credence to it by developing operational systems that demonstrated the potential of the field so much more clearly than abstract reports could ever have done. Important projects during this stage were conducted at the Rand Corporation in California, Imperial College in London, the Norwegian Research Centre for Computers and Law in Oslo, and in England's Open University and Oxford University. It is interesting to note that the work of these projects—during the world's Stage 3—emanated more from institutions than from individuals. The findings and products of these research and development programmes attracted interest not only within the computing and legal communities but also in the popular press. In turn, the commercial world began to take greater interest.

From 1985 onwards, Stage 4 commercial exploitation came about. The findings of earlier research projects were combined with the teachings of traditional data processing and constrained by the pragmatic demands of profit-making organizations. It must be stressed, however, that even on a worldwide basis, commercial exploitation of AI in the legal field is still, in 1990, at a very early phase, for returns on investments so far have been low (with the exception of the use of document modelling systems in the United States).[6]

---

[6] Ten years later, the advent of the World Wide Web and the development of online legal services have clearly injected considerable energy and investment into the field.

It should be said, finally, in this brief history of AI and law, that there have now emerged, quite clearly, two types of worker in the field. On the one hand, there is the 'pragmatist' whose overriding aim is to develop and implement commercial systems that can actually assist in the solving of legal problems. On the other hand, there is the 'purist', for whom completion even of modest prototypes is not always necessary for success. The major goals of the purist are to clarify the nature of legal reasoning, of human and artificial intelligence, and of computational models of law. Live systems are not necessary for this. Generally, pragmatists operate in the commercial world, while purists can be found in research establishments. Pragmatists are at Stage 4 of the evolutionary path just outlined; while purists remain at Stage 3, often with no intention of being involved in Stage 4 activities.

In assessing contributions to the field of AI and law, it is important to bear in mind this distinction between pragmatist and purist approaches. It is crucial to appreciate that workers in these camps have in mind quite different goals and their orientations often diverge radically. There must be room in the world of AI and law for both pragmatists and purists. Indeed it is essential that contributions emerge from both camps. Equally crucial is that neither claims superiority over the other. Above all, perhaps, collaboration between the two is desirable.[7]

3. Practical Issues

This section seeks to offer answers to four questions often asked by persons interested in exploiting the potential that AI and expert systems techniques offer for the law. (Note that hereinafter the term 'expert system' is often used in place of 'AI' as it is this branch of AI that is now attracting the greatest commercial interest.) The four questions are as follows:

- Is it feasible to build artificially intelligent systems in the legal domain?
- What are the benefits of this approach?
- What problems are there for workers in this field?
- What are the keys to success?

This section deals with each of these questions in turn.

---

[7] The distinction between pragmatists and purists is more fully discussed in Susskind, 'Pragmatism and Purism in Artificial Intelligence and Legal Reasoning' (1989) 3 *AI & Society* 28.

Questions of feasibility

People unfamiliar with the field will often say that it is not possible or not feasible to build expert systems in law. Careful analysis of this assertion, however, reveals that there are really five dimensions to this feasibility issue; that there are really five questions to be answered. These questions ask whether building expert systems in law is technically possible, jurisprudentially sound, commercially viable, organizationally suitable, and strategically appropriate.

1. Technical possibility

The key issue here is whether hardware and software in the field of AI has developed to such an extent that sound, reliable, and robust systems can be designed, developed, implemented, tested, and maintained. It is now widely accepted that expert systems have matured to such an extent that technologies and techniques are indeed now available, in 1990, to support the development—at least—of what might be termed 'first generation systems'. Generally, such systems will be stand-alone, will operate in small problem domains, will not be capable of solving all problems that human experts can, but nevertheless will deliver appreciable business benefits.[8]

2. Jurisprudential soundness

Any expert system in law necessarily makes assumptions about the nature of law and of legal reasoning. Accordingly, there is a growing literature on the philosophical implications and presuppositions of building such systems. Some theorists have suggested that building such systems is to misrepresent, distort, and oversimplify the legal problem-solving process. Others have argued that there is a direct match between what the computer can do and what legal reasoning is all about. However, the view that has been most widely supported, and is now gaining even greater acceptance, is that there are no fundamental objections from the point of view of legal philosophy to building expert systems in law of limited scope. These limitations in scope refer to the category of proper user (the lawyer or legally informed person); the way in which such a system should be used (as an 'intelligent assistant' and not a replacement for a legal expert); and the limitations of solving problems on the basis only of legal *rules* (so that these systems currently cannot reason on the basis of legal principle, policy, or purpose).[9]

---

[8] The World Wide Web now enables widespread access to these systems.
[9] The jurisprudential issues are discussed in detail in the following two chapters.

3. Organizational suitability

Even if it is technically possible and jurisprudentially proper to build these systems, it must always be asked whether such a system could actually function effectively in any target organization. Some users of the systems might feel deskilled; others may feel uncomfortable about interacting with computer systems rather than human beings; while still others will lack the confidence to operate any computer system of whatever sort. This question of feasibility is often overlooked by enthusiasts and champions of the field. Yet, from a purely practical point of view, many systems of the future will be regarded as failures precisely because they will not have been integrated with and accepted by the organization for which they were developed.

4. Commercial viability

The costs associated with developing expert systems in law are considerable. Not only are skilled computer professionals required, but extensive time, effort and therefore cost of human experts is also expended. For an expert system in law to succeed in the commercial world, the benefits that accrue from its deployment must outweigh these substantial outlays. A major difficulty here, however, is the notorious difficulty of quantifying the benefits of this technology for many of the benefits, as shall be seen from the next part of this chapter, are of an intangible sort. A major challenge for this field, therefore, is to provide guidance on the compilation of cost/benefit analyses of systems.[10]

5. Strategic relevance

Complete commitment to this emerging technology may be further inhibited by a perception that even if these systems can be built, their operation would not sit comfortably with the nature of the organization for which they are being developed. It may be, for instance, that a firm of solicitors decides not to be heavily involved with any sort of technology, but to offer a distinctively 'human' service. For such a firm, even if systems could profitably be developed, they may be deemed to be strategically inappropriate. The strategic question associated with these systems is, therefore, whether their use supports the wider strategic and business objectives of the organization considering their introduction.

---

[10] It is now recognized that the commercial success of expert systems will be achieved not only through internal efficiency and productivity gains but by packaging the systems as online legal services made available to an entire marketplace.

Significantly, since 1987, the first two questions—about technical and jurisprudential feasibility—have been asked less frequently. Operational systems have themselves, in effect, responded positively. These two questions are the key concerns of those in Stage 3 of the evolutionary path. In the world arena, the focus now is on the third and fourth questions: whether these systems can offer sufficient payback and fit into organizations considering their introduction. Frankly, it is too early to be able to answer these questions with confidence. Early indications of Stage 4 are very encouraging; so what seems certain is that further investment and investigation is necessary. The fifth question, the one relating to strategy, will be the dominant question of the mid- to late 1990s.

The benefits

There are two main categories of benefits to be derived from expert systems. First, there is the benefit from a human resource perspective. Second, there is the impact on quality.

1. Human resources

The central idea of expert systems technology is to allow human knowledge and expertise to be distributed more effectively and efficiently. This dissemination of scarce expertise will give rise to a range of improvements in the way human resources can be managed. Using the technology, complex tasks, which in the past would have required the attention of experts, can now be reliably delegated to less experienced persons. These users will benefit from access to first-rate expertise that would have been possible previously only through direct interaction with human experts (whose time would inevitably have been limited). This possibility of delegating tasks and activities could go some way to overcoming the anticipated skills shortages that are likely to prevail in the 1990s. There are training implications here too: in operating these systems, users will gain considerable insight into the knowledge and techniques necessary and sufficient for first-class performance in the legal problem-solving arena.

Additionally, expert systems will allow the skill and knowledge of many experts to be synthesized and preserved. More than this, they will also perform a liberating function. For it is likely that expert systems will be used largely to assist in the performance of many tasks that for experts are mundane or routine, although in the past required their attention. If expert systems can assist in such tasks, then they will free experts to focus on what they do best and what are likely to be beyond the scope of computer systems for some time yet—namely, the tackling and solving of problems that are complex and difficult even for experts.

2. Quality

Expert systems will also enhance the quality of legal work. By preserving and making widely available scarce legal expertise and in essentially codifying that knowledge, the technology can promote a uniformity of approach to similar problems, a consistency of disposal, and an in-built quality control regime. Moreover, computer systems will not suffer from 'off-days' that so often inhibit the performance of human beings.

It is difficult to quantify with precision the human resource and qualitative benefits just noted. Nevertheless, the major dimensions of financial benefit can easily be identified. For the profit-oriented organization, expert systems will allow greater leverage, that is, a higher proportion of lower-paid to higher-paid employees, while retaining the same quality and quantity (at least) of workload. The technology will also facilitate 'value-billing', whereby the charge for legal services will be based not on the time spent on a task multiplied by some hourly rate; rather, the task itself will have been automated and so undertaken far more quickly or at far lower cost. Value-billing may give rise to charges equivalent to those that would be incurred under conventional billing systems. Yet the task for which the charge is being made will have incurred far less cost for the provider.

For a public service organization, such as a government legal department, the financial benefits of using the technology result from the possibility of substantially reducing the cost of the services delivered by the department. The technology will allow tasks to be undertaken by less costly staff in fewer hours while increasing the quality of the work.

While it is easy to identify the sources of profit derived from expert systems generally, it is far more difficult to quantify these benefits in particular cases. As mentioned earlier, a key challenge for those involved with the commercial exploitation of AI and law is the articulation of techniques for precisely analysing the financial costs and benefits of building systems.[11]

---

[11] See n. 10, however.

Problems and obstacles

A number of problems and obstacles have faced and will continue to confront those wishing to build expert systems in the legal area. Six major problems deserve mention.[12]

1. Lack of knowledge engineers

The person whose task it is to 'mine the jewels' from human experts' heads,
then articulate that knowledge and finally embody it in a computer system,
is known as the 'knowledge engineer'. To be effective in this task, the knowledge engineer must have considerable knowledge both of computer
technology and of the law. Unfortunately, there are few people with training
in both these disciplines. This lack of potential knowledge engineers will
continue to inhibit the number of systems that are developed.

2. Lack of domain experts

The source of knowledge and expertise for any expert system is the human
expert himself. This domain expert must work closely with the knowledge
engineer and this is a very time consuming process. It is not easy to convince
an expert to devote extensive periods of time that could otherwise be
used for chargeable work or more direct legal service. Yet, without the
commitment of the expert to a project, no system can be developed. Understandably, few experts so far have shown the degree of commitment
required.

3. Lack of method

Modern data processing is characterized by the use of so-called 'methodologies'; that is, detailed sets of carefully and clearly formulated standard practices and procedures to guide those developing systems. In contrast, no such
methodology exists for the development of expert systems in the legal area
and so designers of these systems are required to face the same obstacles and
hurdles that others have faced and overcome in the past.

4. Lack of tools

Other than for the development of document modelling systems, there are,
as yet, no commercially available software packages devoted to the development of expert systems in law. Today, designers of systems are compelled to

---

[12] Remarkably, each of these apply equally to today's online legal services.

use tools not ideally suited to the task and inefficiency and inaccuracy inevitably result.[13]

5. Quality control difficulties

A major problem facing the AI community generally is the difficulty of controlling the quality of systems under development. It is enormously difficult to test the reliability and accuracy of the knowledge held within these systems, to test the soundness of the underlying code, and to audit their performance. A fully articulated methodology, of course, would address this issue of quality control.

6. Legal implications

There can be no doubt that some reluctance to develop fully operational systems has its roots in a concern over the legal implications of expert systems in law giving rise to loss. The expert system as a source of information and advice seems to sit somewhere between the professional adviser on the one hand and the textbook on the other. However, there have been no decided cases on the issue of liability for expert systems, and while this uncertainty prevails, so too will some reluctance to develop the technology further.

Keys to success

The fourth and final question often asked of expert systems in law looks for guidance on the successful development of systems. Drawing on international findings, there follows a listing of ten keys to success.

- There must be a management or business problem requiring a solution—too often expert systems are 'solutions looking for problems'.
- A rigorous feasibility study must be undertaken prior to any major development project.
- Quick, inexpensive prototyping of systems can, at an early stage, greatly enhance the understanding of management, experts, and projected users.
- Where possible, existing expert systems development methods and techniques should be used rather than inventing new ones.
- It is crucial for the purposes of development and maintenance, to record and document the knowledge held within a system in some schematic form, usually as 'knowledge base maps'.

[13] This is now no longer accurate for large-scale projects: the impressive Jnana system (see www.jnana.com) is a dedicated tool for the development of sophisticated expert systems in law. The lower end of the market remains without a simple tool, however.

- Conventional data processing skills can and should be regularly used in the course of developing expert systems in law.
- A fundamental, theoretical, jurisprudential understanding of the law on the part of developers greatly increases the likelihood of the development of reliable systems.
- Once in operation, the performance and organizational fit of systems must frequently be monitored.
- The expectations of management, experts, and users must be managed most carefully and developers must not fall foul of 'the fallacy of the successful first step'.
- A system will only be used profitably if there is the commitment of senior management, of domain experts, and of the end users.

In conclusion, it is generally anticipated that the 1990s will be the decade during which artificial intelligence technologies begin to deliver substantial business benefits.[14]

Given careful and sufficient investment, the administration of the law—both in the public and private sectors—is an area of particular promise. The public administration of the law and the provision of private legal services is inherently *knowledge based* and so is especially amenable to AI and expert systems treatment; for these technologies strive precisely to support and enhance knowledge processing tasks.

---

[14] In fact, it was the World Wide Web that began to deliver the benefits I had anticipated. The first decade of the new millennium will see expert systems and the Web converging.

8

A Jurisprudential Approach to Expert Systems in Law[1]

The essay on which this chapter is based was one of the first formal outputs of my doctoral research at Oxford University. My main purpose then was to put down a marker—I was advocating the desirability, indeed the necessity, of tackling the field of expert systems in law through the application of the well-established techniques of jurisprudence (roughly, legal philosophy). I believed at the time that many attempts to computerize legal reasoning had been naïve from a theoretical point of view; and so I attempted to inject greater philosophical rigour into the field—if not to solve the major problems, then at least to clarify their nature and scope. I remain of the view that philosophical insight is similarly important today for those who are working on legal knowledge management and online legal services.

The purpose of the chapter (which, with Chapter 13, is rather more philosophical in tone than the rest of this book) is to offer a general introduction to the field of artificial intelligence and legal reasoning. More specifically, the topic of expert systems in law is addressed, and one approach to the construction of these systems is advocated. In Section I, possible motivations for building expert systems in law are noted. In Section II, the terms 'artificial intelligence' and 'expert systems' are discussed resulting, in Section III, in a

[1] This chapter was originally published as 'Expert Systems in Law: A Jurisprudential Approach to Artificial Intelligence and Legal Reasoning' (1986) 49 *Modern Law Review* 168.

characterization of expert systems in law. In Section IV, projects in artificial intelligence and legal reasoning (from 1970 to 1985) are briefly surveyed and the idea of introducing jurisprudential rigour to the process of building expert systems in law is first advanced. This notion of using legal theory as a point of departure in the construction process is developed in Section V in a discussion of the concepts of legal knowledge acquisition, legal knowledge representation, and legal knowledge utilization. In the concluding Section VI, directions for further research in this field are identified and an interdisciplinary research project, conducted at the University of Oxford, is described. (This project is discussed in still greater detail in the following chapter, where it is referred to as the 'Oxford Project'.)

Although this chapter is intimately concerned with an aspect of computer science, it is intended that the bulk of it will be comprehensible to those who have no knowledge of the new technology. For it is generally not necessary for the lawyer or legal theorist to understand the computer and appreciate the intricacies of logic and mathematics as does a computer scientist, a computer engineer, logician, or mathematician. For the purposes of examining possible functions of computers in the legal world, the lawyer need only familiarize himself with certain crucial matters, such as the potential, the limitations, and the dangers of their introduction to legal practice and research.

I

The first 25 years of research into the application of computer technology to the law, from around 1960 onwards, were devoted largely to the development of what are generally, but, it shall be argued, misleadingly, termed legal information retrieval systems.

Many legal practitioners and academics are now familiar with the operation and capabilities of these systems, the best known of which in the United Kingdom is LEXIS. While the precise sequence of operations to be followed in their actual use varies from system to system, ordinarily the user operates through a terminal and having initially executed various preliminary instructions in order to gain access to the system, then enters one or more keywords, that is, words he considers to be important for, and relevant to, his inquiry. The computer then compares these keywords with the concordance of the full text (or perhaps only headnotes) of that section of the database in which the user has chosen to search. (The concordance is an alphabetical index of almost all the database's words and their addresses.) Seconds later, the number of occurrences of the selected keywords in the material searched appears on the screen. If that number is too great to be easily managed or too small to be of assistance, then the search can be modified by entering additional or alternative keywords or by the addition of further conditions. When the number is deemed convenient, the computer can be instructed to display them on the screen in one of a variety of ways, first, perhaps, by presenting those parts of the text that contain the keywords and then, if the user so chooses, by exhibiting the full text itself. After browsing the user may then instruct the computer to print out any desired portions of text.

In order to appreciate their various shortcomings, it is necessary to have a rudimentary understanding of certain key aspects of these systems' operation. One of the first steps in their construction is the creation of a database which involves the loading of selected materials (for example, statutes and case reports) into the computer, utilizing it as a sort of library. This source material may be stored on a full text, abbreviated text, or headnotes basis. At this stage when the legal material is input, the system assembles its concordance. While in operation, the system identifies and then matches the string of characters (that constitutes the keyword), with this concordance. In more complex search requests, involving several keywords and connectors (for instance, the disjunctive connector, 'or', and the conjunctive connector, 'and') the system compares the addresses of these words in a fashion stipulated by the relationships established through the use of the connectors. The occurrence of the keyword(s) in the full text (or headnotes) of documents, therefore, is the determinative factor with regard to the relevance, or otherwise, of the data retrieved.

While it is now generally accepted that computers can be used in the way just outlined as highly efficient tools for the recovery of legal material, many believe, nevertheless, that this criterion of relevance implicit in the systems is unsatisfactory. As a result, it is argued, many searches deliver an excess of irrelevant documents or fail to produce the bulk of those relevant texts that are in fact stored within the database.[2] To overcome this shortcoming, some

---

[2] In the *LEXIS Handbook* (London: Butterworth Telepublishing, 1981), for instance, it is pointed out (at p. 24) that a hypothetical researcher who had intended to retrieve data containing the words executor and executrix, having entered the search request 'execut!' would be confronted not only by texts carrying those terms he was looking for, but also those holding 'execute', 'execution', and 'executive'. (The use, in this example, of the exclamation mark, known as the super-universal character, results in the computer searching its concordance for all strings of characters with the prefix 'execut'). Another interesting example given (ibid., p. 12) indicates how relevant texts may be missed: the user who entered the keywords 'warehouseman's lien' would miss some of those cases where that concept is referred to as

have endeavoured to develop other methods of searching stored documents (for example by citation vectors[3]) remaining, nonetheless, within the paradigm of what we shall term legal database systems (see Section III). Others, however, with a similar goal in mind—that of improving the performance of computer systems used to recover legal material—have sought to examine the possibility of knowledge-based systems in law.

Still others, for an entirely different reason, have also been motivated to investigate knowledge-based systems. This last group subscribe to the view that the so-called legal information retrieval systems are of minimal utility to the majority of practising lawyers whereas systems that could hold the kind of heuristic knowledge contained in such materials as practitioners' texts and handbooks, might, in contrast, prove to be of inestimable practical value.[4]

There has, then, been a gradual appreciation by many workers in the field that it is now necessary to attempt to develop computer systems in law that can be said to embody knowledge, and even exhibit intelligence. Achievements in the branch of computer science referred to as Artificial Intelligence (AI) over the last twenty years have perhaps now provided the appropriate technological framework within which the construction of such knowledge-based systems in law might now be undertaken. Indeed, although similar such systems were anticipated by Lee Loevinger in 1949,[5] and by Lucien Mehl in 1958,[6] it is unlikely that their aspirations would now be receiving such serious consideration but for the apparently stunning advances that have been made recently by computer scientists involved with AI.

'warehouseman's possessory lien', 'lien of a warehouseman', 'warehousekeeper's lien' or 'warehouse keeper's lien'. It can be forcefully argued, of course, that many of the alleged deficiencies of systems such as LEXIS are in fact no more than users' inability to formulate suitable search requests.

[3] e.g. Colin Tapper, *An Experiment in the Use of Citation Vectors in the Area of Legal Data*, 36 NORIS (Oslo: Norwegian Research Center for Computers and Law, Conplex No. 9/82, 1982).

[4] For evidence of the contention that many lawyers have less need for access to primary legal sources than to lawyers' 'know-how,' see generally *Lawyers and Technology: The Report of a Study of the Use of Technology by Solicitors* (London: National Law Library, 1983) ('The Slot Report'), particularly pp. 33–4, 36–40, and 124.

[5] 'JURIMETRICS—The Next Step Forward' (1949) 33 *Minnesota Law Review* 456–93.

[6] 'Automation in the Legal World—from the Machine Processing of Legal Information to the "Law Machine"' presented at the National Physical Laboratory Symposium No. 10. entitled 'Mechanisation of Thought Processes'; *Proceedings of a Symposium held at the National Physical Laboratory on November 26–7 1958*, Vol. II, pp. 756–79.

II

Perhaps the most intellectually stimulating issue to have arisen from the advent of computer technology concerns the idea of artificial intelligence.[7] This topic has attracted comment from exponents of many diverse disciplines. Many problems of philosophy of mind and of cognitive psychology, for instance, are now being contemplated in a fresh context, relating them to this novel possibility of imbuing a machine, a computer, with artificial intelligence. As a result, much debate on AI, pertaining as it does to the metaphorical relationship between man and machine, can hardly be regarded as an unfamiliar province of academic inquiry. For Western philosophers have puzzled over the nature of intelligence and related concepts for countless centuries and, more recently, even prior to serious AI work of any kind, intelligence had been under thorough experimental and theoretical scrutiny by cognitive psychologists. While many of the issues that are discussed under the rubric of AI are of intense interest to representatives of certain academic disciplines, it is sufficient for those concerned with AI and legal reasoning to characterize AI in a fashion that avoids the many conceivable philosophical, psychological, and linguistic technicalities.

In our present context, the term 'artificial intelligence' can perhaps best be regarded not as derived, by analogy, from the rigorous conceptions of philosophers, psychologists, and linguistic scientists, but as a label used to refer to what it seems that certain computer systems possess to some degree. Such systems, having been so designed and constructed to perform those tasks and solve those problems that together, if performed by human beings, are taken by us to be indicative of intelligence, can be said to exhibit artificial intelligence. On this account, then, the term 'artificial intelligence' connotes a prima facie intelligence and this designation, while perhaps lacking in philosophical rigour, serves simply as an explanatory, and metaphorically framed, classification.[8] Of course, the term 'artificial intelligence' might

---

[7] Despite the current profusion of interest in AI, there seems to be some confusion over the precise date that the term was introduced into our vocabulary. In *The Times* (6 September 1983, p. 8) it was claimed that John McCarthy, of Stanford University, coined the phrase in 1958, whereas Edward A. Feigenbaum and Pamela McCorduck assert, with less conviction, in *The Fifth Generation: Artificial Intelligence and Japan's Computer Challenge to the World* (London: Joseph, 1983), that the name was invented 'around 1956' (p. 38). Many theorists are not impressed by this choice of terminology anyway, often finding it objectionable because it allegedly deprecates a dignity to be associated with human intelligence. It is not clear, however, which constituent word is the offending unit, for some adopt 'machine intelligence' as a substitute epithet while others seek to employ the expression 'artificial thinking' as a more appropriate appellation. In any event, the actual label appended is of little consequence: attention might more fruitfully be paid to the manner in which the term is used and to the problems created by, and the theories discussed in relation to, the concept of AI.

most realistically be regarded not as a label to be appended without due regard to time; for AI research can also be seen as no more than sustained attempts to program computers to exhibit forms of intelligent behaviour, for the production of which we do not seem today to have the necessary computational knowledge.

There are many tasks that computer scientists are currently endeavouring to program computers to perform which are deemed to result in artificially intelligent computer behaviour: the understanding and translation of natural language ('Natural Language Processing'); the understanding of the spoken word ('Speech Understanding'); the recognition of images and objects of the physical world ('Vision and Perception'); the playing of complex games such as chess ('Game Playing'); learning from examples and precedents ('Machine Learning'); the writing of programs, that is, computer programs that can themselves generate programs ('Automatic Programming'); the sophisticated education of human users ('Intelligent Computer-aided Instruction or Tutors'); intelligent problem-solving and reasoning ('Intelligent Knowledge-Based Systems' ('IKBS') or 'Expert Systems'). Moreover, attempts to build intelligent robot systems ('Robotics'), and the study of the human mind using the computer as a means of testing hypotheses and modelling human behaviour, that is, using what is commonly referred to as 'the Computational Metaphor', are also considered to be contributions to the study of AI.[9]

The particular aspect of AI from which the legal profession may well benefit is often regarded as the applied branch and is usually referred to as 'Intelligent Knowledge-Based Systems' ('IKBS'). These are systems that contain representations of knowledge which can be deployed in the solving of given problems. Expert Systems (despite the fact that this term is often considered to be synonymous with IKBS), are, more precisely, a type of IKBS. Expert systems are computer programs that have been constructed (with the assistance of human experts) in such a way that they are capable of functioning at the standard of (and sometimes even at a higher standard than)

[8] We are, therefore, not directly concerned here with the core AI question of whether machines can meaningfully be said to think. The expert systems in law discussed in this chapter will be no more capable of thinking, in the sense of having cognitive states, than legal textbooks. On machine thought, see A.M. Turing, 'Computing Machinery and Intelligence' (1950) LIX *Mind* 236; Ned Block, 'Psychologism and Behaviourism' *Philosophical Review*, January 1981, pp. 543; Douglas Hofstadter and Daniel Dennett (eds.), *The Mind's I: Fantasies and Reflections on Self and Soul* (Brighton: Harvester Press, 1981).

[9] On artificial intelligence in general, see Patrick Winston, *Artificial Intelligence*, 2nd edn. (London: Addison-Wesley, 1984); N.J. Nilsson, *Principles of Artificial Intelligence* (Palo Alto: Tioga 1980); J.E. Hayes and D. Michie (eds.), *Intelligent Systems: The Unprecedented Opportunity* (Chichester: Horwood, 1983); Edward Feigenbaum and Pamela McCorduck, *The Fifth Generation*, n. 7 above; Donald Michie and Rory Johnston, *The Creative Computer* (Harmondsworth: Viking, 1984).

experts in given fields. They are used as high-level intellectual aids to their users; this explains their alternative epithet: 'intelligent assistants'. They differ from IKBS in that the latter may recognize speech, perceive images, or indeed solve problems in a fashion that undoubtedly is dependent on knowledge yet that requires no particular human expertise. Only those IKBS that embody a depth and richness of knowledge that permit them to perform at the level of an expert in a particular (and normally highly specialized) domain, therefore, ought then to be designated expert systems.

The above characterization of expert systems, however, requires considerable refinement in terms of the various attributes that are generally expected of them (although there is some confusion even amongst computer scientists over what programs can correctly be termed expert systems).[10] Expert systems are usually: (1) *transparent*, which means that they can generate explanations of the lines of reasoning that lead them to their conclusions; (2) *heuristic*, by which is meant that they reason with the informal, judgmental, experiential, and often procedural knowledge that underlies expertise in a given field (as well as with the more formal knowledge of the domain in question); and (3) *flexible*, a term that refers to the ability of these systems to allow, without any great difficulty, modifications to their knowledge bases, that is, to their stores of knowledge.[11]

Further insight into expert systems can be gained through appreciation of the three major research issues in this wing of computer science.[12] First, there is the matter of knowledge acquisition. Work on this topic addresses the manner in which the requisite knowledge, particularly the heuristic knowledge, can be extracted from human experts, and then articulated with a view to representing it in the system. Secondly, is the issue of knowledge representation, which concerns the techniques to be adopted in the process of restructuring the body of knowledge of a particular domain so that it can be represented as data structures within the computer system. This has to be done in a fashion that not only facilitates subsequent alterations to the knowledge base, but also makes for easy access during the problem-solving routines. Further, this representation is required to be a configuration, faith-

---

[10] See Bruce G. Buchanan and Richard O. Duda, *Principles of Rule-Based Expert Systems* (Stanford University, Report No. STAN-CS-82–926), p. 1. On expert systems generally, see Frederick Hayes-Roth, Donald A. Waterman, and Douglas B. Lenat (eds.), *Building Expert Systems* (London: Addison-Wesley, 1983), D. Michie (ed.), *Introductory Readings in Expert Systems* (London: Gordon and Breach Science, 1982), D. Michie (ed.), *Expert Systems in the Micro-electronic Age* (Edinburgh: Edinburgh University Press, 1979). See also the Department of Industry, *A Programme for Advanced Information Technology* ('The Alvey Report') (1982), pp. 32–5.

[11] See *Principles of Rule-Based Expert Systems*, n. 10 above, p. 1.

[12] See *Intelligent Systems*, n. 9 above, pp. 37–55. See also *The Fifih Generation*, n. 7 above, ch. 3.

ful in meaning to the original corpus of knowledge. Thirdly, is the question of knowledge utilization. This pertains to the inference procedures, that is, to the methods of reasoning, to be used by the system in the process of problem-solving. For all expert systems require an inference engine, the mechanism by which the knowledge base interacts with the data relating to any problem at hand, so that conclusions may be drawn. The person whose role it is to build expert systems, and, therefore, to consider appropriate methods of knowledge acquisition, representation, and utilization in respect of any project with which he may be concerned, is known as the 'knowledge engineer'.

Applications of expert systems have been many and various.[13] Arguably the first sustained, and ultimately successful, work in this field, was initiated in 1965. This was the DENDRAL project, carried out at Stanford University and inspired by one of the fathers of AI, Edward A. Feigenbaum. By harnessing the formal and heuristic knowledge both of Joshua Lederberg (a professor of genetics and Nobel laureate), and of Carl Djerassi (a physical chemist renowned for having invented the birth control pill), Feigenbaum wrote a program that can infer the molecular structure of an unknown molecule given the mass spectroscopic data that would normally be available to a physical chemist engaged in such a task. The system's capabilities in this sphere are now said to exceed those of any single human being (including its designers), and it is used in university and industrial environments throughout the world. Another expert system, PROSPECTOR, functions as an intelligent assistant for geologists by offering advice on the location of ore deposits based on geological data. As a direct result of its advice (its knowledge base contains the heuristic and formal knowledge of scientists of the US Geological Survey), it is claimed that a molybdenum find, valued at one hundred million dollars, was made in 1982.

Perhaps the most widely known expert systems are those that perform medical diagnoses. MYCIN, for instance, a system developed at the hands of a doctor-cum-computer scientist, Edward H. Shortliffe, provides consultative advice on diagnosis and antibiotic therapy for infectious diseases such as blood infections and meningitis. CADUCEUS (formerly INTERNIST), performs diagnoses (at a level of expertise that permits it to cope with the case studies of the Clinical Pathological Conferences), in the field of internal medicine, 80–85 per cent of which domain is represented in its knowledge base. Finally, CASNET diagnoses, and advocates therapeutic measures for,

---

[13] For details, see *Building Expert Systems*, n. 10 above, and Avron Barr and Edward Feigenbaum (eds.), *The Handbook of Artificial Intelligence*, Vol. 2 (Stanford: Heuristech, 1982).

the disease process of glaucoma, doing so in a fashion, it is averred, that oph-thalmologists have acclaimed to be akin to that of an expert in the field.

Inspired by such successes, some lawyers have suggested the possibility of 'legal diagnostics'[14] and expert systems for lawyers,[15] while various computer scientists, flush with their colleagues' achievements, have turned to the domain of law in order that they might widen their range of conquests.

III

Based on the foregoing, we might expect expert systems in (substantive) law, meaningfully so-called, to correspond to the following tentative character-ization. They are computer programs that have been written with the aid of legal experts in particular, and usually highly specialized, areas of law. (Systems lacking the specialization requirement, yet possessing the other expert systems' attributes mentioned in the previous section, we might more correctly term 'IKBS in law'.) These expert systems are designed to function as intelligent assistants in the process of legal problem-solving (and can also be used as teaching aids). The users of such systems are intended to be gen-eral legal practitioners, who, when faced with legal problems beyond their range of experience and knowledge, rather than always having to turn to appropriately qualified legal specialists, may instead consult their expert systems in law. Such systems ask questions of their users and guide them through the problem-solving process, utilizing the embodied heuristic and formal knowledge of the experts who assisted in their design. Moreover, these systems offer explanations for their lines of reasoning and may be required to provide authority for all assertions made and conclusions drawn.[16]

However, although there are several claims of existing expert systems in

---

[14] Simon Chalton, 'Legal Diagnostics' (1980) 25 *Computers and Law* 13–15.

[15] Bryan Niblett, 'Expert Systems for Lawyers' (1981) 29 *Computers and Law* 2.

[16] In a sense, the forerunners of AI knowledge-based systems in law (see below) are the computer-aided instruction in law systems, by means of whose programmed instructional techniques, it is said that 'the computer can track a student through the process of analysing and solving problems'. See Roger Park and Russell Burris, 'Computer-Aided Instruction in Law: Theories, Techniques and Trepidations' (1978) 1 *American Bar Foundation Research Journal* 1–50, 42. While these CAI systems can be regarded as bridging the conceptual gap between database and knowledge-based systems (see below) it is, without doubt, the techniques of AI that provide the most promising means of developing thoroughgoing knowledge-based systems in law.

law, close examination of the documentation of the systems invariably reveals these pronouncements to be exaggerated. Phillip Leith, for instance, has suggested that his 'legal expert system, E.L.I., produced at the Open University is not only the first legal expert system but one of the few demonstrable expert systems in the U.K.'[17] E.L.I. is indeed a significant program, but according to the paper from which that quotation was taken, it is not transparent and it does not offer explanations for its lines of reasoning (although Leith intends, in the future, to add this facility to his system). More importantly, E.L.I. does not reason with legal experts' heuristic knowledge. The domain of application of E.L.I. is part of the law of the United Kingdom relating to supplementary benefits, chosen because of its simplicity which allowed Leith (not himself trained in law) to 'become "expert" in it'. The system was not constructed, therefore, with the assistance of a legal expert, there could not have been any inclusion of experts' heuristics, and this factor might incline us to doubt whether the designation 'expert system' is appropriate. Moreover, if a non-lawyer could, in a fairly short period, develop expertise in an area of law, then we might justifiably query whether that chosen area is indeed a suitable domain of application. For the chosen legal domain ought to be one whose problems do indeed require expertise (normally acquired over many years) and not relatively brief research, for their resolution. This is not to belittle Leith's achievements, for he was clearly working with limited resources. Where possible, however, legal knowledge engineers should strive to consult extensively with legal experts, and pay heed to the admonition expressed in *Building Expert Systems*: '[it] is very easy to be deluded into thinking one knows a great deal about the domain' but '(r)emember: the expert became one only after years of training and experience.'[18]

It is clear, however, that when fully operational expert systems in law of the type envisaged above are developed (as seems likely) then the output of these systems will be of a very different nature to that of the legal information systems mentioned at beginning of this chapter. In truth, we might question whether these latter machines do indeed offer us 'information' about the law. Much confusion in this field, as indeed in many others, has been occasioned by the ambiguity of the term 'information', a concept in relation to

---

[17] See 'Cautionary Notes on Legal Expert Systems' (1984) 40 *Computers and Law* 14–16. In 'The Emperor's New Expert System (A Reply to Susskind)' (1987) 50 *Modern Law Review*, Philip Leith justifiably challenged my too harsh and sweeping critique of his research.

[18] N. 10 above, p. 165. This text is generally regarded as an excellent contribution to the field.

which two radically diverging analyses are often offered by information theorists.[19]

On one account, information can (logically) come about only subsequent to the operation of the interpretative processes of some cognitive agent on some more basic raw material. In law, Professor Bryan Niblett seems to defend this thesis.[20] He contends that computerized legal information retrieval systems, such as LEXIS, are not, strictly, information retrieval systems at all. Rather, Niblett argues, these are 'document' retrieval systems, because in any search session a user is provided with texts of possibly relevant documents and not with a solution to the problem that he is investigating.

Proponents of the other school of thought in information theory maintain that advocates of the first confuse the notions of 'information' and 'meaning'. If this conceptual error is corrected, they argue, then information can be regarded, in the words of Dretske, 'as an objective commodity, something whose generation, transmission, and reception do not require or in any way presuppose interpretive processes'. He concludes, then, that the 'raw material is information'.[21] This conception of information is favoured implicitly, in law, by all theorists like Lucien Mehl,[22] who consider there to be no attendant linguistic infelicity in the usage of the expression 'legal information' in respect of the produce of LEXIS and other similar systems. In law, however, there is also a third camp, occupants of which seem content to wield the term 'information' wildly and with little discretion.[23] These commentators deploy the title 'legal informatics' on all occasions, exercising it as a generic term for many activities involving the application of computer technology to the law. Thus, they seem to find no difficulty in the practice of referring both to systems such as LEXIS, as well as to systems that might actually solve legal problems, as 'legal information systems'. Yet this practice tends to obscure our vision of what systems have actually been designed to do, how, it is conceived, they should function as aids to the legal profession.

---

[19] See generally Fred I. Dretske, *Knowledge and the Flow of Information* (Oxford: Blackwell, 1981). Also see Michie and Johnston, *The Creative Computer*, n. 9 above, ch. 6.

[20] In 'Expert Systems for Lawyers' in *Computers and Law*, n. 15 above, p. 2.

[21] *Knowledge and the Flow of Information*, n. 19 above, p. vii and passim.

[22] 'Automation in the Legal World from the Machine Processing of Legal Information to the "Law Machine" ', n. 6 above.

[23] e.g. see the collection of articles in Constantino Ciampi (ed.), *Artificial Intelligence and Legal Information Systems* (Amsterdam: North-Holland, 1982). It should be noted, however, that the Italian term *'informatica'* means 'computer science' or 'information science', which perhaps explains the Italian commentators' wide usage of the word information.

It would be advantageous for practitioners and theorists alike, because of the uncertainty of its range of reference, if the word 'information' were to be banished from the vocabulary of all those who profess an interest in computer applications to the law. Instead, it is submitted that a more appropriate distinction of law machines, based on a systems design approach, is between database systems in law and knowledge-based systems in law. Because the term 'information' is so firmly entrenched in the minds of so many, however, by way of compromise, where it would be unavoidable to phrase it otherwise, we might distinguish also between legal database information systems and legal knowledge-based information systems. The former systems are designed to function as non-intelligent supportive components in the general legal problem-solving process, while the latter (which may embody or interface with the former), assist in the more specific interpretative processes requiring a level of knowledge normally associated only with intelligent human beings.

While it would be a premature, and indeed a misconceived, exercise to detail all the conceivable advantages of expert systems in law, one striking and direct consequence of their widespread use bears mention: these systems would provide the legal profession with the possibility of overcoming difficulties resulting from intense specialization in the law. This phenomenon has itself been occasioned, amongst other factors, by the continual expansion of the statute book as well as by the growth in the number of reported cases, as a result of which lawyers are now incapable of keeping pace with many legal developments. Despite the availability and considerable use of database systems in law, many lawyers are undeniably still heavily reliant on the resources of the legal expert and his ability, culled from years of experience in the field, to direct his specialist knowledge to given legal problems.

The general practitioner is less likely now, than in the past, to be able himself to offer counsel to his client and is becoming increasingly dependent on expert advice for problems beyond his range of legal knowledge. The capability of the legal expert to identify, classify, and analyse the problem domain, then adopt an appropriate mode of systematic inquiry, to follow this up by skilful and relevant consultation, and then finally to formulate his opinion, having evaluated various alternatives, is indeed a valuable legal resource. This resource, often transitory, even volatile in nature, surely is worthy of nurture and preservation. Untimely departures of senior partners from law firms, of scholars from the groves of academe, or indeed of members of the judiciary from the Bench can, without adequate educational preparation, wreak havoc in given specialized fields of law. It may now be possible, however, by use of expert systems in law, to preserve indefinitely, and to put at the disposal of others, the wealth of legal knowledge and expertise of various experts, hitherto bestowed upon the legal world in transient and indiscriminate doses. More than this, a 'law machine' may now be able to offer assistance of a quality possibly greater than that of any one individual human legal expert. In the next section, we shall mention various projects that have contributed to the possibility of the development of such machines.

IV

Buchanan and Headrick, in an influential paper published in 1970, were the first to consider, systematically, the possibility of using AI techniques to assist in the process of legal reasoning.[24] Fifteen years later, no more than 25 sustained research projects have been launched in this field, the most important of which shall be mentioned in this and the following sections.[25]

---

[24] 'Some Speculation about Artificial Intelligence and Legal Reasoning' (1970) 23 *Stanford Law Review* 40–62.

[25] Most of the projects noted here have been the subject of many papers presented by the principal researchers at recent conferences, e.g., 'The Advanced Workshop on Computer Science and Law', at University College of Swansea, in September 1979, the proceedings of that workshop are recorded in Bryan Niblett (ed.), *Computer Science and Law* (Cambridge: Cambridge University Press, 1980); The International Conference on 'Logic, Informatics, Law' in Florence, Italy, in April 1981, the selected and edited proceedings of which are presented in *Artificial Intelligence and Legal Information Systems*, n. 23 above, and Antonio A. Martino (ed.), *Deontic Logic, Computational Linguistics and Legal Information Systems* (Amsterdam: North-Holland, 1982); The Sixth Symposium on Legal Data Processing in Europe, in Thessaloniki, in July 1981, the proceedings of which were published as *Artificial Intelligence and Linguistic Problems in Legal Data Processing Systems* (1981); 'Data Processing and the Law', in Leicester, 1982, proceedings in Colin Campbell (ed.), *Data Processing and the Law* (London: Sweet & Maxwell, 1984); and The Second International Conference on 'Logic, Informatics, Law', in Florence, Italy, in September 1985 the pre-proceedings held in *Atti preliminari del II Convegno internazionale di studi su Logica, Informatica, Diritto* (Firenze, IBI, 1985). Many of the projects have been discussed in recent review articles. See, e.g., Garry S. Grossman and Lewis D. Soloman, 'Computers and Legal Reasoning', *Trusts and Estates*, October 1982, pp. 43–8, and in a slightly different article carrying the same title in (1983) 36 *Computers and Law* 11–13; and Mark Morrise, 'Emerging Computer-Assisted Legal Analysis Systems' (1980) 1 *Brigham Young University Law Review* 116–41, in which TAXMAN, the M.I.T. Project, JUDITH and ABF are discussed. Nicolas Bellord in his *Computers for Lawyers* (London: Sinclair Browne, 1983), pp. 141–3, outlines TAXMAN and ABF as well as LEGOL. Carl deBessonet's articles, n. 36 below, are excellent introductions to the general field. In addition to these review articles, in the actual research reports themselves, there are regular cross-references by the authors to the works of the others.

The most thorough and sophisticated contribution so far has been made by McCarty, whose TAXMAN project[26] (initiated in 1972, and now involving both TAXMAN I and II), concerns the development of a program, using classical AI tools, that can perform 'a very rudimentary form of "legal reasoning"' in corporate taxation law. Meldman also commenced his M.I.T. Project[27] in the early 1970s, the prototype of which engages in 'legal analysis' in relation to the torts of assault and battery. (This system was partially implemented by King in 1976.[28]) Two other significant efforts originating in that period are Popp and Schlink's JUDITH,[29] which operates on the German Civil Code, and Sprowl's A.B.F.[30] a computer system that uses regulations to draft legal documents.

Substantial advances in AI led to the launching of many later projects: (1) Hafner's L.I.R.S.,[31] which adopts a knowledge-based approach to the retrieval of documents pertaining to the law of negotiable instruments; (2) Waterman and Peterson's L.D.S.,[32] whose goal is to develop, using expert

---

[26] The following are a selection of L. Thorne McCarty's relevant works: 'Reflections on TAXMAN: An Experiment in Artificial Intelligence and Legal Reasoning' (1977) 90 *Harvard Law Review* 837; 'The TAXMAN Project: Towards a Cognitive Theory of Legal Argument' in *Computer Science and Law*, n. 25 above; 'Some Requirements for a Computer-based Legal Consultant' in *Proceedings of the 1st Annual National Conference on Artificial Intelligence* (Stanford, 1980), pp. 298–300; (with N.S. Sridharan) 'The Representation of an Evolving System of Legal Concepts: I. Logical Templates' in *Proceedings of the Third Biennial Conference of the Canadian Society for Computational Studies of Intelligence* (Victoria, BC, 1980), pp. 304–11; 'A Computational Theory of *Eisner* v. *Macomber*' in C. Ciampi (ed.) *Artificial Intelligence and Legal Information Systems*, n. 23 above; (with Sridharan) 'The Representation of an Evolving System of Legal Concepts: II. Prototypes and Deformations' in *Proceedings of the Seventh International Joint Conference on Artificial Intelligence* (Vancouver, 1981), pp. 246–253; 'Intelligent Legal Information Systems: Problems and Prospects' in *Data Processing and the Law*, n. 25 above; 'Permissions and Obligations' in Hansen (ed.), *Modelling Knowledge, Action, Logic and Norms COMPLEX no. 8/85*. (Oslo: Norwegian Research Center for Computers and Law, 1985).

[27] See *A Preliminary Study in Computer-Aided Legal Analysis*, Report No. MIT/LCS/TR-157, and 'A Structural Model for Computer-Aided Legal Analysis' (1977) 6 *Rutgers Journal of Computers and the Law* 1: 27–71.

[28] 'Analysis and KRL Implementation of a Current Legal Reasoning Program Design' (unpublished, 20 May 1976).

[29] 'JUDITH, A Computer Program to Advise Lawyers in Reasoning a Case' (1975) 15 *Jurimetrics Journal* 4: 303–14.

[30] See 'Automating the Legal Reasoning Process: A Computer That Uses Regulations and Statutes to Draft Legal Documents' (1979) *American Bar Foundation Research Journal*, 1–81, and 'Automated Assembly of Legal Documents' in *Computer Science and Law*, n. 25 above.

[31] See *An Information Retrieval System Based on a Computer Model of Legal Knowledge* (Ann Arbor: UMI Research Press 1981) and 'Representation of Knowledge in a Legal Information Retrieval System' in Oddy et al., *Information Retrieval Research* (London: Butterworths, 1981), pp. 139–53.

[32] See *Models of Legal Decisionmaking*, Report R-2717-ICJ (1981); 'Rule-Based Models of Legal Expertise' in *Proceedings of the First Annual National Conference on Artificial Intelligence* (Stanford, 1980), pp. 272–5, and 'Evaluating Civil Claims: An Expert Systems Approach' in (1984) 1 *Expert Systems* 1: 65–76. Perhaps more than any other work, Waterman and Peterson's L.D.S. establishes the feasibility of constructing fully fledged expert systems in law. Their system, however, is not itself an expert system in law designed to aid in legal reasoning. Rather, they use the techniques of knowledge engineering as a

systems techniques, a rule-based computer model of experts' decision-making in the process of settlement in civil litigation; (3) The PROLOG Projects,[33] the best known of which were developed at Imperial College, London University, where the researchers have translated parts of the British Nationality Act of 1981, and of various DHSS regulations, into a logical formalism which in turn can now be run on a general expert system shell; (4) Michaelsen's TAXADVISOR program,[34] which advises on federal tax planning, and runs on the expert system shell,[35] EMYCIN; (5) DeBessonet's CCLIPS (Civil Code Legal Information Processing System)[36] which is being developed using AI techniques, and one of whose goals is to codify 'scientifically' parts of the Louisiana Civil Code; (6) Leith's E.L.I.,[37] which, as we have said, operates on welfare law; and (7) Gardner's project in Stanford University relating to offer/acceptance law.[38]

Other related projects are LEGOL/NORMA,[39] carried on at the London School of Economics, SARA,[40] developed at the Norwegian Research Center

novel way of examining an aspect of the US system of civil justice. In so doing, they have provided an addition to the methodological weaponry of workers in the fields of sociology of law, sociological jurisprudence, and socio-legal studies. Their system, as they acknowledge, would require considerable refinement before it could help litigants in the process of legal problem-solving.

[33] See Cory et al., 'The British Nationality Act as a Logic Program' (unpublished, January 1984) and Peter Hammond, 'Representation of DHSS Regulations as a Logic Program' in the proceedings of the conference 'Expert Systems '83' held at Churchill College, Cambridge, December 14–16, 1983. Also see Sharpe, 'Logic Programming for the Law' (Master of Technology dissertation, Brunel University, June 1984).

[34] 'An Expert System for Federal Tax Planning' (1984) 1 Expert Systems 2: 149–67.

[35] An expert system shell is a ready-made inference mechanism upon which an expert system may be built. A shell is created by removing the knowledge from an existing expert system, and leaving the inference subsystem so it can be used for other problem domains.

[36] See, e.g., 'A Proposal for Developing the Structural Science of Codification' (1980) 8 Rutgers Journal of Computers, Technology and Law 47–63; 'An Automated Approach to Scientific Codification' (1982) 9 Rutgers Journal of Computers, Technology and Law 27–75; and 'An Automated Intelligent System Based on a Model of a Legal System' (1984) 10 Rutgers Journal of Computers, Technology and Law 31–58.

[37] See 'ELI: An Expert Legislative Consultant' presented at the IEE Conference on Man/Machine Systems, UMIST, 6–9 July 1982, Conference Publication Number 212; 'Hierarchically Structured Production Rules' in (1983) 26 The Computer Journal 1: 1–5; 'Logic, Formal Models and Legal Reasoning' (1984) 24 Jurimetrics Journal 4: 334; 'Cautionary Notes on Legal Expert Systems', n. 17 above, and 'Clear Rules and Legal Expert Systems', Atti preliminari del II Convegno internazionale di studi su Logica, Informatica, Diritto, n. 25 above, pp. 381–97.

[38] See 'The Design of a Legal Analysis Program' in Proceedings of The National Conference on Artificial Intelligence (AAI-83, 1983), pp. 114–18 and 'An Artificial Intelligence Approach to Legal Reasoning' (Stanford University Department of Computer Science, Report No. STAN-CS-85-1045, 1984).

[39] For a general introduction and useful bibliography see R.K. Stamper et al., 'The LEGOL project since 1976' (1980) 23 Computers and Law 10–13. For NORMA, see Stamper, 'A Non-Classical Logic for Law Based on the Structures of Behaviour' Atti preliminari del II Convegno internazionale di studi su Logica, Informatica, Diritto, n. 25 above, pp. 609–27.

[40] See Mette Borchgrevink and Johs. Hansen, 'SARA: A System for the Analysis of Legal Decisions' and Jon Bing, 'Deontic Systems, A Sketchy Introduction' in Jon Bing and K.S. Selmer (eds.), A Decade of Computers and Law (Publications of the Norwegian Research Center for Computers and Law, no. 7) (Oslo: Universitetsforlaget, 1980).

for Computers and Law (NRCCL), and POLYTEXT/ARBIT,[41] conducted under the auspices of the Swedish National Defence Research Institute. Moreover, two lawyers, Bellord of the United Kingdom, and Hellawell of the United States of America, have also written programs that are relevant in this context—ATAXIS[42] and CORPTAX[43] respectively. Finally, worthy of note are the general expert system shells that are currently available, of which ESP/Advisor[44] is an appropriate example: its designers claim that it is suitable for the handling of complex rules and regulations, and, moreover, some of its sample knowledge bases have law as their domain of application.

Despite growing awareness and interest in the application of AI to legal reasoning, and notwithstanding the above research projects, as we have already noted, there has not yet been developed a fully operational expert system in law that is of utility to the legal profession.

If we have regard to the collective achievements of the aforementioned projects, however, it can be seen that significant progress towards the construction of expert systems in law has been made (advances which have benefited immeasurably, it should be stressed, from interdisciplinary activity). Indeed we can now reasonably assert, in terms of the necessary computational tools, such an enterprise (at least of limited scope), is technically feasible. For obvious practical reasons and also for the opportunity of less doctrinaire evaluation (a prevalent feature of many commentaries), it is now desirable that a fully operative and useful system is built—one of the objectives of our project currently being conducted at Oxford University (see Section VI).

Of fundamental importance for workers in this field (despite our present optimism) is the fact that, for almost 15 years now, inquiries into the possibility of knowledge-based computer-assisted legal reasoning have been undertaken and yet have yielded far fewer positive results than comparable efforts in other disciplines. It might seem intuitively obvious that this lack of success stems from the differences between the nature of legal reasoning and the nature of other enterprises such as diagnosing illnesses, mineral prospecting, and inferring chemical structures. The latter, we generally

[41] Staffan Lof, *The POLYTEXT/ARBIT Demonstration System* (Stockholm, FOA Report C40121-M7, September 1980).

[42] See 'Tax Planning by Computer' in *Computer Science and Law*, n. 25 above, pp. 173–82; and 'Information and Artificial Intelligence in the Lawyer's Office' in *Artificial Intelligence and Legal Information Systems*, n. 23 above, pp. 241–49; and *Computers for Lawyers*, n. 25 above, ch. 10 ('Expert Systems').

[43] See 'A Computer Program for Legal Planning and Analysis: Taxation of Stock Redemptions' (1980) 80 *Columbia Law Review* 1362–98. Also by the same author see 'CHOOSE: A Computer Program for Legal Planning and Analysis' (1981) 19 *Columbia Journal of Transnational Law* 339.

[44] See Goodall, *The Guide to Expert Systems* (Oxford: Learned Information, 1985).

agree, are rooted, ultimately, in the empirically based, causal, descriptive laws of the natural sciences, whereas legal reasoning involves the manipulation of the prescriptive laws of the legal order, discoverable, in the main, not from uniformities or patterns in the external world but through scrutiny of the formal sources of the law. No attempts have been made, however, to examine in detail this intuitive reaction to what is regarded by some as an 'epistemological' issue.[45] This lack of interest in such theoretical matters is typified by the paucity of attention exhibited, in the writings pertaining to the projects referred to above, towards the relationship between jurisprudence and AI/legal reasoning.

In the explanatory papers of LDS, ABF, POLYTEXT/ARBIT, as in the writings of Bellord and Hellawell, there are no references to jurisprudence. In the commentaries of the M.I.T. Project, JUDITH, and LEGOL/NORMA, legal theory is mentioned but is not considered as a matter of central significance in relation to the respective enterprises. In short, with the exceptions of SARA,[46] Gardner's work and E.L.I. (and to a far lesser extent, TAXMAN), the relationship manifested in the literature between jurisprudence and the application of AI to legal reasoning has been unidirectional, that is, the projects constitute marginal contributions to, rather than exploitations of, the wealth of jurisprudential resources that are available and indeed invaluable for the would-be scholar or builder of expert systems in law.

In this connection, Professor Bryan Niblett has claimed that 'a successful expert system is likely to contribute more to jurisprudence than the other way round.'[47] Our research (see Section VI) and the remainder of this chapter casts doubt on that suggestion. In any event, if the majority of the projects mentioned above are indicative of quality, then it is unlikely that many commentaries on expert systems will exhibit the analytical rigour and sophistication of argument that characterize today's major contributions to legal theory. More importantly, it is believed that in the first instance jurisprudence can and ought to supply the models of law and legal reasoning that are

---

[45] See Aaron Sloman, 'Epistemology and Artificial Intelligence', *Expert Systems in the Micro-Electronic Age*, n. 10 above, pp. 235–41.

[46] SARA was developed by the Norwegian Research Center for Computers and Law (NRCCL), a body which carries out exemplary interdisciplinary inquiries into the computer/law interface. NRCCL's research is exceptional amongst the projects discussed here in that we find permeating its works an acute awareness of the complexities of jurisprudence and its intimate involvement with the task of designing systems to assist in legal reasoning. Much of their work on legal reasoning and computers is based on the writings of the Norwegian legal theorists Torstein Eckhoff and Nils Kristian Sundby. See, e.g., 'Computers, Discretion, and Legal Decision-making in Public Administration', 'SARA: A System for the Analysis of Legal Decisions', and 'Deontic Systems, A Sketchy Introduction' in *A Decade of Computers and Law*, n. 40 above.

[47] 'Expert Systems for Lawyers', n. 15 above, p. 3.

required for computerized implementation in the process of building all expert systems in law. If this be the case, it is difficult to imagine that any subsequent contribution of expert systems to jurisprudence could be of such import as to overshadow the latter's initial endowment and thereby vindicate Niblett's contention.

No doubt, it may well transpire that, in Niblett's words, 'the value of an expert system will reside not in its conformity to some jurisprudential theory',[48] if by this he means in conformity with a pre-existing theory, such as that of Hart, Dworkin, Finnis, or Raz. It is beyond argument, however, that all expert systems must conform to some jurisprudential theory because all expert systems in law necessarily make assumptions about the nature of law and legal reasoning. To be more specific, all expert systems must embody a theory of structure and individuation of laws, a theory of legal norms, a theory of descriptive legal science, a theory of legal reasoning, a theory of logic and the law, and a theory of legal systems, as well as elements of a semantic theory, a sociology and a psychology of law (theories that must all themselves rest on more basic philosophical foundations).[49] If this is so, it would seem prudent that the general theory of law implicit in expert systems should be explicitly articulated using (where appropriate) the relevant works of seasoned theoreticians of law. Perhaps one reason that there is, as yet, no successful system is that the vast corpus of apposite jurisprudential material has not yet been tapped in the construction process.

It has been naïve to suppose, as we shall see in the next section, that computer scientists could talk unobjectionably and unassailably of issues such as representing legal knowledge and legal inference procedures. These are highly complex matters of jurisprudence that require the attention of workers of that field. It is submitted that we now have sufficient experience of the general field of AI and legal reasoning for the immediate commencement of a systematic jurisprudential inquiry into the various stages of legal knowledge engineering and expert systems in law together with the development of a compatible theory of law, to the extent that such a theory is required in this context. One of the principal goals of our research is to make such an inquiry and develop such a general theory.

The cynical critic of jurisprudence would probably retort, in response to the above proposal, that there is a degree of disagreement and dissent so great between legal theorists themselves that no points of contact between

---

[48] 'Expert Systems for Lawyers', n. 15 above, p. 3.

[49] For a more detailed account of some of these theories, see Gold and Susskind, 'Expert Systems in Law: A Jurisprudential and Formal Specification Approach' in *Atti preliminari del II Convegno internazionale di studi su Logica, Informatica*, n. 25 above, pp. 307–9.

their competing theories could possibly be located and, therefore, legal theory has little to offer for the purposes suggested above. However, it is submitted that the divergence of views within jurisprudence has been unrealistically accentuated by the typical foci of inquiry, in that legal theorists tend to concentrate on the inherently contentious issues while ignoring 'straightforward' matters (which themselves may indeed raise insurmountable difficulties for the less capable). There may very well be consensus over many jurisprudential questions that has remained unarticulated on grounds of it being simplistic or mundane. Indeed, it may be in virtue of this presupposed, unifying substratum of concordance that dialogue between the various schools has been possible. For instance, theorists may all agree on the forms of legal argument that are both possible and desirable in the clearest of cases. This unanimity may not be apparent from the literature because 'hard cases' and not crystal 'clear cases' have invariably been jurists' object of study.

If there is such a concurrence of approach in relation to legal reasoning as well as to legal theory in general, then it is a model culled from that harmony that should be implemented in expert systems in law. If there is not, and if these conflicts affect the expert system enterprise, then a model that clashes as little as possible with the ruling theories should be developed. It is currently being endeavoured to determine if a consensus theory of law (albeit of mundane and limited application), can be propounded. (It would be unnecessary, of course, to repeat such exegeses in respect of all systems in the future if these were all built in accordance with the principles offered in our initial theoretical exposition.)

V

The need for jurisprudential involvement in this field can be appreciated more fully on careful consideration of the various approaches that have thus far been adopted in the design of AI systems in law, in relation to the three major research issues in expert systems that were identified in Section II of this article—knowledge acquisition, knowledge representation, and knowledge utilization.

Most AI theorists argue that knowledge acquisition, the process by which domain specific expertise is extracted from the domain specialist(s), is the major remaining obstacle to be tackled by expert systems research workers.[50] However, with the exceptions of the commentaries on ABF, in which Sprowl proposes an interesting method of acquiring heuristics (and including them in a system), and on LDS, none of the projects that we have noted even approach this hurdle, still less attempt to negotiate it. Waterman and Peterson recognized this lack in their earlier work[51] and suggested techniques that might be used to remedy the shortcoming in their later research. While it seems that they did indeed conduct far more extensive interviews with experts in their subsequent studies, unfortunately we are not told a great deal about the techniques they used, as this was beyond the scope of their paper.[52]

Popp and Schlink also conjectured that their future systems might include heuristic rules. While Bellord and Hellawell are, as it were, their own experts, they too offer little guidance to those who are keen on building expert systems in law but who recognize that they will need to extract the necessary expertise not from their own experience but from that of others. In general, the systems that have been developed to date have minimal heuristic content and no methods have yet been suggested that might eliminate this deficit. The knowledge represented in the systems usually consists of restructured statutory source material (case law has received far less treatment), and even in the statutory domain the researchers remain unsettled over whether superficial coverage of an extensive legal domain should be attempted, as in LEGOL/NORMA, or whether intensive coverage of a far more restricted area is more effective as in, say, the M.I.T. Project.

This last knowledge acquisition related issue is not problematic, however, if the characterization of expert systems in law suggested in Section III of this chapter is adopted. For in accordance with that analysis, there seems little doubt that intensive coverage of a small legal domain is preferable to superficial coverage of an extensive area of law. This is so because expert systems in law ought to be designed to replicate legal experts, the knowledge represented, therefore, necessarily being of a depth, richness, and complexity normally possessed by such a human being. We would, of course, hesitate to call those persons who have a large but nonetheless shallow familiarity with the law 'experts'. This last matter aside, however, the problems of legal knowledge acquisition remain substantially unanswered.

Most of the projects mentioned above are chiefly concerned with legal knowledge representation. This, in our opinion, is the central issue of the study of legal knowledge engineering, a conclusion that is apparent on

[50] See, e.g., *The Fifth Generation*, n. 7 above, p. 75.
[51] See *Models of Legal Decisonmaking*, n. 32 above, ch. 4.
[52] See 'Evaluating Civil Claims: An Expert Systems Approach', n. 32 above.

reflection on the differences between database and knowledge-based systems. In the full text species of the former, the formal legal sources are stored in the computer system in computer-readable format and are retrieved by the user as documents identical in content to the printed statute books and law reports of conventional law libraries. The legal data is not interpreted for this purpose, but are simply fed into the computer as the raw material of the process of legal reasoning. In knowledge-based systems in law, in contrast, these sources must be represented that is, restructured so that they can be stored in the computer and utilized in the reasoning process. The activity of legal knowledge representation, therefore, involves the operation of interpretative processes whereby the legal data of part of a legal system, valid at one particular point in time (that is, the legal data of a momentary legal system)[53] is scrutinized, analysed, and eventually reformulated in a fashion that is both faithful in meaning to the original source materials and that allows for the requisite transparency and flexibility of expert systems in law.

Many different computational methods have been used to represent legal knowledge. In TAXMAN, Hafner's LIRS, the M.I.T. Project, and in King's implementation in KRL, for instance, the knowledge is represented in semantic networks, using frame-based computer languages. In LDS, JUDITH, ABF, the PROLOG Projects, and in the programs of Bellord and Hellawell, in contrast, the knowledge base consists of a system of rules. These rule-based systems themselves differ. For example, in LDS, a generalized, all-purpose language, ROSIE, was used, whereas in the PROLOG Projects, a logic-based language, PROLOG, was deployed. As distinct from both of these 'classical' AI implementation environments, for JUDITH, the science-orientated high-level language, FORTRAN, was chosen, while Hellawell opted for BASIC. The importance of adopting a suitable method of knowledge representation cannot be overstated. For the efficiency of the system depends largely on this matter. In this connection McCarty has argued that: 'the most critical task in the development of an intelligent information system, either for document retrieval or for expert advice, is the construction of a *conceptual model* of the relevant legal domain.'[54] He calls for the development in law of 'deep' systems akin to that of the glaucoma diagnosis expert system, CASNET, in which the disease is represented as a dynamic process structured as a network of causally connected pathophysiological

[53] See Joseph Raz, *The Concept of a Legal System*, 2nd edn. (Oxford: Clarendon Press, 1980), pp. 34–5; Carlos Alchourrón and Eugenio Bulygin, *Normative Systems* (Wien, New York: Springer-Verlag, 1971), pp. 88–9; and J.W. Harris, *Law and Legal Science* (Oxford: Clarendon Press, 1979), pp. 42–3, 49–50.

[54] 'Intelligent Legal Information Systems: Problems and Prospects', n. 26 above, p. 26 (original emphasis).

states, in contrast to the 'shallow rule-based' MYCIN which contains no internal representation of the disease process. Whereas TAXMAN aspires to the CASNET mode of representation, McCarty claims that Sprowl's ABF and Hellawell's CORPTAX can be likened in this respect to MYCIN.

However, no thorough examination of the relative merits of all the various approaches to the representation of legal knowledge has yet been attempted. It might be thought that this is simply a matter for computer scientists to work out. Yet that view reflects a misunderstanding of the enterprise of representing knowledge of the law, as it is quite clear that the fundamental issues involved here are jurisprudential. The object of the exercise is to describe the law in a fashion that can suitably be embodied, together with the experts' heuristics, in the knowledge base. The activity of describing the law while remaining faithful to its meaning has received considerable attention from eminent legal theorists. We need, as Dworkin has admitted, 'a strategy of exposition'[55] and where better to initiate our search for that strategy than, say, the writings of Kelsen and Harris on legal science, Bentham's and Raz's theories of the individuation of laws, and the studies of Ross, von Wright, Alchourron and Bulygin on normative discourse?[56]

It would be bold to question the relevance of the works of Hans Kelsen who in the preface to his *General Theory of Law and State* states that he intends to provide the legal scientist with the 'fundamental concepts by which the positive law of a definite legal community can be described'. Kelsen's general theory of law must be pertinent for theorists of legal knowledge engineering for its aim is said to be 'to enable the jurist concerned with a particular legal order, the lawyer, the judge, the legislator, or the law-teacher' and, we may not unreasonably infer, the legal knowledge engineer, 'to understand and to describe as exactly as possible his own positive law'.[57] When we 'describe' the law in a computer program, we will be engaging, as Alchourron and Bulygin put it, in a 'reformulation',[58] or, as Golding suggests, in a 'rational reconstruction',[59] of an area of law, and the comments of these theorists on these matters cannot sensibly be ignored. Likewise, with regard to the prin-

---

[55] *Taking Rights Seriously* (London: Duckworth, 1977), p. 75.

[56] See, e.g., Hans Kelsen, *General Theory of Law and State* (Cambridge: Harvard University Press, 1946) and *Pure Theory of Law* (Berkeley and Los Angeles: University of California Press, 1967); Harris, *Law and Legal Science*, n. 53 above; Jeremy Bentham, *Of Laws in General*, ed. H.L.A. Hart (London: Athlone Press, 1970), Raz, *The Concept of a Legal System*, n. 53 above; Alf Ross, *Directives and Norms* (London: Routledge & Kegan Paul, 1968), Georg Henrik von Wright, *Norm and Action* (London: Routledge & Kegan Paul, 1963), and Alchourron and Bulygin, *Normative Systems*, n. 53 above.

[57] N. 56 above, p. xiii. See also Harris, Law and Legal Science, n. 53 above, passim.

[58] *Normative Systems*, n. 53 above, p. 71.

[59] M.P. Golding, 'Kelsen and the Concept of "Legal Systems"' (1961) 47 *Archiv Für Rechts und Sozialphilosphie* 355.

ciples in accordance with which we may divide up our formal legal sources, surely we must pay heed to the limiting and guiding requirements with which Raz furnishes us for this purpose.[60] Moreover, once we have individuated our legal rules, we must then decide upon their precise structure for representational purposes. This is no easy task, for as Harris has said, '(t)he law does not announce, on its face, into what units it can be most usefully split up'.[61] We noted previously that many researchers in AI/legal reasoning (for example, Waterman and Peterson, Popp and Schlink, and Sprowl) represented the law as a system of rules. Laying aside the obvious jurisprudential difficulties involved in this process,[62] it is striking that the internal structures of the rules represented in the respective systems are crude in comparison to, say, the components of laws that Ross and von Wright identify.[63] Again, to disregard these theorists would be folly indeed.

Not all legal theorists, of course, agree over the manner in which we ought to describe, individuate, and structure the law. In this respect, Honoré argues that '(t)here is no theoretical way of settling the form, identity or individuality of laws other than to scrutinize them as they appear in professional discourse. To suppose otherwise is to become the victim of a strange form of analytical metaphysics.'[64] However, having surveyed the relevant jurisprudential literature and having noted both the concordance and dissent, we shall surely then be better equipped to discuss with computer scientists how we might build our knowledge base. In that way, we will be able to remove the law from the Procrustean bed into which many computer scientists have remorselessly thrust it in order that they might demonstrate the versatility of their favoured computer programming languages.[65] Furthermore, with our models of law drawn from legal theory, we shall then also be in a position to consider the possibility, desirability and indeed the necessity of following McCarty's claim regarding 'deep conceptual models' and expert systems in law.

To turn now to our third research issue: the challenge of designing the inference procedures of an expert system in law, the problem of legal knowledge utilization, raises interesting questions for the legal knowledge

---

[60] *The Concept of a Legal System*, n. 53 above, pp. 144-7.

[61] *Law and Legal Science*, n. 53 above, p. 92.

[62] The question of whether or not the law is exclusively a system of rules is central to the Hart–Dworkin Debate. See, e.g., *Taking Rights Seriously*, n. 53 above, chs. 2 and 3.

[63] See *Directives and Norms*, n. 55 above, ch. V, and *Norm and Action*, n. 56 above, ch. V.

[64] 'Real Laws' in P.M.S. Hacker and J. Raz (eds.), *Law, Morality and Society* (Oxford: Clarendon Press, 1977), p. 100.

[65] Some of the workers on the PROLOG Projects, for instance, were, in a sense, committed to the use of the language PROLOG prior to the selection of the law as an apposite domain of application. The goal of some of their projects, then, was to represent selected areas of law in PROLOG come what may!

engineer. Commentators Grossman, Soloman, and Morrise[66] all place great emphasis on the distinction between deductive and analogical approaches adopted in the project—a confusion that obscures the actual jurisprudential orientations and functions of the systems. For it is misleading to categorize TAXMAN and the M.I.T. Project as analogical systems. McCarty does not stress in any of the papers cited previously that either TAXMAN I or II are to be conceived as systems that reason by analogy. Moreover, Meldman's definition of 'legal analysis' together with his emphasis that his model simplifies the notion of analogy,[67] imply that he, too, would be reluctant to characterize his system as predominantly an analogical one. (King's implementation of the M.I.T. Project, on the other hand, is principally concerned with analogy.)

Bearing in mind the top-down pattern matching technique used in TAXMAN II, the syllogistic instantiation of the M.I.T. Project, the foward-chaining of LDS and the backward-chaining of both JUDITH and ABF, it seems that the distinguishing characteristic of all these pre-eminent systems (and indeed the others) is their dependence on deductive inference procedures. In consequence, all the objections to deductive legal reasoning that pervade the jurisprudential literature seem to be germane to current research projects in this field. While it is beyond the scope of this chapter to examine in detail the various arguments that are normally marshalled in opposition to the notion of deductive legal reasoning, it is instructive nonetheless to consider several of them very briefly so that we may see their manifest implications for the activity of building expert systems in law.[68]

One argument, 'The Argument from Truth Value', holds that the application of the laws of logic to the laws of the state is precluded because of the normative nature of the law. Because legal norms lack truth value, it is argued, they cannot be related to the facts of case by the logic of theoretical reasoning, that is, reasoning about what is the case.[69] One reply to this argu-

---

[66] In 'Computers and Legal Reasoning' and 'Emerging Computer-Assisted Legal Analysis Systems' respectively, n. 25 above.

[67] 'A Structural Model for Computer-Aided Legal Analysis', n. 26 above, p. 67.

[68] There are many other objections to deductive legal reasoning other than those mentioned in the text. Some theorists have argued, for instance, that the process of selecting legal rules cannot be undertaken deductively. See, e.g., Gidon Gottlieb, *The Logic of Choice: An Investigation of the Concepts of Rule and Rationality* (London: George Allen & Unwin, 1968), p. 17. Wasserstrom has pointed out in *The Judicial Decision: Toward a Theory of Legal Justification* (London: Oxford University Press, 1961), that other critics have suggested that deduction in law presupposes the untenable notion of a gapless system of law (p. 15). Others have said that deductivism precludes purposive interpretation and reasoning (e.g. Harris, *Law and Legal Science*, n. 53 above, ch. 1) while still others have maintained that deductive judicial reasoning is conducive to concrete injustices, e.g. Gottlieb, ibid., p. 18.

[69] This argument has been expressed most lucidly, although not, in the end, espoused, by H.L.A. Hart. See 'Problems of the Philosophy of Law' in *Essays in Jurisprudence and Philosophy* (Oxford: Clarendon Press, 1983), p. 100.

ment involves the development of a logic of norms, or a deontic logic thereby allowing for deduction within a different logical calculus.[70] If it is believed that this is the only satisfactory retort to The Argument from Truth Value, then it follows that the inference procedures used in the inference engine of all expert systems in law must be based on some form of deontic logic.

Another important objection to deductive legal reasoning seems to impose limits on the range of problems that expert systems in law can solve. This challenge is 'The Argument from Open-Texture', introduced to legal theory by H.L.A. Hart.[71] As a result of the semantic indeterminacy[72] of the natural language in which the law is necessarily couched, deduction in law is possible, on the Hartian appraisal, only in the solving of 'clear cases' in law, that is, he says, 'those in which there is general agreement that they fall within the scope of a rule.'[73] Once more, jurisprudence seems to be of central importance, for we can expect in advance, if we accept Hart's analysis, that all expert systems in law whose inference procedures are solely deductive will function exclusively in the clear case domain, and will be of no aid in the solving of 'problems of the penumbra'.

Despite the apparent relevance of legal theory in this context, little cognizance of it has been taken by the leading researchers. Sprowl, for instance, alludes to no complications that arise from the use of deductive inference procedures in his work on AI and legal reasoning. From the thrust of their analyses, Meldman, Popp, and Schlink are aware of several of them but recommend no counter strategies. McCarty, Waterman, and Peterson, on the other hand, suggest how some of the problems arising from the open texture of legal rules might be resolved.

Perhaps the most telling objection to deduction in law with regard to all the projects is what can be termed 'The Argument from Particularity of Facts'.[74] This asserts that the crucial, and non-deductive, stage in legal

[70] See, e.g., Ross, *Directives and Norms*, n. 56 above, ch. VI, and von Wright, *Norm and Action*, n. 56 above, chs. VIII and IX, and 'Norms, Truth and Logic' in *Deontic Logic, Computational Linguistics and Legal Information Systems*, n. 25 above.

[71] See the Introduction and Essays 2, 3, and 12 of *Essays in Jurisprudence and Philosophy*, n. 68 above. See also *The Concept of Law* (London: Oxford University Press, 1961), ch. VII.

[72] See *Normative Systems*, n. 53 above, pp. 31–4.

[73] 'Problems of the Philosophy of Law', n. 69 above, p. 106.

[74] O.C. Jensen, in *The Nature of Legal Argument* (Oxford: Basil Blackwell, 1957) defends this argument: 'the problem in a great number of cases may be expressed symbolically thus: all S is P, but the crucial question is just whether the conduct of the defendant (or of the plaintiff or of the accused) is S. In other words, the problem is one of classification rather than one of deduction' (p. 16). And in respect of classification, Hart has noted that '(f)act situations do not await us neatly labelled, creased, and folded: nor is their legal classification written on them to be simply read off by the judge'—see 'Positivism and the Separation of Law and Morals' in *Essays in Jurisprudence and Philosophy*, n. 69 above, p. 63. See also M.J. Detmold, *The Unity of Law and Morality* (London: Routledge & Kegan Paul, 1984), p. 15.

reasoning is that of classifying the particular facts of the case, a stage in which none of the current computer systems are of support. (All these systems implicitly defend what can be called a weak thesis of deductive legal reasoning, which asserts that it is possible, in some cases, to arrange the factual and legal premises in a way that will yield a conclusion that follows as a matter of logical necessity. A strong thesis would go further and claim that deduction can have a significant role to play in the process of actually selecting these premises.) Only Waterman and Peterson mention the difficulties of classifying the facts, but, even then, just in passing.

The Argument from Particularity of Facts is particularly persuasive if it is further accepted that most of the systems mentioned should be looked upon as intelligent knowledge-based, and not expert, systems in law, for the problems which the described systems are intended to solve do not clearly belong to the expert domain. In that event, the projects can rightly then be subjected also to 'The Argument from Unimportance',[75] which states that the (weak) deductive inference procedure involved is of little significance, for if the systems are operating in an area of law with which general legal practitioners are conversant then they will have little interest in, and hence rare recourse to, a system that when given the facts simply applies the rules and draws the conclusions. Such lawyers, it is generally held, consider the problem in everyday cases to be that of determining just what constitute the facts of the instant case. If this is so, then designers of artificially intelligent systems must embrace one, or more, of the following strategies. First, they must build in the expert domain so that they might evade The Argument from Unimportance (and, also, avoid the criticism—previously directed at Leith— that their system is not indeed an expert system at all). Secondly, if they insist on constructing an IKBS in law, they must then provide sufficient and explicit heuristics and meta-rules (including rules of evidence) within the system so that it assists in the selection of the operative facts, thereby both avoiding the charges of The Argument from Particularity of Facts and also, then, defending a strong thesis of deductive legal reasoning. Thirdly, they must adopt the second strategy in tandem with the first, that is, develop an expert system in law that also aids in the fact-finding process. It is this last possibility that we are currently examining. We are also considering the possibilities both of allowing for open-texture and for reasoning by analogy by

---

[75] Again, Jensen provides us with an instance of this argument: 'if there is a process of logical deduction, it only occurs in the final stage [that is, after the selection of the legal and factual premises] and is so obvious that it need not be, and is not, given explicit formulation ... the deductive process is such a subordinate part of the total argument that the precise determination of its nature is of academic interest only' (*The Nature of Legal Argument*, n. 74 above, p. 16). See also Richard Wasserstrom, *The Judicial Decision*, n. 68 above, p. 23.

using the AI methods of reasoning with uncertainty, such as fuzzy logic and possibility theory, the implications of which have not yet been thoroughly considered in relation to expert systems in law.[76]

And so despite their embodiment of many of the classical tools of AI and their concern with, or their designers' aspirations of, AI, few of the current systems can be said even to approximate to expert systems of the sort with which our work is primarily concerned. We have already noted that the systems do not reason with heuristic, judgmental knowledge. Moreover, not all the systems are transparent, and even those that do offer explanations of their lines of reasoning (for instance, the PROLOG Projects and LDS), do so simply by regurgitating the rules that were fired. If a system is to replicate a human expert in law, it ought to provide more penetrating explanations than these, by clarifying the rules and, as Bellord realizes, also by stating legal authorities for all material propositions advanced. Flexibility, in contrast to heuristics and transparency is well catered for in most of the major systems, particularly those whose knowledge is represented in semantic networks, and it is in relation to this that we can see the limitations of CORPTAX, the tax systems on sale in most leading department stores and, as McCarty has noted,[77] the computer-assisted instruction systems in law.

In the foregoing, the current projects were criticized, from a jurisprudential perspective, within a classification established by AI workers. This critique could be supplemented by examination of the projects, using legal theory as a point of departure. For instance, with regard to the function of legal reasoning, little mention is made in the research reports about whether the systems are intended to assist the user in, say, justifying a legal conclusion, persuading a given audience, predicting the ruling of a court, or in reconciling legal texts with certain values, all functions of legal reasoning that have been dealt with in the jurisprudential literature.[78] Whether the knowledge bases of the

[76] See L.A. Zadeh, 'Fuzzy Sets as a Basis for a Theory of Possibility' (1978) *Fuzzy Sets and Systems* 1: 3–28, in which it is argued that the imprecision in natural language because of open-texture is mainly possibilistic rather than probabilistic in nature. As a result, Zadeh claims that it is possible to develop a universal language 'in which the translation of a proposition expressed in a natural language takes the form of a procedure for computing the possibility distribution of a set of fuzzy relations in a database'. (p. 4). This would clearly be of interest to legal theorists.

[77] 'Intelligent Legal Information Systems: Problems and Prospects', n. 26 above, p. 145.

[78] On justification and legal reasoning see, e.g., Neil MacCormick, *Legal Reasoning and Legal Theory* (Oxford: Clarendon Press, 1978); Harris, *Law and Legal Science*, n. 53 above; and Wasserstrom, *The Judicial Decision*, n. 68 above. On persuasion, see, e.g., Chaïm Perelman, *Justice, Law and Argument: Essays on Moral and Legal Reasoning* (Dordrecht: D. Reidel, 1980), particularly ch. 14. On prediction, see many of the works of the American Legal Realists, e.g. O.W. Holmes, 'The Path of Law' in *Collected Legal Papers* (London: Constable & Co., 1920), pp. 167 and 173. With regard to reconciliation, in civil jurisdictions, one of the functions of legal reasoning undertaken by jurists is considered to be that of reconciling the words of the authoritative texts with the values that the legal system in question is thought to embody.

systems could be manipulated to fulfil all, some, or none of these functions, we are not told. Most of the systems are designed for use by a lawyer. Again, whether the same knowledge base could serve in an expert system for other reasoning agents, by use of a distinct inference engine, is not revealed. This last possibility is of intense importance both to practitioners and theoreticians of the law. Indeed perhaps the most stimulating possibility in this field is that of developing a system that can be used by several classes of reasoning agent for their own very different and respective purposes.

VI

From this chapter, it has emerged that there are many problems research workers in the field of expert systems in law must recognize and confront:

(1) There are no commercially available, satisfactorily operating expert systems in both statute and case law, that have a high heuristic content and that are, moreover, at once transparent and flexible.

(2) No guidelines have been offered by the cognoscenti in the field for those others who are interested in attempting to build such a system but who rightly have little desire to try to overcome problems that have already been successfully tackled.

(3) There has been minimal jurisprudential input to the field, much of the work having been produced from a computational perspective.

(4) The prototypes that are currently in operation cannot be instructed in natural language but require computer language or very restricted English input, and/or 'yes/no' responses to questions asked of the user.

(5) There is little agreement over suitable terminology in the field, to the extent that researchers disagree over what constitutes an expert system in law properly so-called.

(6) No project report has ever addressed the possibility of computer-assisted operative fact finding.

(7) There have been no sustained attempts to employ the AI techniques associated with reasoning with uncertainty and, therefore, reasoning by analogy has not received detailed treatment.

(8) The possibility of expert systems interfacing with existing database computerized legal information retrieval systems has not been sufficiently examined.[79]

---

[79] Because the legal knowledge base of any expert system in law is a representation of the chosen domain, it is desirable, and some would no doubt argue, necessary, that the user has direct access to the

The above eight problems will require decades of attention from the most skilful exponents in the field. It is the object of our interdisciplinary research project, currently being conducted at the Programming Research Group of the University of Oxford, to examine some of them, although problem 4, for example, is clearly beyond the scope of our study as it constitutes a major AI research topic in itself—natural language processing.

Our point of departure has been jurisprudence and a systematic inquiry into two of the stages of legal knowledge engineering has been made.[80] Having surveyed the relevant literature, we have developed methods of describing, individuating, and structuring all laws (not merely statutory material) with a view to engaging in legal knowledge representation. With regard to legal knowledge utilization, we have examined many commentaries on the notion of deductive legal reasoning in order to determine the utility and limitations of a deductive inference engine.[81] Thus equipped with coherent but nevertheless relatively informal models of laws and legal reasoning, we are now attempting to write formal specifications of these using appropriate mathematical tools.[82] On completion of this task, we hope then to have at hand accurate and concise formal models that will be suitable for use in the construction of expert systems in law in any domain, and will therefore constitute the foundations of a shell for expert systems in law. To demonstrate our findings, we are endeavouring to build an expert system in law of the sort outlined in Section III of this paper. Our chosen domain belongs to Scottish law of divorce, whose sources are to be found both in

primary sources which have actually been represented. This could be achieved by interfacing expert systems in law with already existing database systems in law such as LEXIS. In no discussions of expert systems (or aspiring expert systems) in law, however, has this possibility been given serious consideration.

[80] The emphasis of our project is on legal knowledge representation and utilization. Legal knowledge acquisition will not be given detailed and separate consideration, as we believe, in the legal domain, that this activity is inextricably related to legal knowledge representation. Any detailed study of legal knowledge acquisition and heuristics might best be undertaken by someone whose expertise is in the field of socio-legal studies.

[81] To date, the inference procedures chosen by knowledge engineers for expert systems (not in law) have been relatively simple, often based on classical first-order logic. Because such deductive procedures have been favoured (see, e.g., Nilsson, *Principles of Artificial Intelligence*, n. 9 above), it seemed appropriate to start our investigation of legal knowledge utilization with an examination of deductive legal reasoning.

[82] On formal specification, see, e.g., Bernard Sufrin, *Formal Specification of a Display Editor* (Oxford University Computing Laboratory, Technical Monograph PRG-21, June 1981): 'The purpose of a formal system specification is to capture precisely and obviously the requirements of the system designer and his client—independently of whether the structures and functions embodied in it are immediately implementable ... It should be an adequate basis both for judgements about the correctness of implementations of the system to be made, and for conclusions about system behaviour to be drawn independently of (and preferably in advance of) implementation' (p. 1). Also see Gold and Susskind, 'Expert Systems in Law: A Jurisprudential and Formal Specification Approach', n. 49 above, pp. 305–16.

statutes and judicial precedents. A portion of the Scottish legal system is particularly appropriate, as the law in that jurisdiction manifests features of both civil- and common-law systems.[83]

The findings, accordingly, are conceived as both a guide to anyone interested in building an expert system in law, as no such guide can presently be found, and, further, as a contribution to the study of legal theory as it is apparent that traditional questions of jurisprudence, and in particular, of analytical jurisprudence, are of relevance in this context. We will, moreover, as McCarty claimed in 1977, be able 'to test out the implications of our theories' using the computer as 'the most powerful tool for expressing formal theories and spinning out their consequences that has ever been devised.'[84] There can be little doubt, then, that the successful construction of expert systems in law will be of profound theoretical and practical importance to all those whose concern is the law.

[83] Thus, our findings will be of relevance to the construction of expert systems in law in most, if not all, legal systems.

[84] 'Reflections on TAXMAN: An Experiment in Artificial Intelligence and Legal Reasoning', n. 26 above, p. 840.

9

Expert Systems in Law:
From Theory into Practice[1]

This chapter builds on the previous two, by linking the theoretical side of expert systems in law with the practicalities of implementation. We are concerned once again, therefore, with a type of computer system that can be said to solve legal problems and offer legal advice. The first part of the chapter offers a non-technical introduction to artificial intelligence and expert systems, while the second provides a theoretical defence of the field of expert systems in law. The third part is practical in orientation, describing an expert system that operates on the English law on latent damage. This system is thought to have been the world's first commercially available expert system in law, properly so-called. The final part presents some concluding observations.

---

[1] This chapter was originally delivered as one of the Cambridge Lectures in 1987. It was published as 'Expert Systems: Theory and Practice', in Frank McArdle (ed.), *The Cambridge Lectures* (Montreal: Yvon Blais, 1989). Earlier parts of some of the chapter appeared in my conference paper, 'Expert Systems in Law: Out of the Research Laboratory and into the Marketplace' (ACM, Proceedings of 1st International Conference on 'Artificial Intelligence and Law', (1987)).

I

Artificial intelligence, as discussed in Chapters 7 and 8, is the branch of computer science devoted to the design, development, and implementation of computer systems that can perform tasks and solve problems of a sort for which it is normally expected human intelligence is required. Examples of such systems are those that understand the spoken word and translate limited subsets of natural language.

Expert systems are one type of artificially intelligent computer system. They are computer applications that have been built with the help of human experts in such a way that they are able to offer advice, draw conclusions, and solve specialized problems within limited fields of discourse. Expert systems are designed to reason at the standard of, and even sometimes at a higher level than, human experts in given subjects. They act as sophisticated intellectual aids for their users: that is why they are also known as 'intelligent assistants'. Ordinarily, the users of expert systems are not expected to be laymen, but rather should be persons of general training within a discipline who are seeking answers to specific problems that require expertise for their resolution.

For the purpose of this chapter, an expert system can be said to have two major components. First, there is its knowledge base, its store of knowledge. This is the part of the system that holds specialized expertise and knowledge about its domain of application. Related research issues here are those of *knowledge representation*, which pertains to the techniques and problems of representing the knowledge of a domain within a computer system, and of *knowledge acquisition*, concerning the way in which expertise can be drawn from human beings and then articulated with a view to embodying it in a knowledge base.

The second component of any expert system is its inference engine, the reasoning mechanism which applies the knowledge in the knowledge base to given problem data and thereby generates conclusion and advice. The research topic of *knowledge utilization* is relevant here, because scholars of this issue concentrate on the development or identification of reasoning methods suitable for given fields.

Persons who actually build expert systems are known as 'knowledge engineers'.

Generally, as we have seen earlier in the book, expert systems are:

1. *transparent*, by which is meant they can generate explanations of the lines of reasoning that lead them to their conclusions;

2. *heuristic*, which means they reason with the informal, judgmental know-ledge that is gained from experience, and that underlies expertise, in a given field (as well as reasoning with the more formal knowledge of the domain in question); and
3. *flexible*, a term that refers to their capability of allowing modifications to their knowledge bases without great difficulty.

Although the best publicized achievements in expert systems have concerned mineral prospecting, chemical analysis, and medical diagnosis, since 1970 both computer scientists and lawyers have recognized the suitability of law as a domain of application for research and development in this branch of computer science. In principle, wherever human expertise is required in the administration of law, there is scope for the development and installation of an expert system. The expert systems in law discussed in this chapter, however, are more specialized applications: systems that reason with, solve problems of, and offer advice on the basis of, the law as held in legislation and judicial precedents. The ability to interpret statutes and case reports and apply such interpretations to help solve concrete legal problems is the hallmark of legal expertise, and, therefore, its implementation is the province of expert systems in law.

On this account, then, expert systems in law are computer programs that have been developed, with the help of human legal experts, in particular and usually highly specialized branches of the law. These systems are designed to perform as intelligent assistants in the processes of legal reasoning and legal problem-solving (and are also useful teaching aids). The users of such systems are intended to be general legal practitioners or legally informed persons, who, when confronted with legal difficulties beyond their range of knowledge and experience, rather than always having to turn to appropriately qualified legal specialists or to unwieldy textbooks, may instead consult their expert systems in law. The systems ask questions of their users, exposing them to all and only those parts of the law that bear on the problems being investigated. They guide their users through the problem-solving process, using the embodied formal and heuristic knowledge of the experts who assisted in their design. Furthermore, these systems offer explanations for the advice they offer, they can indicate what avenues they are exploring, and may be required to provide legal authority for all assertions made and conclusions drawn.

The major goal of workers in the field of expert systems in law can be summarized in another way. The goal can be said to be that of making scarce, human legal expertise and legal knowledge more widely available and more easily accessible through the use of computer technology.

In the UK, as at the middle of 1987, there were very few operational systems that met the specifications just offered. Other than the system discussed here—The Latent Damage System—no such systems at that time had emerged from the legal profession.[2] What has emerged is that there are both theoretical and practical problems associated with the field. The remainder of this chapter addresses these problems. From a theoretical point of view a research project carried out at the University of Oxford is described while, from a practical perspective, The Latent Damage System is introduced.

II

In 1983, a collaborative research project on expert systems in law, involving the Law Faculty and the Programming Research Group, was initiated at the University of Oxford. The project, some background to which was outlined in the previous chapter, was carried out by two investigators: the current author (then a law graduate who had specialized for several years in jurisprudence) and David Gold (then a computing science graduate with experience in industry). Both had already been working in the field of computer applications to the law since 1981 and had quickly recognized the desirability—indeed, the necessity—for concentrated, interdisciplinary research in the field.

The Oxford Project, as it shall be called, had three fundamental goals. The first objective was to build an expert system in Scottish divorce law. A prototype of this system was in fact rendered operational. The second aim of the project was to consider the use of certain mathematical techniques for the formal description of expert systems in general, and of expert systems in law in particular.[3] The project's third goal was to enquire into the process of building expert systems in law from the point of view of jurisprudence (legal philosophy or legal theory). Although the value and point of jurisprudence has frequently been doubted by legal practitioners, students, and academics alike, one aspect of the discipline—analytical jurisprudence—is of central

[2] An exception here is document assembly systems, which have enjoyed commercial success and serious usage in several jurisdictions. It still remains the case that very few expert systems have been developed; although expert systems modules for online legal services are emerging as a priority; and some notable successes have also been achieved in the regulatory field (see www.softlaw.com.au).

[3] That work is discussed in some detail in David Gold and Richard Susskind, 'Expert Systems in Law: A Jurisprudential and Formal Specification Approach' in Antonio Martino and Fiorenza Natali (eds.), *Automated Analysis of Legal Texts* (Amsterdam: North-Holland, 1986).

importance to expert systems in law. For that part of legal theory strives to promote a systematic, theoretical, and general understanding of issues such as the structure of legal rules and legal systems, the nature of legal reasoning, the role of logic in the law, and the interpretation of legislation and case law. And, of course, each of these issues is crucial for building expert systems that reason in law.

This discussion of expert systems theory focuses on some of the jurisprudential matters addressed during the Oxford Project. A complete exposition of the jurisprudential conclusions of the Oxford Project is provided in my book, *Expert Systems in Law*.[4]

As a matter of necessity, all expert systems in law make assumptions about the nature of law and the nature of legal reasoning. It is apparent, then, that the enterprise of constructing these systems is laden with jurisprudential (particularly analytical) implications. To be more precise, the work of the Oxford Project confirms that jurisprudence is pertinent for legal knowledge engineering in two significant ways. First of all, jurisprudence can be deployed as an invaluable source of practical, sound guidance for those developing expert systems in law. Secondly, through jurisprudential discussion and argumentation, the latent theoretical implications, presuppositions, and assumptions of existing systems can be articulated and thereby the potential, as well as the practical and jurisprudential limitations, of these systems can be pinpointed.

These applications for jurisprudence are now becoming accepted. Yet several words of caution should be offered in this context. It should be stressed, in the first place, that while it is argued that it is both possible and desirable for jurisprudence to be used in the two ways just outlined, it is not suggested that it is in any sense logically necessary for all engineers of legal knowledge to have recourse to legal philosophy as their touchstone and guide. In the same way as it is not necessary for writers of texts on the law to use jurisprudence explicitly while preparing their prose, similarly, expert systems in law in the future may possibly be developed in absence of reliance on sources of legal theory. However, it is likely that any such systems will be of lowish quality. Accepting that the sound engineering of legal expertise requires extensive familiarity with the nature of legal reasoning and the law, it is hardly imaginable that such an acquaintance could be gained other than by extensive exposure to jurisprudence of some sort.

However, there is a great range of often conflicting theories and schools of thought within the jurisprudential literature. It might be thought, because of

---

[4] Oxford: Oxford University Press, 1987.

this feature of legal theory, that perplexity and confusion—and not inspiration and clarification—would result from recourse to the writings of legal theory. The Oxford Project sought to rebut this suggestion by seeking to identify (limited) consensus over many relevant questions of jurisprudence and to demonstrate that expert systems in law both could and should be developed on the basis of that body of agreement. Approximately fifty leading texts and one hundred major articles were studied in the quest for consensus. On the strength of that survey, it is suggested that in the past the divergence of opinions and theories within jurisprudence has been misleadingly accentuated by the tendency of legal theorists to concentrate on the most contentious matters without stopping to articulate those issues over which few of them would reasonably argue. An initial step in the project was that of clarifying why theorists examining the nature of law and legal reasoning have failed to agree. Several factors were pinpointed and awareness of these helped the search for consensus.

The approach of the Oxford Project can be summarized as follows: with a view to locating consensus within those aspects of jurisprudence relevant to expert systems in law, a wide range of jurisprudential writings were surveyed, on the strength of which it was endeavoured to articulate models and theories of law and legal reasoning of use as guidance to those building and evaluating systems.

With regard to the sources examined for the Oxford Project, while analytical jurisprudence was identified as being crucial, because the writings on this one aspect of legal theory are so extensive, it was, of course, necessary to be selective; this inevitably gave rise to those perennial problems of subjectivity and bias that fetter workers in all disciplines. With the prominent exceptions of the writings of Hans Kelsen and Jeremy Bentham, the vast proportion of the sources examined were writings of analytical jurisprudence and philosophy composed since the mid-1950s and early 1960s in the United Kingdom.

Since that time, there have emerged exceptionally erudite and penetrating legal analyses, focusing in particular on the nature of reasoning and rules, most of which work was inspired by H.L.A. Hart. It was considered that the most rigorous and formal of these works were the sources with the greatest potential given the major goals of the Oxford Project. The recommendations and conclusions reached in respect of the jurisprudential part of the Oxford Project are, therefore, open to falsification in light of research that accounts for a wider range of legal philosophies.

Seven issues of analytical jurisprudence in particular were addressed in the course of the Oxford Project:

1. the nature of legal reasoning;
2. the relationship of logic to the law;
3. the nature of legal knowledge;
4. the structure of legal rules;
5. the activity of legal science;
6. the individuation of laws; and
7. the nature of legal systems and legal subsystems.

The major jurisprudential finding of the Oxford Project is that there is nothing inherent in the process of legal reasoning or in the nature of law that constitutes a theoretical or practical obstacle to the development of rule-based expert systems in law of restricted scope. This view is supported by consensus within analytical jurisprudence as shown in detail in my book, *Expert Systems in Law*. The following paragraphs offer a brief overview of one of the central arguments.

It seems that legal theorists agree—although they do not always do so explicitly—that *rules* both do and ought to play a central role in descriptive legal science (roughly speaking, describing the law) and in legal reasoning. On careful analysis, it turns out that even a legal theorist such as Ronald Dworkin, who is automatically associated with doubt over the sufficiency of rules for legal decision making, does nevertheless seem to assume a predominant place for them. Rules are central to the administration of law: they are the fundamental building blocks with which all the legal profession operate.

Yet any rule-based model of legal reasoning is clearly vulnerable to the criticism that, in arriving at legal decisions and conclusions, legal reasoning agents frequently receive insufficient or unacceptable guidance from rules alone and so both do, and ought to, apply non-rule standards ranging from policy, principles, and purpose through to social justice, political morality, personal preference, and even mere whim. In reply to this charge, the consensus model responds in the following way: while it may well be the case that the guidance rules offer in many cases is either insufficient or unacceptable, surely it is only once rules have been applied that the insufficiency or unacceptability of the guidance they offer can be gauged. In other words, all legal reasoning agents strive in the first place to apply possibly applicable rules and when some conclusion is inferred in that way they then proceed to assess the resultant conclusion. Reasoning with rules, therefore, according to consensus within jurisprudence, is a necessary but not always sufficient component of the process of legal reasoning. If this is so, rule-based expert systems in law, prima facie, should be able to help in the execution of that component part of the activity of legal reasoning.

No one could sensibly contend, however, that rules are flawless and complete entities. Consensus in jurisprudence suggests that rules can always be subject to implied exceptions—mainly on grounds of purpose of principle—and conclusions reached through their application to sets of facts are, accordingly, conditional in kind. Furthermore, rules are expressed in natural language and so suffer from being 'open-textured' and often vague. Rules themselves cannot be said to be clear. All that can be clear is their application in certain cases: hence the well-worn phrase of legal theory, 'clear cases'.

What is unclear, however, is precisely what constitutes a clear case. This issue is addressed at length in my book, *Expert Systems in Law*, which offers a 'semantic' theory of clear cases. This theory is best understood if the idea of 'acontextual meaning' is first clarified. Ronald Dworkin, formerly the Professor of Jurisprudence at the University of Oxford, introduced the notion of 'acontextual meaning' to jurisprudence. It denotes the meaning we would assign to words 'if we had no special information about the context of their use or the intentions of their author.'[5] According to the semantic theory of clear cases, then, these cases are, roughly, those in which the facts of the case can, in accordance with the conventional and 'acontextual' use of legal and ordinary language, be subsumed unambiguously within the terms of valid legal rules.

In short, rule-based expert systems in law can assist in the solving of such clear cases and can identify the literal interpretations of rules as they apply to the facts of cases.

The utility of systems that can solve only semantically clear cases by offering conditional conclusions might be questioned. However, when a lawyer is faced with a problem of a highly specialized sort, requiring a familiarity he lacks with obscure and detailed areas of law, he has no idea whether the case is one that would present difficulties for relevant experts. It may be that the problem is indeed a very hard case which even a legal expert would be hesitant about, but frequently it will be one to which the expert has an immediate answer. The latter case can be called a 'clear case of the expert domain': its resolution, I argue in *Expert Systems in Law*, is dependent not on intricate reasoning techniques but on extensive domain-specific knowledge applied to the problem data using some variant of deductive logic. And by solving clear cases of the expert domain, rule-based expert systems in law will provide access to scarce legal expertise.

The Oxford Project confirmed to the satisfaction of the current author that the enterprises of building rule-based expert systems in law (with their vari-

---

[5] See *Law's Empire* (London: Fontana, 1986), p. 17.

ous restrictions and limitations) is both jurisprudentially and computationally feasible. Why, then, have there been so few operational systems available for purchase and deployment by lawyers?

III

Rule-based expert systems in law are not available widely in the marketplace for two main reasons.[6]

In the first place, there is a human resources problem. Simply put, there is a lack of appropriately skilled knowledge engineers and willing domain experts available to develop the systems. Constructing expert systems in law is extremely labour intensive. Ideally, it demands a knowledge engineer with considerable experience or training in law: there are, however, very few such people. Although legal knowledge engineering may emerge in the future as a career in its own right, in the interim, there is a regrettable shortage of individuals with suitable backgrounds in both computers and the law.

Yet, even if we had large teams of eager and qualified legal knowledge engineers, unless designers of systems have direct access to human legal experts, expert systems in law will not be developed. If the legal knowledge engineer is particularly knowledgeable about the domain of application, expert(s) may not be required throughout the entire construction process. Rather, they will be needed only to 'tune' the system. But even this itself can be a time-consuming process. In summary, until now, legal experts have been unwilling to contribute significantly to the development of expert systems. As long as this remains so, progress in the field will be very slow.

The second reason for the lack of commercially viable and marketable expert systems in law is the absence of carefully and clearly formulated standard procedures and practices for their development. Little has been written, for example, on the management, staffing, planning documentation, co-ordination and evaluation of projects in this field. It has rarely been possible, therefore, for anyone embarking upon the development of an expert system in law to benefit from the findings and recommendations of others. Rather, would-be legal knowledge engineers invariably have been

---

[6] I would add a third today—that the advent of the World Wide Web (several years after this essay was originally written), moved many researchers from using rule-based systems techniques to deploying the Web to capture and disseminate knowledge and expertise.

confronted with the same obstacles and pitfalls as have fettered their colleagues in the past.

The advantages of having a body of legal knowledge engineering standards—a methodology, as it is known—are clear. Such a methodology promotes considerably more speedy and effective construction of systems; ensures quality and consistency of products; makes for ease of maintenance of systems; controls the development process; and, more generally, allows systems to be developed in a far less haphazard fashion than in the past.

During 1987, I was involved in an intensely practical project in the course of which the difficulties just mentioned were overcome. For the project had the co-operation and commitment of an expert and a legal knowledge engineer, and a methodology was to hand. Before discussing the system, it is appropriate to say a little about the area of law in which it operates.

Until September 1986, English law gave rise to remarkable injustice: the owners and occupiers of buildings and the clients of professional advisers could lose legal rights even before they could have known they had them; and advisers, designers, and builders could be exposed to liability for long, uncertain periods of time extending to decades. The problem was to be removed by a short Act of Parliament. The Lord Chancellor told the House of Lords: 'The Bill does two things and two things only. The first is to give a plaintiff who may have suffered damage without his knowledge and which was beyond his power of discovery, a further period within which to obtain his rights . . . [and secondly] to fix a long stop as it is called, beyond which the architect or whoever could not be sued.'

Although the intention of the Bill could be described so simply, the implementing provisions in what became the Latent Damage Act 1986 were cumbersome and convoluted and were couched in a multitude of cross-referenced subsections.

Even for the most adept legal practitioner, the Act seemed to be a dense web of barely intelligible, interrelated rules. And these rules themselves introduced a range of overlapping and interrelated time periods. Moreover, the Act could not be understood without extensive knowledge of other relevant pieces of legislation and case law. In short, the field of latent damage was a challenging testing ground for expert systems work.

The project to build an expert system to advise on latent damage law was a collaborative venture involving Ernst & Whinney (now Ernst & Young), the international accounting and consultancy firm, and the Law Faculty of the University of Oxford. Knowledge engineering skills were provided by Ernst & Whinney and the legal expertise came from Keble College, Oxford. The goal of the project was to develop an expert system—'The Latent Damage

System'—that advised on legal provisions relating to the law on latent damage.

The project's domain expert was Phillip Capper, then a full-time Fellow of Keble College, Oxford, and chairman of the Oxford University Law Faculty. Furthermore, he was an ex-IBM programmer. An acknowledged expert on the Latent Damage Act 1986, he had written the first book on the statute. For the purpose of lecturing to lawyers and other professionals, he had developed a model of what the legislation was trying to achieve. He then recognized that his model could perhaps be implemented in an expert system, and so got in touch—at Ernst & Whinney—with me, as someone who had originally trained in law and had spent the previous six years working on expert systems in law and engineering legal knowledge.

There was never any intention of directly translating the Latent Damage Act 1986 into some computer formalism: the goal, rather, was to implement in a system a leading expert's conception and interpretation of the Act and related law. (Notice also that the Latent Damage Project was distinct from the Oxford Project discussed earlier.)

The expert system that was developed, the Latent Damage System, offered advice and drew conclusions in relation to the Latent Damage Act 1986 and related statutes and judicial precedents. The system was for use both by professional advisers and by persons working in the construction, manufacturing, and supply industries. The system assisted in identifying when a breach of duty occurred, on what date the cause of action accrued, and when the plaintiff had knowledge of the damage suffered. The implications of fraud, deliberate concealment, contractual liability, personal injuries, successive ownership, and many other related matters were also taken into account. The key piece of advice offered by the system was the date after which the claimant could no longer commence proceedings. The discovery of this date was the product of a sophisticated reasoning process.

It was estimated that a competent lawyer would have taken about five to ten hours to understand the Act and its implications. (Non-lawyers would almost certainly have been unable to fathom its consequences, unless they were familiar with the fundamental principles of the law of negligence.) By using the Latent Damage System, however, the lawyer or legally informed person was able to find solutions to latent damage problems in about five to ten minutes. The system was an intelligent assistant—it guided a user through all but only those legal rules that bore on the problem at hand.

The user needed to have no knowledge whatsoever of computer science, as the system offered friendly prompts and guidance throughout the consultation. The system offered explanation facilities: it clarified questions, and indicated what line of reasoning it was exploring. Final touches included the facility to examine, onscreen, extracts both from judgments and legislation, and the option of requesting a printed summary of any consultation.

The Latent Damage System, on two 5¼-inch floppy discs, was published together with a book in 1988.[7] Many law publishers perceived this form of multimedia publishing—a book with a disk in the back—as the next step forward in legal publications.

The most challenging and important part of the system development process was acquiring and structuring the expertise. (The formulation of precise wordings for questions, messages, and prompts, and the compilation of explanation screens, was not tackled at the stage of structuring. This was postponed until the knowledge had been entered.) Central to the knowledge acquisition process was the Latent Damage Act itself. This meant tackling and representing the following legal complexities.

In solving latent damage problems, even before attempting to apply the Act to any particular case, two matters have to be clarified: the nature of the loss suffered; and the nature of the duty that has been broken. In neither instance will this be straightforward. These are matters of legal classification, and in both areas there had recently been remarkable and fast-moving changes to the law as a result of decisions in the courts, even during the very period when the Latent Damage Bill was passing through Parliament. The case law that underpinned the Act was, therefore, the subject of considerable uncertainty.

The whole Act, as we interpreted it then, turned on the concept of damage, but it did not even define 'latent damage' explicitly. This actually represents a wide cluster of ideas with some vital distinctions. Is the loss financial or physical? When did it occur? Can a defect be damage? Was the remedial work carried out in order to remove a defect or a danger?

In law, the likelihood of recovering a particular loss depends on the kind of duty that was broken. Professional advisers' duties can be different from those of contractors, suppliers, and manufacturers. The extent of a surveyor's liability is different from an architect's. Financial and legal advisers are treated in some cases as a category distinct from other professionals. Local authority liabilities for building control have been narrowed considerably. A duty which when broken causes latent damage may arise in the law of tort, the law of contract, or under a statute. Each may have different conse-

---

[7] Phillip Capper and Richard Susskind, *Latent Damage Law: The Expert System* (London: Butterworths, 1988). This is a full case study of the development of the system. It can be seen from the book that many of the suggestions in the third part of Chapter Seven of this book were applied in developing The Latent Damage System.

quences as to the range of losses protected, and to the timing of the limitation period applicable to a claim. Moreover, the Latent Damage Act applied only to 'negligence': but this is not defined in the Act. The principle of the '15-year longstop' was particularly novel: that in the law of negligence the time period should be reckoned as starting from a breach of duty. Hence, past case law concerned with establishing a breach of duty is focused more on the point *that* it happened, rather than *when* it happened.

For clarity, these legal complexities required a modular approach in structuring the expertise, that is, each of the above issues had to be addressed in a separate portion of the system. But the conceptual interrelationships precluded complete independence of the modules.

The knowledge acquisition sessions themselves—the discussion sessions between expert and knowledge engineer generally focused on particular sections of the Act, what they meant, and how they related both to other provisions of the Act and to related statutes and cases. Given that the expert had already articulated much of his expertise for the purposes of his book, written material was to hand; and the structure of the knowledge base reflects the approach in the book. Although being involved in the design of the expert system urged the expert to think in a different and perhaps more precise and structured fashion than had been demanded of him in the past, the existence of his writings in the field rendered the problem of knowledge acquisition less acute than is normally the case.

The major structuring of the system was usually undertaken on paper—through flowcharts, tables, diagrams, and notes—and refined at the computer itself. The knowledge engineer and the expert always worked together in building up and structuring the knowledge base. Both parties found this to be an intellectually stimulating and enormously enjoyable activity.

IV

The success of the Latent Damage System project was due in large part to the particular combination of skills that were brought to bear on the project. The expert was not only an excellent specialist in the domain of application but was trained in computer programming and therefore was more involved technically than domain experts tend to be in expert systems projects. Very little about the technology of expert systems needed to be introduced to the expert. As the knowledge engineer, my experience in building expert systems in law was also crucial for the project, and my training in law allowed the development to progress unhindered by law tutorials by expert to engineer. In sum, because both the expert and knowledge engineer had strong backgrounds in computers and law, it was possible to avoid spending extensive periods of time familiarizing the expert with computers and the knowledge engineer with law.

It should be stressed too that there is no substitute for having the undivided attention of an expert for considerable periods of time. The expert devoted extensive portions of time to the project, and without his continued interest in and involvement with the system, progress could not have been made. One of the principal reasons for there being comparatively few expert systems is that human experts are not prepared to allocate substantial periods of time to work with knowledge engineers. And this is especially true in the legal domain.

In conclusion, because legal knowledge and expertise is such a valuable and scarce resource the potential for expert systems in law is considerable. The Oxford Project established the jurisprudential propriety of such systems, while the Latent Damage System demonstrated the feasibility of building them.

10

An Early Case Study in Packaging the Law[1]

This chapter is something of a curiosity. It is a review of an early and fairly unimpressive attempt to package the law as a consultative service. Although the system in question was thought to be wanting in various dimensions, the issues raised remain instructive today. When I reread the original article, I was struck by two apparently contradictory thoughts. The first is how far we seem to have travelled in IT and law over the past 15 years. And the second is how, in some ways, comparatively little has been achieved. In a short post-script to the chapter, I try to make sense of this contradiction in the context of several very recent attempts to package the law.

As with the other essays in this part of the book, the main body of the chapter concerns computer systems that offer legal advice. Section I is a non-technical introduction to the topic of expert systems in substantive law, and Section II reviews what was claimed to be an expert system guide to the Data Protection Act 1984.

---

[1] This chapter was originally published as 'Expert Systems in Law and the Data Protection Adviser' (1987) 7 *Oxford Journal of Legal Studies* 1: 145.

I

Most legal practitioners and academics are now familiar with the idea of computerized legal data retrieval systems such as LEXIS. These systems constitute a significant addition to the research armoury of the lawyer by providing the facility under favourable conditions for the swift retrieval of the formal sources of our law (as well now as some secondary material). The operation of these systems can be summarized quite briefly. In their databases, they hold, in full-text format, large bodies of legislation and case law, and these can be retrieved by the user and presented to him in the same form as they appear in the statute books and law reports. The user instructs the computer system by typing in a single keyword or several keywords in combination: that is, a word or sequence of words he considers to be relevant to any legal problem at hand. The computer then effectively searches the selected part of its database for occurrences of these keywords, informs the user of the number of documents holding such words, and presents these texts to him when instructed to do so.[2] Although legal database systems, particularly in the USA, are being used widely, their utility for legal research has been questioned: the criterion of relevance implicit in the keyword search strategy can result in the retrieval of irrelevant data or in a failure to locate all pertinent documents within the database. More 'intelligent' systems have been called for, and, in this connection, the possibility of building what are known as expert systems in law is now being given serious consideration. (A detailed introduction to these systems is given in the previous three chapters.)

As we have seen in earlier chapters, expert systems are computer programs that have been written with the assistance of human experts in such a way that they are capable of drawing conclusions and solving highly specialized problems within limited fields of discourse. They are designed to reason at the level of, and sometimes even at a higher standard than, human experts in given subjects. They function as high-level intellectual aids for their users, which explains one of their alternative names: 'intelligent assistants'. The users of expert systems are not usually expected to be laymen, but persons of general training within a discipline who require answers to specific problems that demand expertise for their resolution.

For present purposes, an expert system can be considered to have two major components. First, there is its knowledge base. This is the portion of the system that contains specialized knowledge and expertise about its domain of application. Associated research topics here are those of *know-*

---

[2] Many modern, Internet-based legal retrieval systems operate in much the same way today.

ledge representation, which concerns the problems and techniques of representing the knowledge of a domain within computer memory, and of *knowledge acquisition*, pertaining to the way in which expertise can be extracted from human beings and articulated with a view to embodying it in a knowledge base. The second component of any expert system is its inference engine, the problem-solving mechanism which allows the knowledge base to interact and reason with any problem data. The research issue of *knowledge utilization* is also relevant here, because students of this matter focus on the identification or development of reasoning methods appropriate for given fields.

Expert systems are usually: (1) *transparent*, which means that they can generate explanations of the lines of reasoning that lead them to their conclusions; (2) *heuristic*, by which is meant they reason with the informal, judgmental, experiential, and often procedural knowledge that underlies expertise in a given field (as well as with the more formal knowledge of the domain in question); and (3) *flexible*, a term that refers to their ability to allow, without any great difficulty, modifications to their knowledge bases.

Although the best-known work on expert systems has concerned medical diagnosis, chemical analysis, and mineral prospecting, for fifteen years now both lawyers and computer scientists have recognized the suitability of law as a domain of application for research and development in this wing of computer science. Much attention has been directed towards the design of systems that can reason with, and solve problems of, substantive law (although a lawyer's expertise will invariably extend well beyond purely legal knowledge).

On the basis of the discussion so far, expert systems in substantive law should be expected to correspond roughly to the following tentative characterization. They are computer programs that have been developed, with the aid of human legal experts, in particular and usually highly specialized areas of law. These systems are designed to function as intelligent assistants in the processes of legal reasoning and legal problem-solving. The users of such systems are intended to be general legal practitioners, who, when faced with legal problems beyond their range of experience and knowledge, rather than always having to turn to appropriately qualified legal specialists or to unwieldy textbooks, may instead consult their expert systems in law. Such systems ask questions of their users and guide them through the problem-solving process, using the embodied heuristic and formal knowledge of the experts who assisted in their design. Moreover, these systems offer explanations for their lines of reasoning and may be required to provide legal authority for all assertions made and conclusions drawn.

It must be stressed that such an outline today constitutes the research aspirations of workers in the field of expert systems in law, and is not a description of any single computer system currently in use by legal practitioners. It is likely, however, that fully operational systems of the sort envisaged will be developed in the next ten years, given that sufficient resources are directed to this end. This prediction[3] is made on the basis of: (1) the achievements of current projects in this field, which collectively demonstrate the computational feasibility of constructing such systems; and (2) the findings of the current author's research, which indicate the jurisprudential feasibility (and limitations) of building rule-based expert systems in substantive law. (From 1983 to 1986, the author was involved in a collaborative research project concerning expert systems in law, involving the Law Faculty and the Programming Research Group of the University of Oxford. One product of the project was an aspiring expert system that solved some problems relating to Scottish divorce law.[4])

From 1970 to 1985, about 25 university research projects were involved (directly or indirectly) with expert systems in law, but from none of these emerged a system that could be purchased and used by the legal profession or indeed the general public. However, work in the field was not confined to the academic world: interest in expert systems that operated on legislation has also been evinced by several software houses. And it was one such company that marketed a program claimed to be an expert system guide to the Data Protection Act 1984. In the remainder of this chapter, that program is described and evaluated.

II

The *Data Protection Adviser* (DPA) was written and marketed by a software house called Intelligent Environments Ltd (iE). It is understood that iE released several versions of DPA. This chapter reviews the first release that was available to the public, although some relevant updates are acknowledged.

DPA was the first of a projected series of low-cost advisers designed for business users, and was described as 'An Expert System Guide to the Data

---

[3] Made in 1985.

[4] For a description of that project, see Chapter 9; and for a description of other projects of that era, see Chapter 8.

Protection Act'. (Systems offering advice on statutory sick pay and on loans to company directors were also available from iE.) DPA cost £20, and this price included a second disk on which the user could store relevant information relating to registration under the Act. Over 500 copies of DPA were sold. It is interesting to note that in the small leaflet that accompanied the program, iE explicitly excluded liability for loss resulting from users' reliance on the advice of DPA: the question of liability for defective advice given by expert systems remains a pressing issue for computer lawyers, and one to which there has been little serious attention paid.

DPA was developed using a type of software tool that is commonly referred to as an expert system *shell*. Shells are ready-made problem-solving mechanisms upon which expert systems may be built. Broadly speaking, they provide a general-purpose framework into which knowledge may be put, and they eliminate the need for the redesign of inference engines each time a new expert system is built. The shell used for the creation of DPA was CRYSTAL, also a product of iE. CRYSTAL, written in the programming language C and costing £395 (CRYSTAL II, the updated version, was priced at £695), was a shell that assisted in the development of *rule-based* expert systems, those systems whose domain knowledge is represented within the knowledge base as a system of rules. DPA held 400 rules and could present the user with a total of 200 questions (though clearly not during every consultation). The bulk of the knowledge, derived from the 1984 Act and the Data Registrar's publications, was entered into the system by one man in three days. Although it was intimated that the knowledge base was refined by data protection experts, the incompleteness and (as we shall see) often poor quality of the represented knowledge suggested that experts' direct involvement was minimal.

The DPA program was purchased as a small (5¼-inch) computer disk that operated on IBM PCs or compatible machines. The system ran under PC-DOS and MS-DOS operating systems, with a minimum of 256kb RAM. DPA was presented in a small envelope together with a leaflet with several paragraphs of introductory remarks, a licence agreement, and related sentences that sought to minimize iE's liability. The system was remarkably easy to use. After inserting the disk, two simple commands—'A' and 'DPA'—rendered it ready for immediate operation. The user interacted with the system either by reading one of the many assertions stored within the program and then by pressing any key to continue the consultation; or by giving positive or negative answers to questions posed by the system. The direction of the dialogue was partly dictated by the responses given by the user, and partly by the system's reasoning mechanism which made it move backwards through the knowledge base in search of premises that led to desired conclusions. The system, as we said, was rule-based, and the rules were connected to one another by the standard connectors of propositional logic. On the basis of the user's answers and the rules held in the program, intermediate and final conclusions could be drawn by DPA. In short, the advice given by DPA was either in the form of direct informative statements, or of inferences made on the strength both of its knowledge and of the data presented to it. As well as being able to reply 'yes' or 'no' to questions asked, the user could ask 'why' any question was being asked. In reply to this, the line of reasoning the system was pursuing was revealed, although not in an illuminating way. In general, DPA was not particularly transparent: its explanation facilities did not promote any clear understanding of its reasoning processes.

DPA offered advice (made assertions and drew inferences) on four aspects of data protection law. (A familiarity with this area of law is assumed in the following.) First, it dealt with registration, and did so in two stages. Initially, the system presented a series of assertions that constituted non-legal but prudent advice for the data user on sensible procedures to be adopted by any institution that may be affected by the legislation. These assertions were based on the Data Protection Registrar's first guideline to the 1984 Act. Thereafter, DPA asked a long series of questions about the user's deployment of computer systems, and eventually, in accordance with the Act, concluded whether the user was a data user who 'processes' data about 'data subjects'. Exemptions were allowed for, and persons carrying on computer bureaux also received advice. The system finally concluded whether or not the user ought to register. Unfortunately, at that stage, in contrast with most expert systems, the user did not seem to be offered an opportunity to ask *how* the final conclusion was inferred. (Later versions of DPA were supposed to overcome this deficiency in transparency.)

The second area in which DPA offered advice was in relation to the legislation's implications for business. This was not a particularly subtle part of the system, as it consisted solely in a long series of assertions (about 15), and no interaction was allowed. No menu was offered, and so the user had to proceed through the statements sequentially.

Thirdly, DPA was designed to advise on the question of subject access. It did so not from the point of view of a potential data subject, but from that of a data user. (It was understood that future releases of the system were to give direct advice to both data users and data subjects.) This portion of the system was fettered by an early yet unintelligible prompt that: 'If you are uncertain of the answers to any of the questions answer NO to continue to find other possibly strong access denial conditions.' This part of the program sought to indicate whether access to the user's data had to be given to sub-jects and once more it allowed for the user to answer positively or negatively, or to ask why queries had been posed. Exemptions were dealt with, but the lawyer would have found unacceptable the implicit conflation of paragraphs in the questions. For example, one question merges paragraphs (a), (b), and (c) of subsection 28(1) of the Act, each of which had a distinguishable subject matter and should, according to any sensible theory of the individuation of laws, constitute the bases of three separate questions.[5] Furthermore, the sys-tem was sometimes misleading: its assertion that '[Note: the Act does not mention doctors]' did not sit comfortably with subsection 29(1) of the Act that pertains to 'physical or mental health'.

Fourthly, DPA offered a rather restricted summary of the data protection principles. Again this was presented not in the form of a menu but as a series of (eight) propositions. These were derived from Part I of Schedule I to the Act, but were offered in an unnecessarily abbreviated form. For instance, the system omitted 'at reasonable intervals and without due delay or expense' from its rendition of the seventh principle. Moreover, no mention was made of Part II of Schedule I which offered some crucial guidelines regarding the interpretation of the principles.

Turning now to an evaluation of the system, in its favour, DPA was simple and quick to use, it was very inexpensive in comparison to many commer-cially available (non-legal) expert systems, and it lacked the extensive and tiresome documentation that normally accompanied computer software. (DPA's documentation was equivalent to one short paragraph of text.) Moreover, it seemed to be the first attempt to market a system that pur-ported to offer expert legal advice.

However, it could be criticized on many grounds over and above those that have already been mentioned. DPA was poorly structured in that the user was given no idea of what stage he was at in his consultation: the 'why' facil-ity was far from helpful and offered no substantial help through its produc-tion of the propositions whose truth-value the system may have been seeking. Interactions with users who knew little of the law or of expert sys-tems would inevitably have lapsed into mindless exercises, particularly as the user often had very little control of the search and problem-solving processes. (Greater control was introduced in later releases.)

There was no sense in which one felt that one was communicating with a human expert as should have been the case according to the prevailing

---

[5] On the relevance of the jurisprudential question of the individuation of laws, see Chapter 8 of this book; and on individuation in general, see Joseph Raz, *The Concept of a Legal System*, 2nd edn. (Oxford: Clarendon Press, 1980), pp. 140–7.

expert systems orthodoxy and to theories of the role of heuristics in expert decision-making. Indeed it would surely have been inaccurate, on any reasonable interpretation of the term, to have said that DPA held legal *expertise*. A 'don't know' facility was also sadly lacking. That would have allowed the system perhaps to reason to hypothetical conclusions in the event of the user not knowing whether to answer 'yes' or 'no' to given questions. There was little to recommend this system for business users' purposes; for many of the currently available textbooks and pamphlets on data protection were as user-friendly and informative as DPA, but offered fuller coverage of the pertinent details.

From a legal point of view, given that DPA was described as a guide to the Act, it was far from satisfactory. The statute was given exceptionally scanty treatment: there was little or no mention, for example, of the Registrar, the Tribunal, implications of application (refusal and so forth), enforcement notices, de-registration notices, transfer prohibition notices, appeals, details of liability to prosecution, or rights of data subjects (to compensation and so forth). Further, the system never stated the provisions of the Act, from which the questions were often taken. An expert system in law should state 'authority' for all assertions made and conclusions drawn.

The system could not then be recommended to law students or legal practitioners. It was apparent from its many defects that DPA was hastily constructed with little regard to the quality of the resultant legal advice. Such haste in development was surely inappropriate in respect of a system that purported to offer advice in a field as profoundly important as the law. It may be contended in its defence that later releases of DPA would have overcome many of the shortcomings just identified. Yet this argument surely does not hold in respect of any system, being sold to the public, that allegedly offered useful advice to its users. Surely any commercial product, upon whose output people may rely immediately after purchase, should be a more polished item than the first version of DPA. (We would of course tolerate rough edges in experimental research prototypes, but iE did not present DPA in that category.)

In years to come,[6] it is likely that legal journals will devote separate portions of each of their issues to reviews of the latest computer programs that claim to offer legal advice, just as today book reviews are allocated their own sections. With advances in software engineering, the evolution of succeeding generations of hardware, and, most important of all, with increased jurisprudential understanding of how best to represent legal knowledge and design legal inference mechanisms, expert systems in law of the type envis-

---

[6] Said in 1985.

aged in Section I will no doubt be developed. It is hoped that reviewers of the future will be able to evaluate the systems more favourably than the present writer has been able to assess DPA.

Postscript

Writing in mid-2000, I said at the start of the chapter that when I look back on this review of DPA, two apparently contradictory reactions spring to mind. The first is that we have come a long way since 1985 when I wrote the piece; and the second is how little progress we have made. I can reconcile these views in the following way: technically, we have made enormous progress; whereas, commercially, the legal world has barely begun to exploit the opportunities.

In 1985, the machines on which DPA would run look remarkable in retrospect. These were large, heavy, stand-alone computers, not networked to anything; running from floppies (few users of today would actually recognize these genuinely floppy, 5¼-inch disks); functioning under a far-from-intuitive operating system known as DOS; with an average random access memory of 256kb. And, of course, hardly anyone used PCs anyway. The average kid of today would be embarrassed to have that kind of specification associated with his or her hand-held. These machines of yesteryear bear very little resemblance to the Windows-based, compact PCs (with about 250 times the amount of memory) that we have today. Above all else, we now have the World Wide Web, so that all users can connect with one another. I marvel at this technical progress.

How have lawyers exploited these astounding technical developments? Until recently, they have hardly exploited them at all; and that is why I feel little progress has been made. Looking specifically at expert systems, while it is true that The Latent Damage System, as described in Chapter 9 of this book, did fulfil my prediction that a fully operational expert system in law would be developed, there have been precious few other such systems, save for some document assembly systems and regulatory applications. The reality is that, in 1985, lawyers were using IT for word-processing, accounts, and other administrative applications—and not much changed for a decade after that. Following my thinking of Chapter 1, lawyers invested almost exclusively in back-office technology until 1995—in the 'plumbing'. Only since then have the bolder and more imaginative firms sought to harness the power of

Internet-based personal computing and develop client relationship systems, internal knowledge systems, and online legal services.

Nonetheless, I am more optimistic than ever. As I am fond of saying—I have been working in IT and the law for twenty years and have seen more progress in the last two than in the previous eighteen. I find it satisfying that I can back up my optimism in the very domain of law—data protection—that was the subject matter of this first review. For I know of no less than four online data protection services developed by UK law firms.[7] The most sophisticated is NextLaw by Clifford Chance. This online service helps its users (mainly large, international organizations working in financial services) to assess their compliance with over 30 data protection regimes around the world. It is comprehensive, easy to use, frequently updated and has a formidable collection of subscribers. At several thousand pounds sterling per jurisdiction, it is a far cry from the £20 cost of DPA but, as users attest, its value to them can be considerable. NextLaw is not an expert system in the sense in which expert systems were conceived in the 1980s—as stand-alone, rule-based, diagnostic systems. But its ethos is the same: it is about using IT to make scarce expertise and knowledge more widely available and more easily accessible. Ironically, for the systems are so wildly different—in terms of sophistication, content, and utility—DPA and NextLaw share this ethos. And it is that ethos that will transform the legal marketplace.

---

[7] Clifford Chance's *NextLaw* service at www.nextlaw.com; Paisner & Co's *ComplyToday* package at www.complytoday.com; Manches' *Data Protection Compliance Service* at www.manches.com/dpa; and Hammond Suddard Edge's *dataedge* at www.edge.co.uk/dataedge

Part IV

IT in the Justice System

11

IT and the English Civil Justice System[1]

I am often asked about the various public sector projects with which I have been involved, especially those that relate to the civil justice system in England and Wales. What have been the most significant initiatives? How do they relate to one another? And how do they bear on the use of IT by practitioners?

To answer these and other questions, I have written this personal perspective on past, current, and future uses of information technology in the civil justice system of England and Wales. I start with a brief historical analysis that identifies some key events in the development of IT-based civil litigation: the founding of the Society for Computers and Law in 1973; the establishment of the ITAC committee in 1985; and the innovations in the Official Referees Courts in the early 1990s. I suggest thereafter that in the decade from 1994 the major influence in the development of IT for the civil courts will be Lord Woolf's *Access to Justice* Inquiry and its various recommendations on IT (summarized in this article). I then show that the Bowman Report on reform of the Civil Division of the Court of Appeal encourages and develops similar applications of IT. Thereafter, I seek to describe and evaluate English lawyers' exploitation of litigation support technology.

[1] An earlier version of this chapter appeared as 'IT in the Civil Justice System of England and Wales' (1999) 10 *Computers and Law* 1: 6. In turn, that paper was based on a report, dated December 1998, for the XIth World Congress on Procedural Law, held in Vienna, on 23–8 August 1999. That report was entitled 'The Challenge of the Information Society: Application of Advanced Technologies in Civil Litigation and Other Procedures—Report on England and Wales'.

Penultimately, I summarize the consultation document known as *civil.jus-tice*—the government's initiative to develop a five- to fifteen-year IT strategy for the civil justice system in England and Wales. Finally, in a postscript, I draw attention to a number of initiatives that were emerging or bearing fruit as this book went to press. It is a measure of just how quickly civil justice technology is developing that the postscript draws attention to a wide range of recent developments.

1. A Brief History of Civil Litigation Technology in England and Wales[2]

In England and Wales, there has been strong interest in the use of IT in support of civil litigation at least since the Society for Computers and Law was founded—on 11 December 1973. Although a handful of pioneers had worked in the field prior to that date, it was only thereafter, with a formal body in place, that it was possible for English lawyers, judges, and officials to work together in a systematic and sustained way in assessing the actual and likely impact of courtroom and litigation support technologies.

After a decade of experimentation and modest progress, the next milestone was the establishment in 1985 by Lord Mackay (the then Lord Chancellor) of ITAC, the Information Technology and Courts Committee. ITAC was inspired and then chaired for the first eleven years or so by the immediate past-president of the Society for Computers and Law, Sir Brian Neill. The chair then passed to the current holder, Lord Saville (who also chairs the Judicial Technology Group, which focuses on the short- and medium-term IT needs of English judges). Lord Saville works closely on IT matters with Lord Justice Brooke, Senior IT Judge, who takes on much of the day-to-day responsibility for judicial IT. Strong leadership from top judges is and always has been crucial for securing support for IT in the justice system.

Still very active today, the purpose of ITAC has always been to provide a forum at which a very wide range of participants in the justice system (civil and criminal) could come together and exchange news about their respective investments in IT and their plans for the future. I joined ITAC in 1990, while I was chairman of the Society for Computers and Law and have repre-

[2] For another appraisal of the impact of IT on the justice system in England and Wales, see Lord Justice Brooke, 'IT and the English and Welsh Courts: The Next Ten Years' (Keynote Speech, 13th Bileta Conference, March 1999), at www.open.gov.uk/lcd/judicial/speeches/dublin.htm

sented the Society on the committee since then. Although ITAC has never had executive powers, it remains, for me and many others, an invaluable body, whose very existence encourages collaboration and compatibility across the civil justice system—around the ITAC table, solicitors are represented by The Law Society and barristers by the Bar Council, while they are joined by judges representing all levels of courts and by senior officials from numerous government bodies, including the Lord Chancellor's Department, the Court Service, and the Legal Services Commission.

In the late 1980s and early 1990s, one part of the civil justice system that always came to ITAC with exciting news of innovation was the Official Referees Court (now The Technology and Construction Court). It was in this court that much of the speculation about civil litigation technology became reality. The early success in these courts is a case study worth recounting. In 1991, The Official Referees Solicitors' Association (ORSA) set up an IT subcommittee to establish some standards for the use of litigation support systems (document management systems) in the courts of the Official Referees (those judges in England who specialized in technical disputes, largely in the construction, engineering, and IT industries). While these courts had frequently been facing huge document loads which were ideal for litigation support, law firms had been tending to argue with one another over the selection of systems, with each boasting unrivalled merit for their own preferred packages. The subcommittee, with representatives from a number of major litigation practices, sought to cut through these debates and wrote The ORSA Protocol which laid out standard formats for various aspects of litigation support.

Along with John Bishop and Martin Telfer, I was one of the main authors of the original Protocol and its publication was during my time as chairman of the Society for Computers and Law. The Society decided to support the initiative and indeed funded the printing and widespread distribution of the document.

Although it was in no sense binding, a number of the judges strongly encouraged its usage, most solicitors accepted its recommendations and it motivated those who were previously unaware of litigation support to take it far more seriously.[3]

As I mentioned, The Official Referees Court is now known as The Technology and Construction Court. A new protocol, known as the TeCSA (The Technology and Construction Court Solicitors Association) Protocol, is currently being prepared. Of considerable support in this exercise is the

---

[3] Version 2.0 of The ORSA Protocol can be obtained at www.courtservice.gov.uk/notices/tcc/tcc_it.htm

Masters dissertation of Richard Honey, whose work focused on analysing the problems associated with documentary evidence in civil litigation (using construction disputes as a benchmark of complex, technical, document intensive litigation). In the course of that research, he investigated the practical impact of the ORSA Protocol. Through a questionnaire survey, Richard Honey found that 87 per cent of construction solicitors who were surveyed were aware of the Protocol. Of these, 95 per cent said they felt that it was useful. 36 per cent of the respondents, 27 in number, had actually used the Protocol in the course of a dispute; of whom, three quarters stated that it had been successful in achieving co-operation. There can be little doubt that his findings were sufficiently positive to encourage further work on the Protocol; and not just for technology and construction disputes, in my view, but for civil litigation generally.[4]

Also in the Official Referees Courts, just after the ORSA Protocol was published, an important experiment was conducted in relation to what has become one of the most successful uses of IT in the English courts—computer-assisted transcription (CAT). Again under the auspices of the Society of Computers and Law, a short study was commissioned, which sought to explore the impact of this technology. As is now widely known, through CAT, the words spoken in the courtroom as captured by the keystrokes of stenographers are converted into text that appears almost instantaneously on the judge's monitor. Additionally, there is a facility to annotate text as it appears. The original study suggested[5] that the use of this technology could reduce the length of hearings, a finding supported by later projects and by the widespread anecdotal evidence of judges who have used such systems.

Elsewhere in the civil justice system at that same time, there was also some acceptance and exploitation of the same techniques and technologies that had been used in the Official Referees Courts. Some larger law firms and technologically enthused barristers began to work with litigation support technologies (inspired often by their counterparts in the USA), while judicial technology received a boost in 1992 with the launch of the JUDITH (Judicial IT Help) pilot project—the Lord Chancellor's Department provided the funding for the provision of computers and training to 25 judges.[6] The

---

[4] Richard Honey, 'Managing Documentary Evidence in Civil Litigation' (M.Sc. dissertation, King's College, London, 1999).

[5] Joyce Plotnikoff and Richard Woolfson, 'Replacing the Judge's Pen? Evaluation of a Real-time Transcription System' (1993) 1 *International Journal of Law and Information Technology* 90.

[6] See His Honour Judge Michael Mander, 'The Judith Report' (1993) 1 *International Journal of Law and Information Technology* 249.

JUDITH experience valuably laid the foundations for the gradual adoption of IT by the English judiciary—there are just over 1000 judges in England, of whom about half were IT users by the end of 1998.

Nonetheless, although there were some law firms, barristers, and judges embracing IT in the early 1990s, the general uptake of the technology across the civil justice system was neither rapid nor enthusiastic. Most acknowledged (often with some reluctance) that it was in some sense inevitable that IT might at some time come to pervade the lives of everyone involved with civil litigation. No one knew that that time would come as soon as 1994.

2. Lord Woolf's Reforms and IT

In March 1994, the Lord Chancellor, Lord Mackay, appointed Lord Woolf to review the rules and procedures of the civil courts in England and Wales. At that time Lord Woolf was a Lord of Appeal in Ordinary in the House of Lords (a Law Lord). From 1996–2000, he was the Master of the Rolls. In mid-2000, he was appointed the Lord Chief Justice of England and Wales.

I was delighted to be appointed as Lord Woolf's IT Adviser in early 1995. It seemed to me then, as now, that the very appointment of someone who specialized in IT in the law was of itself significant. I did not know of any other prior law reform initiative in the UK that had taken IT particularly seriously.

An overview of the Woolf reforms

The aims of Lord Woolf's review were, in summary: to improve access to justice; to reduce the cost of litigation; and to reduce the complexity of the rules and terminology. Lord Woolf's review became known as the *Access to Justice* Inquiry. In June 1995, he produced an Interim Report.[7] In July 1996, he published his Final Report[8] together with a set of draft rules, proposing a unified body of rules to replace the Rules of Supreme Court and County Court Rules.

Lord Woolf proposed a radically new landscape for civil litigation. In the new world he advocated, he suggested civil litigation should be: avoided wherever possible; less adversarial, and more co-operative; less complex;

[7] Lord Woolf, *Access to Justice—Interim Report* (Woolf Inquiry Team, June 1995). Also available at www.open.gov.uk/lcd

[8] Lord Woolf, *Access to Justice—Final Report* (HMSO, July 1996). Also available at www.open.gov.uk/lcd

more certain with shorter timescales; and more affordable, predictable and proportionate. He recommended that parties should be placed on more equal footing (financially); that there should be a clearer division of judicial and administrative responsibilities; that the courts and judges should be more litigant-oriented; that there should be a more effective deployment of judges; and that the civil justice system should be more responsive to litigants' needs.

When the Labour Party came to power in England in May 1997, the new Lord Chancellor, Lord Irvine, invited Sir Peter Middleton to review Lord Woolf's recommendation alongside other proposals for the reform of the Legal Aid system.[9] The new government's general approach was captured in a White Paper, published in December 1998, entitled 'Modernising Justice'.[10] In summary, the first phase of the civil justice reforms, as proposed by Lord Woolf, were to begin on 26 April 1999 and these were to include the coming into force of the new Civil Procedure Rules, signed by the Lord Chancellor on 10 December 1998.

And so, the most fundamental reforms to the English civil justice system for centuries, as proposed by Lord Woolf, were to be taken ahead. For current purposes, it is vital to know that the introduction of new and improved information technologies were central to Lord Woolf's main recommendations. IT was to be a key part of the civil reform process.

IT and the Woolf reforms

Taking his interim and final reports together, Lord Woolf made a wide range of recommendations in relation to IT.[11] Most fundamentally, Lord Woolf proposed the introduction and use of what are often known as 'case management systems'. Before detailing the proposals themselves, it should be said that there has been some considerable confusion over the very term 'case management system'. In an attempt to clarify the issue, it has been found helpful in England to recognize that there are at least five categories of system, each of which can meaningfully (but unhelpfully) be called case management systems. Each, in fact, is best regarded a subsystem of the next generation of court systems:

---

[9] Sir Peter Middleton, *Review of Civil Justice and Legal Aid: Report to the Lord Chancellor* (September 1997). Also available at www.open.gov.uk/lcd

[10] *Modernising Justice: The Government's Plans for Reforming Legal Services and the Courts* (December 1998, Cm 4155). This can be found at www.open.gov.uk/lcd

[11] See Chapter 13 of the *Interim Report*, n. 7 above, and Chapter 21 of the *Final Report*, n. 8 above. This chapter does not seek to address all of Lord Woolf's recommendations on IT. The main focus here is on case management technologies because these are the most vital for the reforms.

- *management information systems*—to help (politicians, officials, judges, and others) monitor the throughput and performance of our courts (consistent with the recommendations of Sir Peter Middleton);
- *case administration systems*—to support and automate the formidable back-office, administrative work of court staff;
- *judicial case management*—including case tracking, case planning, telephone and videoconferencing, and document management, intended for direct use by judges;
- *judicial case management support systems*—being the systems used by court staff in support of judges who are involved with case management; and
- *non-judicial case management*—to help court staff progress those many cases which are not disposed of judicially.

Absolutely fundamental to the Woolf reforms are two quite different categories of case management system. First, for the 'fast track' (very broadly, for claims up to £15,000 in value, other than small claims), it is vital that the Court Service has efficient, reliable, and effective ways of monitoring and administering all those cases that are following fixed timetables. In terms of the classification above, this requires first-rate case administration systems. Such systems continue to be evolved.

Secondly, it is central to Lord Woolf's new landscape that judges are more proactive in the management and progression of cases on the 'multi-track' (also, broadly, cases worth more than £15,000). In this respect, looking to the medium to long term, a range of technologies are envisaged for direct use by judges in support of their new case management responsibilities, largely on the multi-track. In the language of above, what is needed here are judicial case management systems. This is a rather radical new departure and worthy of special attention here.

Lord Woolf recommended four broad categories of judicial case management system:

1. *case tracking systems*—producing daily reminders, progress reports, lists of outstanding tasks, and notices of who has responsibilities for further actions, thus supporting judges in supervising, monitoring, and controlling their cases from start to finish;
2. *case planning systems*—simple, PC-based, project management software to enable judges to generate their own plans/charts for cases, depicting timescales, key events and activities;
3. *telephone and videoconferencing*—as important tools for judges in maintaining the progress of cases and keeping in direct contact with parties where formal meetings would be impractical; and

4. *document retrieval systems*—to allow judges to gain access to documents relating to the individual cases on which they are working: including full case histories, pleadings, affidavits, orders, and document bundles for example; and to be able to retrieve these, either as images or as searchable text, from some central location.

More generally, he stressed that there must also be coherent programmes for training the judges in IT and adequate technical support in place as well, for he recognized that new judicial users would inevitably be less comfortable with the technologies than the pioneers.

These recommendations on judicial case management technology raise a fascinating range of further issues.

In the first instance, as stressed above, it must always be borne in mind that the different kinds of case management systems are *interrelated*, such that judicial case management systems are not entirely separate systems. An emerging objective is to move towards unified court information systems across the country that support all five case management applications noted above. Case management systems for judges will not, therefore, be separate and distinct applications. Instead, they will draw on much of the same information that is needed for judicial case management support systems and for non-judicial case management systems. It is perhaps best to regard the English court information system of the future as one single system, with a range of different users; and judges will be one category of user with their own specific requirements.

Early experience of the reforms in action suggests that case tracking is a priority for judges in the short term. However, it is vital to bear in mind that we are currently at the beginning of an evolutionary path which will lead in due course to an inevitably highly automated court system, under which the administration of cases will flow from start to finish in a largely automated environment, with human (largely judicial) intervention only for judicial decision-making and management decision-making. Judges involved with analysing requirements are therefore being encouraged to regard their current work as being the first building blocks towards such fully integrated case flow management systems.

Consistent with the spirit of the reforms which seek to simplify, unify, and rationalize the civil justice system, work on systems today is seeking to reflect the objective of developing court information systems which, in so far as possible, are common across all civil courts in England. To this end, at this stage, the underlying database technology should be the same across all courts and the 'front-end' for all judicial users should be similar in design and content. Inevitably, different courts and specialist jurisdictions will have some different requirements but there should be a strong common element across all modules of the unified system.

As for the fast-track, while IT is absolutely crucial, the case administration technology which will be so vital there must be able to operate without regular consultation or use by judges themselves. Failure to meet deadlines on the fast-track must automatically trigger appropriate action. Court staff enter data regularly and the systems should be designed to monitor progress and initiate activity. In contrast, to manage cases effectively on the multi-track, judges will need to have direct access to systems themselves (or to the output of systems as used by the court staff).

Implementation issues

Given that not all judges will be willing or able to use any new systems, there seems to be general agreement that there must be parallel systems (IT and paper-based systems) for judicial case management for some years to come, to accommodate non-users of technology. It is a moot question of policy whether a target date should be set for all (or at least the overwhelming majority of) judges to be direct users of judicial case management systems. What is especially encouraging, in any event, is that the current government seems willing to supply equipment, applications, and training to any judge who wants the new technology.

And yet, it will not all be down to judges. The benefits of a managed system will not be realized simply by grafting judicial case management on top of the current organizational infrastructure (court staff with their existing roles and responsibilities). Given that some judges will use the systems directly while others will not and that some will be more active case managers than others, it is clear that court staff will play a crucial and new role in working alongside judges who are managing the flow of their cases.

Much further thinking needs to be done here but there are strong arguments in favour of reorientating the work of court staff and adopting a 'team-based' approach.

In the medium to long term, I believe that the creation of *electronic files* will be central to the operation of the civil justice system under the reforms. These files will be able, effectively, to flow quickly and cheaply through the system. Once set up in the first instance, perhaps by court staff, such a file should contain and record information about each particular case. Eventually, all the documents relating to each case will also be attached to the file. At any time, the file should be available, under strict access controls, in electronic form, to authorized users—as an accurate, complete, and up-to-date record. The Woolf reforms point, therefore, to the need for an electronic filing system but this has not yet been specified in any detail.

As for the actual introduction of the new technologies, this was the subject of some minor controversy. Some of the press noted that the IT which is so vital for the reforms was not available in April 1999 and so, it was argued, the very future of the reforms was at risk.

In fact, there has been some confusion here over the readiness of the fast-track as opposed to the multi-track technologies. Generally, the fast-track technology was always expected to be ready before the range of judicial technologies; and, in any event, the latter will not come as one monolithic system but should be phased in over a number of years. Nonetheless, it is true that the new systems for neither were completed by 26 April 1999. However, interim systems were up and running: indeed for law firms that struggle for months with new office systems, it should be a sobering thought that at 9am on 26 April 1999, out of 226 court locations, the interim systems were operating successfully in all but four (and the problems there were unrelated to the reforms).

Yet, no one closely involved with the IT for Woolf ever believed that any of the serious technology would be ready by then. The projects involved are relatively complex and take time. A robust view was that it was right not to wait for the IT to start the reform process. Almost all major IT projects are late; and few systems meet all users' requirements in their first versions. Decision-makers were right if they had been nervous about the start date for the reform being wholly dependent on IT. Such pressure would inevitably have led to corners being cut (for example, insufficient acceptance testing and training).

When the IT is introduced over the next few years, there is cause to be optimistic that it will bring about huge efficiencies and productivity gains.

As for the multi-track, in the absence of judicial case management systems, it is regrettable that the judges did not at the outset have advanced tools at their disposal to help tackle their new responsibilities; but it was by no means fatal. I say this with some confidence because it was always known that some judges would not be using IT in any event; and so that there would have to have been parallel (paper and IT-based systems) in place at the very least.

As for the management of the introduction of the new technologies, this is very much a joint effort, led by the Head of Civil Justice, working closely with both the Lord Chancellor's Department and with the Court Service. Two further factors bode well. The first is that the current Chief Executive of the Court Service, Ian Magee, and the Director-General of Policy at the Lord

Chancellor's Department, Joan MacNaughton, have strong backgrounds in technology and IT management and are already personally supportive of many of the IT initiatives. Secondly, the Court Service and the English judiciary now have a very strong working relationship.

3. IT and the Review of the Court of Appeal (Civil Division)

It should not be thought that the computerization of the civil justice system ends with Lord Woolf's recommendations on IT. On the contrary, in many ways the Woolf reforms can be regarded as the starting point, as laying the foundations for further investment and development. Two initiatives support this proposition. The first is the work of the Civil Justice IT Strategy Development Group (discussed in the final section of this article). The second, the subject of this section, was a review of the Court of Appeal (Civil Division), which was published in September 1997.[12]

In late 1996, Sir Jeffery Bowman (former worldwide senior partner of Price Waterhouse) was asked by the Lord Chancellor (Lord Mackay) to carry out a comprehensive review of the Civil Division of the Court of Appeal. The context of this review was concern over the increasing number of applications and appeals and consequent delays in the hearing of appeals in England. I was appointed to join Sir Jeffery's formidable and yet very good natured team. The other members were Lord Woolf (by then appointed Master of the Rolls), Ian Burns (then the Director-General of Policy at the Lord Chancellor's Department), Michael Huebner (then the Chief Executive of the Court Service), and Baroness Wilcox (a consumer specialist). The work that followed was, for me, immensely stimulating.

The recommendations of the Bowman Report were intended to ensure that the Civil Division dealt with cases of appropriate weight for a Court consisting of senior and very experienced judges; to improve the way the Court worked so that it could deal with its caseload more quickly; and to achieve better access to justice.

Once again, a central role was identified for IT.[13] To manage the Court's workload more effectively and to be able to evaluate its performance more

---

[12] Sir Jeffery Bowman, *Review of the Court of Appeal (Civil Division)* (September 1997). Also available at www.open.gov.uk/lcd

[13] Chapter Eight of the Bowman Report, n. 12 above, makes detailed recommendations on IT.

easily, the development of management information systems was recommended. More fundamentally for the work of the Court itself, it was proposed that judicial case management systems be introduced to support the broader recommendation of the report that case management techniques (as originally introduced to the English legal system in Lord Woolf's *Access to Justice* reports) be adopted within the Court of Appeal. In particular, there were recommendations for the introduction of case tracking systems, case planning systems, telephone, and videoconferencing systems, and document retrieval systems.

Much of the chapter on IT focused on the systems for the judges. Especially interesting are the results of a survey which was conducted during the review 'to determine the disposition of the Lords Justices towards IT'. It transpired that (in early 1997) more than half of the Lords Justices already used IT in the course of their work (one-third had been using IT for seven years or more). The great majority of the remainder expressed a willingness and enthusiasm to learn. This gave Sir Jeffery's team confidence to recommend 'an ambitious programme' for the introduction of a substantial IT infrastructure (internal network linked to other court systems, Internet access, and videoconferencing) and a wide range of applications for the judges—electronic communications, document creation, document management, external information systems (on the Internet and on CD), and internal information systems (a Court of Appeal Intranet).

In all, the report anticipated that greater usage of IT in the Civil Division of the Court of Appeal would result in: improved usage of the Lords Justices' time; greater productivity; greater consistency of approach; compatibility between the Lords Justices and other parts of the Justice System; improved internal communication; new and improved methods of communicating with parties and their legal representatives; and an environment which would support case management.

The Lord Chancellor, Lord Irvine, supported most of the general recommendations of the Bowman Report. Indeed, some were articulated as government policy in the White Paper, 'Modernising Justice'.[14] In relation to the technology, implementation of much of the IT that was advocated in the Bowman Report is ongoing. From a judicial point of view, this is under the able stewardship of Lord Justice Brooke.

The success of the introduction of the new technology in the Court of Appeal is of wide interest in the English legal system. For, as is pointed out in the Bowman Report, the Civil Division is a particularly interesting test-bed

---

[14] See n. 10 above.

for many of the general suggestions for judicial technology that have been put forward in the last few years. This is precisely because it is atypical: it is highly influential and widely respected; it is populated by a manageable number of users (judges, lawyers, and administrators) with (in IT terms) a manageable size of case load; and the judges themselves are exceptional in their abilities and commitment. If IT cannot work well here, this would be challenging indeed for other courts and judges. Although it was not an objective of the exercise, the Review may well give rise to the Court becoming an influential pilot site for new technologies.

4. Litigation Support for Practising Lawyers

What do practising lawyers think of all this new technology and the enthusiasm of both government and the judges? In many ways, the numerous developments sit comfortably with much that is already going on in law firms and chambers. Indeed, one of the first front-office applications for lawyers (solicitors and barristers) was litigation support. Primarily for direct use by legal advisers themselves, litigation support convinced many practitioners in England and Wales in the early 1990s that IT could be central to legal practice and to the actual delivery of legal service. The term 'litigation support' can be a little confusing, however, because it is used by lawyers in a variety of contexts and can refer to one or more of three applications of technology in the arena of dispute resolution.[15]

First, and most commonly, litigation support is the use of IT to help manage and control the document load which lawyers have to master to advance and prepare their client's case. This is the type of litigation support system that Lord Woolf recommended lawyers embrace more extensively.[16] It is the main focus of attention in this section of the chapter but it may be helpful to introduce and say a few words about the others before delving into any further detail.

The second category of litigation support, then, is the use of IT to store and make readily available the work product of lawyers as they progress through a case and generate their own sets of documents. This can be called work

---

[15] On litigation support generally and the underlying technologies that are used, see Richard Susskind, *The Future of Law* (Oxford: Oxford University Press, 1996 and 1998 (revised paperback edition)).

[16] See especially Chapter 13 of Lord Woolf's *Interim Report*, n. 7 above.

product management. Hypertext (the enabling technology which underlies the document browsing capability of the World Wide Web) is a most useful technology in this connection—for linking relevant documents to one another and so enabling users to browse across crucial work product (including pleadings and witness statements) and evidentiary material (files of correspondence, for example).

The final sense of litigation support is where it refers to the use of IT in the courtroom itself. This embraces laptop computers for judges, computer assisted transcription (CAT), displaying documents on monitors across the courtroom, graphics for the presentation of evidence, and even video simulations of events at issue. Judicial IT and CAT are dealt with elsewhere in this chapter. As for the use of IT in presenting evidence, this has caused far greater stir in the United States and other jurisdictions in which civil juries are more commonplace than in England, where interest in this kind of technology has been confined to criminal cases. Even in criminal cases, however, it is interesting to note that many senior advocates and judges in England harbour reservations about the lack of relevant court procedures to control this use of IT and are alive to the possibility of technology being misused and misleading jurors and judges. At a Society for Computers and Law litigation support conference in 1990, this hesitation was captured by Lord Griffiths who—paraphrasing one of Disraeli's aphorisms—suggested that 'there are lies, damn lies and graphics'. What lawyers will think of virtual reality applications, which will surely come to the courtroom in due course, one can only begin to guess.[17]

Returning to the most common usage of the term litigation support (in the sense of document management), it should be added immediately, despite the local literature and bravado, that much (although not all) litigation support is still in its infancy in England and Wales. In contrast, it was first introduced in the United States in the mid-1960s and has been embraced more extensively there since then. This is not to say that there are not advanced users and sophisticated suppliers in England. On the contrary, some are as leading-edge as can be found anywhere. However, the technology is very far from pervasive: a comparatively small number of English practices use the technologies. There is considerable depth, therefore, but surprisingly little breadth of usage.

[17] We will not need to guess for much longer. In July 2000, at an American Bar Association meeting in London, Lord Saville demonstrated the virtual reality being used in the Bloody Sunday Inquiry that he is chairing (www.bloody-sunday-inquiry.org.uk). A computer model of Londonderry in 1972 has been developed on the basis of historical plans and photographs. Using touch-screen technology, witnesses (and others) are able to walk through the streets as they appeared at the time. In this way, virtual reality is proving a powerful tool to help the Inquiry understand as accurately as possible the events of 28 years ago.

To put the application still further into context, the main thrust of litigation support is to *automate* various aspects of trial preparation. Rather than having teams of paralegals and junior lawyers thumbing through mountains of files and photocopying extracts well into the small hours of the morning, litigation support technologies streamline these manual processes. Searching, retrieval, cross-referencing, and annotating can all be automated using IT. Lawyers can locate relevant papers more quickly than when using manual methods alone. While the cynics are right in saying that litigation support is simply coping with the chaos IT created through photocopying technology, it is still an improvement that is long overdue.

Whether the facilities reduce the cost of litigation for English clients is in doubt. A common view is that this application generally enables lawyers to do far more for their clients (more thorough and comprehensive work) in the available time and so for the same (but not less) fees.

For the avoidance of doubt, litigation support does not obviate the need for an initial appraisal of each document. In the absence of natural language processing technologies, it is hard to see how any competent lawyer can avoid looking through case documents once, for it is only then that the relevance or otherwise of the documents can be assessed. The point of litigation support is that the full document load should not need to be read or searched through manually, in its entirety, more than once.

The potential of this technology is particularly clear in complex technical cases, such as construction or computer disputes, where the party that has mastery of the documents can enjoy a clear strategic advantage over others. But lawyers invest for other reasons as well: the overriding aim for some is to control the costs of the dispute by handling the documentation more efficiently; while others are motivated by a desire to keep apace with opposing parties who have indicated that they are using IT (or it is suspected that they are).

Three techniques have dominated litigation support over the past decade. One approach is to compile a computerized index of all documents relating to a case. Each document can be represented in a database as a collection of 'objective' features (e.g. date of document, author, recipient) as well as subjective features, requiring lawyers' classifications (such as whether a document is privileged or prejudicial to the client's case or raises a particular point of law). Once set up, such a system can sort all documents, for example, in date order or by authors' name.

A second and complementary approach to litigation support uses document image processing technology. This is the process which can be likened to taking 'photographs' of individual documents and so this technology can

cope well with materials which are neither printed nor typed, such as draw-
ings or documents with handwriting, signatures, marginal annotations, date
stamps, and so forth. Users of systems that hold images cannot search for
individual words within the imaged documents (the text is not in machine-
readable form). Rather, they can view these images as if perusing microfiche
on a computer screen.

The third technique is to build a retrieval system that holds not an index
but the full text of a collection of papers. This should enable lawyers to search
quickly and easily within the entire text of documents for the occurrence of
single words (for example, names of individuals, companies, places, or terms
such as 'warranty' or 'delay') or for words in combination (for instance, the
name of a company within a specified number of words of the name of an
individual or a phrase such as 'defective software').

More advanced users have found that the real benefits of litigation support
come with a subtle combination of these three techniques and with hypertext-
based work product management systems as well. The sophistication needed
here is in selecting one or more of the three appropriate technologies for any
case at hand, a decision over which lawyers often agonize. While it is commonly thought in addressing the needs of particular matters that the same
selected techniques should be applied to all the documents, in reality this is
unworkable and commercially inappropriate and leads either to overkill or to
missing an opportunity of full analysis of vital materials. A convincing argument can be made to support the view that the selection of techniques should
be dictated very largely by the *relative significance* of the documents themselves. In any dispute, the documents can be categorized according to their
likely impact (which, to make matters difficult, can change as a case pro-
gresses); in light of which appropriate enabling techniques can be allocated to
each category (for example, vital documents may be subject to all available
techniques, while peripheral ones may only enjoy superficial indexing).

Perhaps the most common combination of techniques currently favoured
in England (and generally favoured by me) is indexing together with imag-
ing—useful but not prohibitively expensive.

For clients, developments in litigation support raise challenging questions
about the suitability of the lawyers they instruct. A further set of criteria in
selecting legal advisers now emerges, relating to the extent to which lawyers
have appropriate technology skills and support. If in major cases of the future,
all parties have the documents held in litigation support systems (loaded perhaps by some external bureau), a key point of differentiation amongst practices will be law firms' relative proficiency in exploiting the data in these
systems. Are the lawyers adequately trained in advanced searching tech-

niques? What practical experience and track record do they have with litigation support? Do they have permanent, first-rate support staff? Are they using advanced techniques, such as conceptual searching, augmented 'front-ends', and hypertext to enhance the basic systems? Are they capable of advising proactively on versatile document management systems? Do they understand the complex legal questions, regarding issues such as admissibility and authentication of evidence, that litigation support systems raise?

Certainly, a question today for all clients is whether their current lawyers are investing sufficiently in IT in preparation for the central role it is destined to play. The stage is set for major change in the world of litigation. Within a very few years, large-scale or complex litigation without IT will be virtually unimaginable.

5. Long-term IT Strategy for the Civil Justice System—*civil.justice*

The last observation leads neatly to the penultimate topic addressed in this chapter—long-term strategy.

One of Lord Woolf's recommendations on IT was that a group should be set up to consider and formulate a long-term IT strategy for the civil justice system as a whole. This idea was taken up in earnest in late 1997 by the Minister of State at the Lord Chancellor's Department, Geoff Hoon MP (who was the Shadow IT Minister during the previous Conservative administration and is now the Secretary of State for Defence). Under the Minister's chairmanship, a Group was set up (known as the Civil Justice IT Strategy Development Group), with the broad idea of making recommendations for the role of IT in civil justice over the long term. The Society for Computers and Law was well represented on the Group, with Sir Brian Neill and I appointed as members.

The first, main piece of work undertaken by the Group was the publication of a consultation paper in September 1998. Entitled '*civil.justice*' and subtitled 'Resolving and Avoiding Disputes in the Information Age', the paper expressly states that it relates to the civil justice system, 5 to 15 years hence (suggesting that Lord Woolf's recommendations on IT set the agenda for the coming five years).[18] In short, *civil.justice* takes up where Lord Woolf's work on IT ends.

[18] www.open.gov.uk/lcd

The terms of reference for the group can be paraphrased as follows: to discuss the future of the civil justice system and its use of IT post-Woolf; to look at the future prospects for the development of IT and consider their potential for innovation in the civil system; and to consult relevant groups, individuals, and businesses with an interest in civil justice, including the judiciary, the legal profession, other government Departments, and others.

In the preface to *civil.justice*, Geoff Hoon explains why it was considered important to take a long-term view: to ensure that money spent now on short- and medium-term IT is not wasted in years to come; to help produce a long-term vision that will lead the way for the civil justice system; to engender greater public confidence; and to attract private sector investment.

In its 40 or so pages, *civil.justice* covers an enormous amount of ground. Only a flavour of its contents can be given here.

Perhaps the most provocative part of the consultation paper is the second chapter, which identifies some 16 assumptions that are frequently made about the civil justice system; and, to some extent, each is challenged in the light of the possible impact of IT. The following four assumptions indicate the type of debate that is being encouraged:

- civil justice involves the resolution and not the avoidance of disputes;
- the work of civil courts must be conducted in physical courtrooms (it is asked: is a court a service or a place?);
- presentation of legal arguments orally is central to the administration of justice;
- not all cases can be reported.

Each of these (and 12 more) are called into question.

New directions in legal services are also identified in *civil.justice*. It is postulated, consistent with some of the central arguments in my book, *The Future of Law*,[19] that high-value and complex legal work of today's lawyers will not be fundamentally changed through IT but will certainly be rendered more efficient (optimized and streamlined). At the same time, legal work that is frankly routine and repetitive work will in due course come to be systematized and, later, delivered online. Finally, and most radically, IT is regarded as a vital tool to overcome the grave social ill of 'unmet legal need': the report envisages, for example, online legal guidance systems accessible to non-lawyers through the next generation of televisions; and online legal information systems to support and empower voluntary legal workers.

Disputes and the court system are, of course, central to the consultation paper. Acknowledging that the problems and challenges facing the low-

---

[19] N. 15 above.

value, high-volume cases are quite different from those of the high-value, low-volume matters, *civil.justice* does seek to address both categories. A variety of topics are addressed: the need for an Intranet for the Court Service and the judiciary which is connected to the wider GSI (the UK Government Secure Intranet); unified case management; multimedia electronic files; litigation support systems; courtroom technology; alternative dispute resolution and IT; judicial technology; and 'virtual hearings'.

This last possibility goes to the heart of all serious questions about the future of civil litigation and dispute resolution—will children of today feel it vital to congregate together in one physical location to enforce their entitlements or might they find it more natural to 'appear' through videoconferencing, or have their disputes resolved through some kind of online adjudication service?

So, what was the reaction to *civil.justice*? By the closing date, around 60 responses were received. In very broad terms, I believe they fall into two camps. One camp, occupied exclusively by lawyers and judges, expressed the view that the civil justice system is in good shape and the only role for IT is to render it a bit more efficient. The other camp (occupied by users of the court system, legal publishers, IT specialists, and non-lawyers generally) put forward the view that the system is in dire need of modernization and fundamental change through IT. (Neither camp tended to make it clear whether they were referring to the pre-Woolf or post-Woolf civil justice system.) Only a handful of responses took a balanced view between the two extremes. One of these was that of the Society for Computers and Law, which in my view was especially constructive.[20]

What is vital, however, is that some of the most difficult issues are now being debated publicly. In the context of this ongoing discussion, it is crucial that we continue to remind ourselves of the benefits that can reasonably be expected from IT in the English civil justice system in the long term. A powerful pointer here is given in *civil.justice* (in the preface). There, it is said that the major benefits should be:

- increased efficiency and so cutting of costs;
- better productivity and so reduction in delays;
- improved justice and access to justice; and
- greater public confidence in the justice system.

If this is achieved, IT will indeed help to transform the civil litigation process in England and Wales in the twenty-first century.

---

[20] 'civil.justice: The SCL Response' in (1998) 9 *Computers and Law* 5: 4.

The field of computers and law has never been more action-packed and exciting.

6. Postscript: Developments in 2000

It is a measure of just how rapidly IT is impacting on the civil justice system that there have been a significant number of relevant developments since I originally wrote this chapter in mid-1999. To give a flavour of progress, consider the following initiatives of the first half of 2000.

March 2000 saw the launch of the first web site to offer free access to an integrated body of British and Irish legislation and case law.[21] The service is a pilot and is known as BAILII (British and Irish Legal Information Institute). It was developed by the Australasian Legal Information Institute[22] in co-operation with steering groups in Britain and Ireland. Aside from BAILLI's immediate utility, the pilot service must be seen in its wider context as one of two strands in an ongoing initiative whose aim is to ensure that there is Internet access to British and Irish legislation and case law at no cost. The other strand is as important and that is to conduct a six–nine month study to analyse longer-term implications and needs. David Lock MP, now the Minister at the Lord Chancellor's Department with responsibility for IT issues, intends that the study be undertaken as part of the *civil.justice.2000* initiative (as discussed below). The establishment of a full-scale service beyond a pilot raises innumerable and complex questions that the study must answer—questions not just of IT but also of public policy, project management, utility to the public, intellectual property law, and funding. It is currently envisaged that the BAILII pilot will remain operational for about two years, after which it will be displaced by some more sophisticated, world-class service. Whether that will be an enhanced version of BAILII, a new service altogether, or a variation on some existing commercial service, will not be settled until the study has been completed.

In April 2000, 'Just Ask!' was launched. This is the web site of the Community Legal Service.[23] With legal sites proliferating on the Internet, the Lord Chancellor's Department set itself a formidable challenge in seeking to produce a site that it hopes will become the first port of call for people looking for legal information and help on the Internet. Polished in appearance,

---

[21] www.bailii.org   [22] www.austlii.edu.au   [23] www.justask.org.uk

imaginatively named, laudably uncluttered and intuitive to use, the service is undoubtedly impressive. The core services are a sophisticated directory of over 15,000 solicitors and advice agencies, an advice search facility which takes users to relevant help held on 300 linked sites, and useful basic introductions to various areas of law. Just Ask! has been designed for various categories of user who tend otherwise to be excluded from the online world—it is presented in eight different languages, it conforms with standards for disabled Internet users, and it runs not only on PCs, but also on digital TV and games consoles too.

In May 2000, the Lord Chancellor announced a wide-ranging, independent review of tribunals in England and Wales.[24] The review is being led by Sir Andrew Leggatt, a retired Court of Appeal judge, and Dame Valerie Strachan, a past Chairman of HM Customs and Excise. With almost 100 tribunals in operation, affecting almost half a million citizens every year, I believe the potential for the use of IT is considerable. I was therefore very pleased to be appointed an expert consultee to the review; and still happier to report that technology is indeed being taken very seriously. However, as with the Criminal Courts Review, under the chairmanship of Lord Justice Auld, which was announced in December 1999[25] (to which I am also an expert consultee), it is clear that one of major challenges is not just to put technology in place in particular parts of the justice system but also to ensure that the systems operating in civil justice, administrative justice, and criminal justice are appropriately compatible and interoperable with one another. This is a formidable challenge.

In June 2000, it was announced that over 1000 English judges will soon be able to surf the Web from their laptops. The catalyst for this investment by the Court Service was the urgent need for judges to have ready access to comprehensive sources and updates relating to the Human Rights Act. The solution is LEXicon, a web site that provides links to a wide range of Internet resources relating to human rights. Also, but for judges only, there is a customized version of *Butterworths Direct*, offering access to legislation, cases, commentary, and e-mail updates.[26] The take-up of the service is likely to be high. Hundreds of judges are already regular users of an e-mail, conferencing, and bulletin board known as FELIX.

Finally, also in June 2000, coinciding with this book going to press, *civil.justice.2000* was issued by the Lord Chancellor's Department.[27] This is the final report of the Civil Justice IT Strategy Development Group,

---

[24] www.tribunals-review.org.uk   [25] www.criminal-courts-review.org.uk
[26] See www.courtservice.gov.uk/lexicon. The service was due to go live on 17 July 2000.
[27] www.open.gov.uk/lcd

anticipated earlier in my discussion of *civil.justice*. The completion of the report was led enthusiastically by Geoff Hoon's successor, David Lock MP, Parliamentary Secretary at the Lord Chancellor's Department. A full analysis of this latest report will have to wait for another occasion. Suffice it to say that it is an ambitious attempt to plot an overall direction for the civil justice system for the period, 2005–15, with a strong emphasis on dispute avoidance and on ensuring that citizens have ready access to guidance on their rights, responsibilities, and the best ways of securing their entitlements and pursuing their remedies.

The report is not just a strategy for government. It also puts down a marker for the rest of the legal world. It should leave no lawyer in any doubt that the civil justice system will be transformed through IT.

12

The Electronic Pillars of Justice[1]

How should a national government, faced with the task of modernizing its justice system, meet the challenges of the future, given the formidable array of technical options that have emerged over the last decade? This is an increasingly important question for governments around the world, many of whom are currently seeking to prioritize amongst a bewildering array of information technologies. The main difficulty here is that it is barely conceivable that *all* the possibilities and opportunities outlined in Chapter 5 could be implemented in the course of, say, the coming ten years. How can balanced choices be made?

The argument presented in this chapter is that to meet the challenge squarely, any justice system that is taking IT seriously must develop its own long-term IT strategy. In the absence of a strategic approach, some of the systems outlined in Chapter 5 would no doubt be put in place, but this would probably happen in a rather haphazard and random way.

[1] This chapter is a revised version of a paper published under the same title in (2000) 4 *The Jersey Law Review* June: 117. It is an updated statement of my position as presented in the revised paperback version of *The Future of Law* (Oxford: Oxford University Press, 1998).

1. The Need for a Strategic Approach

Rather than leave the evolution of much of the justice system to chance, I believe passionately that some systematic strategic planning should take place so that technical possibilities and opportunities are prioritized in an informed, structured, and controlled way; and, further, that the choices between the various possible options are made on sound policy grounds. When I speak of strategy in this context and of adopting a strategic approach, I must stress that I am not suggesting the development of highly detailed plans, with finely calibrated milestones and budgets, articulated a decade in advance. Rather, I am referring to what I call 'strategic direction'—clear, overall direction (a point on the horizon), with well-established high-level priorities, a shared sense of purpose and strong linkage to overarching policy objectives or business strategy. This is to be contrasted with short-term IT thinking, driven either by a desire only for 'quick wins' or by IT enthusiasts within organizations who make their demands more forcefully than others.

If a strategic approach is indeed preferred, one vexed question that immediately follows is whether it is desirable that the approach should, in so far as is possible, be an overarching one, applying to numerous bodies, agencies, and individuals across the civil and criminal justice systems; or whether various parts of the system should be left to develop their own independent strategies. In finding a response to that question, it is worth reflecting first on the wide range of systems that are currently possible in the law (again, for further detail, see Chapter 5 of this book). It becomes clear, on reflection, that many of the current and impending technology-based changes share two significant features. On the one hand, many of the possible applications of IT (for example, desktop videoconferencing) are generic, in that they actually apply to, or are relevant for, most (if not all) individual parts of the justice system. On the other hand, many of them are instances of innovation rather than automation. This means that their deployment would result not just in the streamlining of specific organizations but instead would often bring fundamental change well beyond the component of the justice system to which they most obviously apply. In turn, this would impact heavily on neighbouring bodies, agencies, or organizations.

Computerization across the life cycle of a criminal case which goes to trial, for example, would impinge on the technology of a wide variety of bodies (police, prosecution, court, prison, and many more). The partial introduction of IT across that life cycle, which would come about if new systems were implemented in one agency but not in several others would be unlikely to deliver maximum benefits. Future uses of IT are likely to apply across the entire justice system and establish new relationships between parts of the justice system. Major IT initiatives will challenge and perhaps even eliminate traditional boundaries. Accordingly, it would be sensible for at least some IT strategy and planning work to operate at the macro level across the entire justice system (civil and criminal).

This is not the place to delve into the details of strategic planning (Chapters 1 and 2 should be helpful for that process), but I think it might be helpful to explain that I have, in the last few years, refined my own position in this context in one important respect—I now believe that we have some considerably greater control over the future than is often supposed. This is crisply captured by those who say that the best way to predict the future is to invent it. The future is not out there like some foggy day, pre-existing and waiting to be revealed once the mist lifts. Instead, I now like to think of it more as a lump of clay—It has the potential of being fashioned into a fine sculpture but, equally, it could end up an unstructured mess. Within the confines of what is technically possible, it is up to human beings to create the future just as though it were malleable clay.

There is a difficulty here, however: although IT is now attracting far more attention across the justice systems of the globe than ever before, it is still doubtful that most top opinion formers and decision-makers, in either the public or private sectors, have grasped just how fundamentally and rapidly the administration of justice might be transformed through technology in the next five to ten years. Thus, the world over, those who are best placed to create the future of law are often not yet fully engaged when it comes to IT.

Yet empirical evidence of the benefits of IT for justice is mounting and the impact is becoming hard to ignore on any level. Ongoing work on the potential of IT for many of the courts in England, for example, confirmed what for proponents of IT had never been in doubt—that the introduction even of modest technologies could bring enormous efficiency gains and costs savings to the court system. The justice system in England is a vast, document intensive and labour intensive operation, most of whose administrative and management systems were developed at a time when the throughput and workload of the courts and lawyers was far smaller. Many of the systems are crude, paper-based, orientated towards the process of administration and not the public, and few are able to cope with the increasing demands placed upon them. This currently brings high staffing costs, inefficiencies, error, delay, poor reputation, and dissatisfaction. The time for computerization is long overdue.

And yet, rendering the current system more efficient through automation is only to begin work on bringing the administration of justice into the information age. More radically still, given the inevitably pervasive impact of the Internet, and as the nation's education, health, welfare, taxation, and employment services, for example, come to be administered electronically, it is reasonable to assume that there will also be pressure for the legal system to be available online and for legal services to be delivered electronically. This will bring not just efficiency gains but fundamental changes to entire justice systems.

2. A Model to Form the Basis of Strategic Thinking

I would like now to propose a simple model for thinking about the place for IT in any justice system of the future. Diagramatically represented in Figure 12.1, the model assumes there will be three vital roles for IT in the justice system. These will be in providing and enabling:

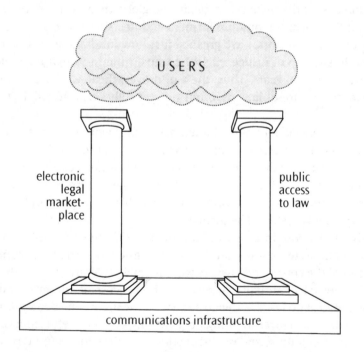

Fig. 12.1

- an internal communications infrastructure for justice workers;
- the provision of electronic legal information and services within the justice system; and
- public access to the law and legal guidance.

Each of these is addressed below, with special reference, at this stage, to the justice system in England.

An internal communications infrastructure for justice workers

At the core of tomorrow's justice system should be the whole set of justice workers (including judges, solicitors, public officials, voluntary workers, and support staff).

Following from my earlier analysis of what is possible and likely, in Chapter 5, I would anticipate that, in less than two years, the overwhelming majority of justice workers in advanced legal systems (more than half a million in England, excluding the police who should be included in a fuller analysis) will be able to communicate electronically with one another and with the outside world.

While in one sense the infrastructure can be thought of as one big network, it is better imagined as a collection of innumerable 'virtual private networks'. Thus, each justice worker will have her own portfolio of what can be regarded as 'affiliations', all accessible through one mail box. A typical solicitor, for example, might be affiliated to a general court system network, to the Intranets of a series of professional bodies, to networks set up for particular cases, to her own firm's systems, and so forth. Each virtual network would, in effect, be discrete and separate. The key point, however, is that each would function in accordance with common and appropriate standards and the user herself would have only one point of entry to her entire portfolio. There will be no need to log in and out of separate systems and no complex file conversion processes.

Advances in telecommunications technologies (including optical fibre, mobile, and satellite) and the introduction of widely accepted standards will enable the transfer of files and of funds and provide common areas to visit to hold public and private, online, and off-line, discussions and forums, all under conditions which will be sufficiently secure, confidential, private, reliable, and capable of authentication.

This telecommunications infrastructure will carry not only electronic mail and conventional data, but will also support the transmission of bundles of documents, which are connected to one another through hyperlinks, so that, on arrival, recipients will immediately be able to navigate through them following explicit cross-references. These bundles will come to be delivered in multimedia format, so that users will not just read the documents in textual form but also be able, on screen, to view, for example, relevant photographic evidence and sound recordings and even video as well.

Finally, that same telecommunications infrastructure will, in due course, support videoconferencing directly from the personal computers of all justice workers.

The provision of electronic legal information and services within the justice system

That same internal telecommunications infrastructure for justice workers will also serve as the basis for the provision of innumerable electronic systems and services for lawyers, judges, and others. Across this infrastructure, for example, users will be able to gain access to edited legal source materials made available by legal publishers and other providers; and they will have direct access to services such as land registration and to agencies such as the legal aid bodies. Crucially, a good deal of court business (for example, the lodging of documents, the tracking of the status of cases, and videoconferencing with judges) will also be mediated through the new systems. And high-speed broadband access to the World Wide Web will also be available for the legal profession across this infrastructure.

One pillar of the justice system, as shown in Figure 12.1, will therefore be the new *electronic legal marketplace*—conventional legal services and new forms of legal service will be available here on a commercial basis. As the business of both the courts and of lawyers becomes increasingly dominated by IT, this electronic legal marketplace will in due course become the focal point of justice workers. But on this model, justice workers will only be part of the user community. The rest, who will dispose of their legal business electronically, will be those who today fall into category of 'clients' as well as those other users who belong to what I call the 'latent legal market'. What all these users have in common is that they will need to pay for legal services delivered from this first pillar.

My notion of the latent legal market needs some elaboration. I start from the premise that there are innumerable situations, in the domestic and working lives of all non-lawyers, in which they need and would benefit from legal guidance (or earlier and more timely help) but obtaining that legal input today seems to be too costly, excessively time-consuming, too cumbersome and convoluted, or just plain forbidding. This is the latent legal

market, which I believe will be liberated by the availability of straightforward, no-nonsense, online legal guidance systems. They will not replace
conventional legal services, but they will provide affordable, easy access to
legal guidance where this may have been unaffordable or impractical in the
past. I see particular benefit here for small- to medium-sized businesses who
are willing to pay for legal help today but not perhaps as much as lawyers
want to charge them. (The latent legal market is discussed in further detail in
Chapters 3 and 4 of this book.)

Public access to the law and to legal guidance

In contrast to the first, the second pillar of the justice system, as depicted in
Figure 12.1, will be accessible by everyone in society; and at *no direct cost* to
these non-legal users. Alongside all manner of other bodies of freely available public information, legal guidance and legal services will inevitably, I
believe, be accessible on the World Wide Web, providing *public access to the
law.*

In England, this is entirely consistent with the government's commitment
to the electronic delivery of government services, within the broader context
of an ambitious programme to modernize government.[2] But more particularly, the model fully supports the government's commitment to the establishment of a 'Community Legal Service'.[3]

IT could help in offering public access to law in at least ten ways, by
enabling the provision of:

1. *A 'portal' offering public access to law*—this would be a master web site
   or gateway for all legal services in a country: the definitive, first port of
   call for anyone who has a legal problem or worry. From this portal, there
   would be links to all appropriate legal sites which essentially would be
   authorized, authenticated, and regulated (an IT-oriented version of
   'quality mark' will be needed here). At the portal, for example, users
   would find directories of voluntary legal services and law firms, guidance
   on using the courts, as well as links to professional bodies and to primary
   source materials. Consistent with the UK's 'Modernising Government'
   ethos, the links and guidance would not be listed under conventional

---

[2] See *Modernising Government*, a White Paper published in March 1999, at www.cabinet-office.gov.
uk/moderngov; 'e-government', the UK Government's strategy for public services in the information
age, at www.citu.gov.uk/iagc/strategy.htm; and related reports on electronic delivery of public service
at www.citu.gov.uk.
[3] See www.open.gov.uk/lcd for the Community Legal Service generally; and www.justask.org.uk for
the web site of the Community Legal Service.

legal classifications but be oriented towards real-life events (for example, wanting to move house, recover a debt or complain about a lawyer). The portal should offer a range of working facilities (as below) and provide a framework for future services (such as online adjudication and video-conferencing).

2. *Systems to support voluntary workers together with a network of legal practitioners*—online legal information systems to support and empower voluntary and other legal advice workers, so that they have usable legal know-how at their fingertips which would greatly extend their areas of competence and confidence, accessible on the World Wide Web (through the portal just mentioned). There could also be a facility for advice and voluntary workers that would provide e-mail links to lawyers who have volunteered their help (online via e-mail, and so with no commitment to being at a particular place at a particular time) in specified areas of law. The support of professional bodies would be invaluable here, with a view perhaps to committing every practising lawyer, in due course, to providing a minimum number of hours each year.

3. *Facilities for citizens to ask legal questions online*—again available on the portal, this would be a simple e-mail facility, whereby any citizen with access to the Internet could ask a legal question (perhaps in clearly defined areas) and be assured of a response within a specified period. The questions could be assessed initially by lawyers or advice workers who could then route the queries to advisers familiar with the particular areas of law in question.

4. *Online help on how to use the courts*—building on any existing materials (written and online) this assistance would again be made available on the portal (not just as a link to other sites). Easy to use and presented in punchy and graphical form, the focus here would be on the *process* of pursuing a claim (that is, *how* to pursue a claim)—designed both for those who are already involved in a dispute as well as those contemplating action.

5. *Online legal guidance systems*—directly accessible through publicly available services, perhaps through kiosks or terminals in courts or shopping malls but, far more significantly, in the home and the workplace through the Internet and the World Wide Web. These systems could help users understand their rights and obligations, appreciate how to enforce their entitlements, and even offer preventative legal guidance as well (as I am fond of saying—'putting a fence at the top of the cliff rather than an ambulance at the bottom'). On this model, incidentally, the role of 'local communities' becomes less central.

6. *Online dispute resolution*—the resolution of disputes through online adjudication or mediation, whereby cases are settled not by assembling parties together but through online submissions and settlement. (In the UK, if even a fraction of today's 1 million small claim arbitrations and tribunal hearings could be settled in this way, the savings could be enormous and the capacity to handle a greater number of cases—which increased access to justice will entail—could be increased considerably.)

7. *Videoconferencing*—through the said portal again (in due course via the next generation of televisions perhaps), offering direct video access to workers in the voluntary legal sector, to lawyers, and indeed to judges, as appropriate.

8. *Preventative legal services*—by analogy with preventative medicine and health promotion (as more fully discussed below), the portal could provide a vital means by which citizens could improve their general wellbeing; and not only by helping to resolve or avoid problems. The law can often confer benefits and advantages even when there is no recognized legal problem. And yet, many people are not familiar with many advantageous legal facilities that are available today (from obscure welfare benefits to tax planning schemes) such that there is often little possibility of achieving legal health promotion. Access to justice should surely include access to the opportunities that the law creates. Again the portal could help users—by guiding them to sources of preventative legal guidance (collaboration across departments and other agencies would be needed here).

9. *Electronic case files*—when all the documents pertaining to cases before the courts are in due course accessible online, and when much court business (for example, interaction between lawyers and judges) is conducted electronically, the 'place' where users will congregate should be the portal.

10. *Free access to primary source materials*—a facility offering access to an integrated body of legislation and case law.[4]

All ten facilities could offer legal help to individuals and organizations that may otherwise have to go without. In so doing, IT would genuinely enable greater 'access to justice'. But technology has caused me, as the eighth suggestion above shows, to look more carefully at that much used and oftabused phrase.

---

[4] The best example of such a system is AustLII, the Australasian Legal Information Institute, at www.austlii.edu.au while in Great Britain and Ireland there is now a substantial pilot known as BAILII (www.bailii.org)—see Chapter 11.

The thrust of Lord Woolf's seminal reports, which bore this phrase as their title,[5] was on access to improved, cheaper, and fairer means of resolving disputes and tackling legal problems which have already arisen. For Lord Woolf, and for most lawyers who speak about access to justice, they could equally be said to be referring to access to much improved dispute resolution. In the information society, however, access to justice may well also come to have two further dimensions.

First, if I am right and the Internet will realize a latent legal market that will come to mean that legal guidance will be at everyone's fingertips to an extent that has not been possible in the past, then this readier, cheaper, and more widespread access to legal counsel will give rise, I argue, *not* to improved dispute resolution but to *dispute pre-emption* instead. And my experience is that non-lawyers would generally prefer the prevention or avoidance of legal problems to the dispute resolution process no matter how much it is over-hauled. In law, as elsewhere, prevention is better than cure; and access to legal guidance will give rise to a more just society, in the same way that immunization leads to a healthier community.

As mentioned earlier, the medical analogy helps identify a third sense of access to justice. I have in mind relatively recent work on health promotion—we are advised nowadays to exercise aerobically for at least 20 minutes, three times a week, not just because this will reduce our chances of, for example, coronary heart disease but because it will make us feel a whole lot better. The idea is not only to prevent ill health but to promote our physical and mental well-being. The law also surely provides us with the means by which we can improve our general well-being; and not only by helping to resolve or avoid problems. Instead, there are many benefits, improvements and advantages that the law can confer, even when there is no perceived problem or difficulty. And yet, as I said earlier, many people are hopelessly unaware of the full range of facilities available today (from welfare benefits through to tax planning schemes; from making a will to undertaking corporate restructuring), such that there is not much chance of putting in place legal health promotion facilities. Access to justice, in this third sense, means access to the opportunities that the law creates. This underlies one of the themes of my work—that in legal systems of tomorrow the law will come to be seen as empowering and not restrictive. Looking ahead, then, governments that are committed to public access to law and to community legal services, akin perhaps to community medicine programmes, should be aiming to improve access to justice in three senses and not just one.

---

[5] *Access to Justice* (2 volumes, June 1995 and July 1996).

3. The Benefits of a Justice System Supported by IT

If realized, I believe this model of tomorrow's justice system, with a sound communications infrastructure and the two pillars of electronic legal marketplace and public access to the law, would bring a variety of benefits, including:

- *a more efficient justice system*, by making what is a highly information-intensive system more productive and less costly (in terms of the unit costs of transactions within the system if not the overall cost);
- *provision of greater access to the law*, legal guidance and so to justice, through publicly available legal information services (available, for example, in kiosks in courts; or public access terminals in shopping centres; or—vitally and soon—in the home through the Internet) which may come to be at the core of a community legal service;
- *reduction in the delays, costs, and time* associated with resolving disputes, by equipping the courts and judges with systems which will manage resources and documents more effectively, enhance productivity, and reduce the length of hearings;
- *greater empowerment of the voluntary sector*, by providing legal information facilities which will extend the capability and areas of competence, for example, of citizens advice bureaux and legal advice centres, and community legal services generally; and
- *stimulation of greater confidence in the justice system*: in individuals, for whom the law is too often regarded as antiquated; and for the business community whose dissatisfaction with delays is compounded by exposure to court practices that are primitive in comparison to those found in most modern offices.

4. Who should Develop and Finance the New Technology?

Who might develop and fund the implementation of the vision just outlined, given that the infrastructure and the two pillars envisaged would undoubtedly be costly and complex to put in place?

There are compelling reasons, in the UK at least, for proposing that the new technology should *not* be financed and developed from within the public sector. In the first place, in the current climate of strict control of public expenditure, it is simply unrealistic to expect that funds would be allocated to such a costly and long-term investment. Moreover, the infrastructure, systems, and services that are anticipated constitute a formidable technical challenge for which the public sector of today's justice system is not technically resourced or sufficiently experienced to undertake.

The alternative is to procure appropriate systems and services from private sector suppliers. This is the approach being adopted in the UK, where it is intended that a series of major IT programmes for the courts and justice system be introduced through the government's Private Finance Initiative. It is still relatively early days yet for this scheme in relation to the justice system, and so a reliable progress report cannot be given at this stage.

Thinking about this approach in general terms, however, it seems to me, from a public sector point of view, that the main challenge of privately financing IT in the justice system is to identify a range of IT projects which, when outsourced (for this is what it amounts to), would lead not only to increased productivity and to improved access to legal and court services but to keeping a good deal of IT off the government's balance sheet. At the same time, from a commercial angle, the projects must also offer sufficient return for the private investors and result in net cost to the state and the citizen which is less than is currently possible.

I am optimistic that this can be achieved. The reason for my confidence is that I am convinced that the current system is woefully inefficient and that there is scope for a vast array of projects that can give rise to gains in efficiency, productivity, quality, and range of service. Beyond being optimistic, I also find myself excited by the possibility of first-rate private sector suppliers introducing and maintaining a state-of-the-art IT infrastructure for the justice system. But my model and its funding does assume three further requirements.

First of all, unless there is commitment by the government in question to a clear, *10-year vision* of an IT-based justice system, then the projects in question simply will not attract private sector investment. If investors (banks and IT suppliers, for example) do not see where the justice system might be going with IT they will not fund the ventures. I have spoken to numerous potential investors and suppliers and know this to be true.

Second, and leaving aside the less concrete latent legal market, the real attraction for hard-nosed private investors in the justice system is surely not just in the courts but in their hinterland as well—in the wider electronic legal marketplace of lawyers (many hundreds of thousands of potential users, including the support staff as well as the practitioners). These investors will want to feel confident that they might be able to capture this wider market's need for IT. And so, for example, they will find the entire internal communications infrastructure for justice workers, as outlined here, to be a more attractive target than, say, a mere Intranet for judges. But if indeed these private sector suppliers will engage only if they can capture a big slice of the courts' hinterland, then the collaboration and support of various professional bodies will, in turn, need to be sought.

In the past, sadly, the many legal organs and bodies that constitute the justice system have tended not to collaborate and have instead developed incompatible systems, or at least systems which were not designed to operate easily with one another. The justice system has generally been treated as a collection of quite separate information systems. IT may have brought benefits to individual parts of the system but the lack of co-ordination has inhibited the realization of benefits for the whole. Yet, to achieve the vision outlined above, collaboration as well as funding will be vital. Is it realistic to expect it? Here again, there is cause for optimism but not for the noblest of reasons. The stark reality today is that most government agencies and professional bodies of the justice system tend to struggle with IT and would welcome some clear direction, the establishment of standards, and the use of common systems. If a standard solution (with shared infrastructure, service providers, and even applications) could be identified and made available to their constituencies, for most top managers this would be one major headache removed at a stroke and they would warmly welcome such an initiative. Again I know this to be case, having taken various soundings.

But third, and the final requirement for my model to work, decision-makers across the justice system and the public in general would all no doubt agree that with such vital functions in the hands of private sector suppliers, it would be necessary to have some methods in place to manage the risks of outsourcing the technology of the justice system. Judges, lawyers, and consumer groups, for example, have been understandably nervous about the IT of the English courts being managed by a powerful private supplier. They have rightly recognized that control over the court infrastructure in the future could mean having huge impact on in the administration of justice.

There are strong arguments here, then, for the establishment of some kind of regulatory body, or at least structure—to control the potentially excessive zeal or even the expansionist tendencies of the kinds of major suppliers who are likely to be involved, to determine and control pricing and service levels, to set strategy and monitor performance, and generally to manage the whole process rigorously.

The individuals or bodies involved could also assume, or encourage others to assume, a further regulatory function: that of setting standards for the provision of legal information systems or services, whether as part of the electronic legal marketplace or by way of public access. The issue here, as mentioned earlier, is that users of such systems (especially non-lawyers) must be given confidence from the face of any system itself that the legal knowledge and experience embodied in it was indeed engineered by duly qualified lawyers. I worry about non-lawyers relying on legal guidance systems which have been put together by individuals with no legal training. We need, therefore, some process of certification of systems, together with regulation that sets out and requires good practice in the discipline of legal information engineering.

5. My Recommendations

Bringing my various threads of thought together now, the widespread use of information technology in the justice system, as envisaged here, can be seen to support two fundamental commitments:

- to a society in which computers and telecommunications greatly enhance all aspects of life; and
- to a justice system under which access to the law and the legal process is widely available and affordable.

Promotion of sensible investment in IT for the justice system has the further attraction of projecting an image of a forward-looking, innovative, and modern legal system able to compete effectively with other jurisdictions across the world.

Despite the likely benefits, as I speak to judges and lawyers across the world, concerns are invariably expressed about the absence of overall co-ordination of the wide range of legal bodies and individuals involved in justice systems. In particular, I hear it frequently said that, although numerous applications and solutions have been proposed, there is no agreed overall direction for IT across their justice systems in the medium and long terms. At the same time, they worry that there is considerable duplication of effort across their justice systems, in research, development, requirements analysis, and development activity. Worse, they confirm that the many legal organs and bodies which make up their justice systems have developed incompatible systems or at best systems which have not been designed to be interoperable.

In summary, it is apparent to many that there is therefore a need the world over not just for a strategic approach but also for greater vision, direction, leadership, collaboration, co-ordination, and consultation in relation to the use of IT in justice. This is certainly the case, in my view, in the UK; although I am more confident than ever before that this is now recognized by relevant decision-makers across the profession.

It must be recognized, however, that the introduction of IT in most walks of life is both technically challenging and emotionally forbidding. Success in other industries and jurisdictions, however, suggests there is a range of well-accepted, non-technical factors (keys to success, it might be said) which are likely to be critical for those seeking to overhaul the justice system using IT. There is, in sum, a need for:

- a clearly articulated *vision* of a justice system under which access to the law and the legal process is made far more widely available and affordable through IT;
- a centrally co-ordinated IT strategy for the entire justice system, developed in conjunction with all relevant interest groups, indicating what investment is necessary, identifying the anticipated benefits and embracing the vision of how the legal system will function with the new technologies in place;
- unambiguous and explicitly articulated support for an IT-based justice system, from relevant, senior political figures and civil servants;
- recognition that substantial financial investment is vital if the vision is to be realized and yet acknowledgement that this funding may not be sourced directly by central government;
- commitment to ongoing, well-targeted research and development pro-grammes, aimed at generating results which will ensure that the available IT is being exploited to the full and that technical innovations are being recognized and deployed as early as possible;
- acceptance that many of the most substantial and beneficial influences of IT will come from *innovation* rather than *automation*; and
- realization that the Internet and the World Wide Web are fundamentally changing the nature of communications and information dissemination in society and so are likely to exert a massive influence on the development of the law.

These keys to success could provide the basis for a systematic and publicized programme for reform which in turn would help immeasurably in easing the justice system's transition into the information age.

6. A Case Study—Jersey

What is actually happening in practice? Are justice systems around the world embracing IT and doing so in a strategic manner? Or do the law and its institutions remain resistant to change? While it is a little misleading to generalize, I find there is, in fact, far greater interest in IT than ever before. Whereas ten years ago, I encountered huge resistance to the introduction of IT—from lawyers, judges, and officials—I now perceive in most advanced legal systems that IT is moving steadily up the agenda of decision-makers. That said, the methods of forward-planning often fall well short of the strategic approach advocated in this chapter.

There are several examples of governments that, in my view, are tackling the challenges sensibly and systematically. In England, for example, the *civil.justice* initiative, led by the Lord Chancellor's Department, is an illustration of good practice—a small team has been set up to explore possibilities and make recommendations for the role of IT in civil justice over the next five to fifteen years. A consultation paper was published in September 1998 and the final report should appear in mid 2000.[6]

Also impressive is the approach adopted in Victoria, Australia. There, the Victorian Law Reform Committee, after extensive assessment of all major international initiatives, produced a report in May 1999, entitled *Technology and the Law*.[7] Of particular interest is that the report addressed the entire justice system (and not just the civil aspects) and even integrated their thinking with some of the major substantive legal issues (for example, privacy) that our legal systems must adapt to accommodate.

For the purposes of providing a case study, however, I have chosen not to focus on England or Australia but instead have selected a much smaller jurisdiction—that of Jersey—in which there are currently a number of exciting developments.[8]

By way of context, Jersey is the largest of the Channel Islands. It is neither a part of the UK nor a colony of it; but it does have allegiance to the British Crown, although it is not represented in the United Kingdom Parliament. UK legislation applies to Jersey only if the Island expressly agrees that it should do so. Jersey has its own legal system and courts of law.

---

[6] See Chapter 11. The final report was published as this book was going to press. It appears, together with the consultation paper, at www.open.gov.uk/lcd

[7] Available at www.parliament.vic.gov.au/lawreform

[8] I should state a personal interest and acknowledge that I have had the good fortune to have acted as an external adviser to the Jersey Legal Information Board in respect of the work discussed here.

In November 1999, the Bailiff of Jersey[9], Sir Philip Bailhache, announced ambitious plans for the development of the island's legal information systems. Previously, he had set up the Jersey Legal Information Board, a body that he chairs and at the outset was charged with the task of creating a legal information strategy for Jersey. The announcement in November 1999 took the form of the publication of the Board's strategy and the launch of a pilot web site.[10]

The strategy document stated that the Board's general aim was to create a Vision, and set the direction for, Jersey's legal information systems for a five-year period, ending in 2004. To paraphrase the Vision, it is: to help ensure that Jersey's legal system is recognized as a global leader amongst small jurisdictions, providing outstanding service to the peoples and businesses of Jersey as well as to those who interact with the island from beyond.

To achieve the Vision, the Board recommended an approach (a 'spirit') that is at once 'progressive and forward-looking, exploiting emerging technologies' but that builds appropriately on the 'Island's unique historical and social status'. Here, then, is an island, widely regarded as a hub for various financial services, as an attractive location for tourists, and as a homeland that provides a high standard of living—that is responding proactively to global shifts being brought about by electronic commerce and electronic government.

Consistent with this, to achieve the Vision, the Board identified three key elements for its legal information strategy:

- to strengthen continuously Jersey's position as a leading financial centre through refinement and development of the Island's legal processes and infrastructure;
- to capitalize on and continuously develop, through intelligent exploitation of IT, the accessibility of law and legal process to the public; and
- to provide an integrated legal system, that is, one that is co-ordinated, connected, and unified and inclusive of the courts, legal processes, the professions, and government departments.

The Board made a number of assumptions in setting the strategy. First, it was assumed that the island generally would have an ambitious and well-supported strategy for IT, the Internet, and telecommunications (in relation to the work of Information Society Commission, see below). Second, it was taken for granted that e-commerce would indeed burgeon, both in Jersey

---

[9] The Bailiff is the Chief Judge and President of the Royal Court, President of the Court of Appeal, and President of the States of Jersey. He is the Civic Head of the Island.
[10] For full details, see www.jerseylegalinfo.org

and around the world. Finally, it was presumed that sufficient security, data protection, and other privacy measures could be put in place.

As for the main objectives of the entire initiative, these also numbered three: the enhanced reputation of Jersey; ever-improving access to justice; and ever-increasing public confidence in the legal system. It was also recognized that two important by-products would arise: increased efficiency and so reduced costs; and better productivity, fewer delays and more efficient use of manpower.

Implementation of the strategy was given serious attention. In the end, the Board opted for a 'divide and conquer' approach—dividing the implementation process into a series of manageable (and, admittedly, interrelated) projects, to be conducted concurrently but each with its own allocated champion, manager, milestones, timescales, budget, and business objectives. Each is to be reviewed regularly and adapted where necessary. This approach recognizes that in the rapidly changing Internet-based world, it is not possible to map out all details in advance. Instead, it is vital to be able to be flexible and refine projects as circumstances require. By managing them separately, problems in one project will not necessarily destabilize the entire initiative. Had the Board opted to manage the initiative as one monolithic whole, it would have reduced its flexibility and been open to the danger of failure in one aspect of the venture prejudicing the entire programme.

There are fourteen projects in all, each grouped under one of the three key strategic elements noted earlier. Some of the projects are short term (0–1 year), others are medium term (0–3 years), while still others are long term (0–5 years). For example, there is a project devoted to creating an information map of the legal system and its connected agencies and users—this falls under the heading of creating an integrated legal system and is a short-term project. Or, again, there is a project assessing the need for a preventative legal health programme on the island—this falls under the rubric of increasing accessibility of the law and is a long-term project.

It is important that the legal information strategy is seen in the broader context of Jersey's more general response to the challenges of the information age. In mid-1999, the government created its Information Society Commission to take direct responsibility for the island's overall IT strategy. The Commission intends that Jersey should become a leader in its exploitation of information and communications technologies; that IT be integrated across all aspects of Jersey society; and that the island nurtures a range of prosperous businesses in the IT and Internet fields.

To achieve this overall vision, the Commission has set four strategic priorities: the creation of integrated, online government; the development of an information economy wherein technology is an integral part of all business and industry; the evolution of a community that has access, through technology, to ongoing learning and training opportunities; and the establishment of a world-class telecommunications infrastructure to support all aspects of the information society. Moreover, the government is giving high priority to the enactment of legislation that will support and not hinder e-commerce in Jersey.[11]

Clearly, then, Jersey is adopting a strategic approach, in respect both of its justice system and its society more generally. Focusing now just on its legal information strategy, will it succeed? One way of answering that question is to compare Jersey's approach with the critical success factors (for IT in justice systems) that I put forward earlier. I identified seven and have recast them in summary form below, together with brief assessments of Jersey's position in respect of each.

1. *Is there a clearly articulated vision?* There is undoubtedly such a vision for Jersey and it is one in which IT is regarded as central to offering greater access to justice.

2. *Is there a centrally co-ordinated IT strategy that applies across the entire justice system?* Again, the answer must be positive. Indeed, such central co-ordination is at the very heart of the Jersey strategy.

3. *Is there recognition that substantial investment is needed and that private sector funding may be appropriate?* The Jersey Legal Information Board certainly appreciates that the initiative will cost a lot, but it has not yet fully assessed the role that private sector funding might play.

4. *Is there support from the top?* In this respect, Jersey is stronger than any jurisdiction I have encountered. Not only is the initiative being led by the Bailiff but he has assembled in his Board the key decision-makers within government, from whom considerable support is forthcoming.

5. *Is there commitment to ongoing research and development?* Given the size of the jurisdiction involved, it would not be feasible for Jersey to conduct basic research into legal information systems. However, the Board is committed to monitoring all relevant developments worldwide and exploiting existing and emerging best practice.

6. *Is it accepted that the main benefits will come from innovation and not just automation?* The fourteen projects represent a mix of automation and innovation. Rightly, however, the emphasis on innovation is in respect of the medium- to long-term projects.

[11] For further details on the work of the Information Society Commission, see www.jerseyisc.org

7. *Is there appreciation of just how radically the Internet will change Jersey society generally and the justice system in particular?* The work of the Information Society Commission confirms that Jersey is taking the Internet very seriously indeed. Whether all members of the Legal Information Board appreciate just how radically IT will transform Jersey's legal system over the next decade is unclear.

Overall, and certainly compared with other jurisdictions, Jersey fares well in this brief analysis. Of course, any number of human factors or technical hitches may yet intervene and derail part or all of Jersey's Legal Information Strategy. But, at this stage, there can be little doubt that the vital signs are good.

I said earlier that the developments in Jersey were exciting. For my own part, the excitement lies in the relative manageability of the initiatives and so the likelihood of success. It is, quite simply, easier for smaller jurisdictions to meet the challenges of the information age. It would be possible for Jersey in months and not years, for example, to jump from its pilot legal information web site to facilities as sophisticated as anywhere in the world. The population of Jersey is akin to the number of employees in one of the world's leading accountancy firms. The formal sources of law in Jersey can be stored on a modest number of shelves. In larger jurisdictions, with millions of people and vast libraries of materials involved, the task is more formidable. Indeed they invariably suffer from 'supertanker syndrome'—the inability to change direction quickly and cheaply.

As in the private sector, the threat to the very large players in the information age is that they might be out-manoeuvred by small entrepreneurs, whose ability to make decisions quickly and respond easily to external change is better suited to the fast-moving Internet world. In that context, Jersey and other small jurisdictions may be able to gain competitive advantage over other countries.

13

The Computer Judge: Early Thoughts[1]

Lurking near the surface of many debates about computers and legal reasoning lies the profound question of whether or not computers might ever replace judges. A little further investigation reveals a wide array of difficult issues: some technical; others philosophical; and still others social. Is it technically possible for the behaviour of judges to be simulated computationally? Is judicial legal reasoning deductive in nature? Even if it might become possible for computer systems to replace judges, would this ever be desirable? I have found such questions raise ideal issues for discussion at postgraduate seminars.

When first published, this chapter was an early attempt by me to explore but one set of related topics—the jurisprudential ones. I did so, as will be seen, in the context of reviewing (quite harshly, in retrospect) a provocative book which, in my view (then and now) proposed an untenable model of the notion of a computer judge.

My focus here, therefore, is on the nature of judicial legal reasoning, on the relationships between logic and the law, and on the connection between law and morality. (Readers interested only in the notion of the computer judge have to wait until the third section of the essay.)

The subject matter of the chapter might be said to be rather more academic than the other essays in the book. Certainly, I wrote the essay in the tradition of post-war analytical jurisprudence and so the style and approach

[1] This chapter originally appeared in (1986) 49 *Modern Law Review* 125–38.

may not be familiar to legal practitioners. Nonetheless, I hope that readers will be intrigued, as I continue to be, by the complexity of the issues and by the range of philosophical problems that are thrown up by the concept of the computer judge.

I

In his book, *The Unity of Law and Morality*, according to the subtitle that it bears, M.J. Detmold falsifies the positivist thesis.[2] It is, however, only one aspect of the positivistic posture that Detmold attacks: the separation of the law and morals doctrine. He goes about his assault on this widely accepted principle in a rather mystical manner, painting on a vast canvas with a very broad brush; but all too often, he fails to cover the necessary material thoroughly. In certain aspects of style and metaphysics, Detmold often resembles the early Wittgenstein: for example, in his usage of short and esoteric sentences, and in his awe at the very existence of our world. Yet unlike an encounter with, say, *Tractatus Logico-Philosophicus*,[3] which leaves one with the impression that there has been a mammoth, unresolved but no doubt worthwhile struggle between a remarkable intellect and intractable philosophical problems, one feels a little disappointed after a careful reading of *The Unity of Law and Morality*, for Detmold leaves many crucial gaps unattended, and does not successfully collect his arguments together into a coherent whole. Tantalizingly, Detmold frequently leaves the reader to guess how some of his yawning cavities might be filled.

At the outset, Detmold tells us of his method of analysing the concept of law. He does not intend to confront the positivist thesis directly, and propound his theory on the basis of its failures (as, say, Hart does with Austin's jurisprudence in *The Concept of Law*[4]) but, rather, he prefers 'the taking of problems as they come,'[5] an approach which allows him—with some subtlety—to avoid some crucial questions. The end result, as I have said, is disappointing because the book lacks coherence. It is all the more frustrating because his ideas about legal judgments and particulars, and the nature of

---

[2] M.J. Detmold, *The Unity of Law and Morality: A Refutation of Legal Positivism* (London: Routledge & Kegan Paul, 1984).

[3] Ludwig Wittgenstein, *Tractatus Logico-Philosophicus* (London, 1922).

[4] H.L.A. Hart, *The Concept of Law* (London: Oxford University Press, 1961).

[5] Detmold, n. 2 above, p. xix.

facts in general, are stimulating and well worth the more detailed and sustained consideration that a direct confrontation of legal positivism might
have yielded.

Like anyone who eschews a version of positivism and seeks to espouse an
anti-positivist position, Detmold sets himself a daunting task that necessi-
tates not only a profound examination of the concept of law, but also regular
encounters with moral philosophy and metaphysics. A glance at the useful
seven-page synopsis that prefaces the study reveals that Detmold covers a
great deal of ground. As has come to be expected in a contemporary work of
analytical jurisprudence—which, amongst many others things, is what *The
Unity of Law and Morality* is—Detmold offers an examination of Hart,
Dworkin, and Raz, all of whose general jurisprudential orientations he criti-
cizes heavily (although he does follow and acknowledge many of Raz's arguments in the latter's *Practical Reason and Norms*[6]). Remarkably Detmold
never refers to the writings of J.M. Finnis and J.W. Harris, treatment of whose
works might well have enhanced the study. Beyond the three standard figures of modern Oxford legal theory, Detmold summarily considers features
of other prominent philosophers, not all of whose writings are popularly
regarded as belonging to mainstream legal theory—Searle's derivation of
'ought' from 'is'; Anscombe's notion of brute facts; Hare's work on univer-
salizability; Kant's notion of a priori concepts; Plato's cave metaphor—and
not all of whose writings seem entirely germane to Detmold's enterprise.

Fundamental to Detmold's concept of law, and indeed central to many of
his arguments, is the notion of 'reasons for action'. In this he owes much to
Raz's general account of normativity in terms of reasons for action in
Practical Reason and Norms. In light of reasons for action, Detmold analyses
rules, principles, case law and precedent, statute law, constitutional law, and
even the world itself (no less). He expends a great deal of energy in discussing
weighing of reasons in relation to Dworkin's principles and in this there are
to be found many penetrating insights. But it is one of his, as he puts it, 'consistent themes',[7]—that of refuting legal positivism—that most who are interested in legal theory will be eager to know about and in what follows, having
briefly reflected on Detmold's metaphysical inclinations, I shall examine his
rejection of the separation of law and morals thesis, first, in relation to
descriptive legal science, and, second, in connection with the idea of a computer judge.

Detmold's ventures into metaphysics (secular jaunts, it should be noted)
are undoubtedly obscure and often constitute no more than unsubstanti-
ated stipulative assertions. The following may serve as examples:

[6] London: Hutchinson, 1975.   [7] Detmold, n. 2 above, p. xix.

The pure existence of the world is mysterious. The importance of this for moral philosophy is that it identifies what in the world requires respect. Mystery requires respect.[8]

The moral sceptic who denies this, Detmold tells us,[9] is committing a logical error. He suggests that the same point can be expressed in terms of beauty and love:

the correlative of beauty is love. It is not possible to affirm the beauty of a particular but deny love. But is that not what the moral sceptic is doing when he denies respect? The affirmation of the mysterious particularity of the world is an affirmation of beauty. The denial of respect for that world is simply a denial of love.[10]

This kind of discourse is, to say the least, enigmatic: and, it should be added, it is no less abstruse when encountered in context. The same has to be said of his concluding chapter entitled unambiguously 'The World', a 32-page discussion in which he propounds his world view. Detmold is, I think, a naïve metaphysicist, and while he perhaps deserves praise for confidently and boldly laying out his fundamental philosophical premises where others leave theirs unarticulated, his mystical conclusions would perhaps have been better left for another more detailed text.

II

Turning now to the central theme of Detmold's book—his refutation of positivism—we should be cautioned at the outset that there are, of course, many ways of being a legal positivist. H.L.A. Hart, in his influential article—'Positivism and the Separation of Law and Morals' (to which, stunningly, in light of his book's sub-title and general argument, Detmold does not allude) identifies five meanings of legal positivism 'bandied about—in contemporary jurisprudence', only one of which is 'the contention that there is no necessary connection between law and morals.[11] Yet it is this thesis that

---

[8] Detmold, n. 2 above, p. 4.   [9] ibid., p. 7.   [10] ibid., p. 8.

[11] See *Essays in Jurisprudence and Philosophy* (Oxford: Clarendon Press, 1983), pp. 57–8. See also see Hart, n. 4 above, pp. 253–4. The term 'legal positivism' has of course promoted a plethora of confusions in jurisprudence. N.E. Simmonds in *The Decline of Juridical Reason: Doctrine and Theory in the Legal Order* (Manchester: Manchester University Press, 1984) has sought to clarify matters by using 'the term "legal positivism" to refer to theories which claim that all laws emanate from authoritative sources in the sense that they have been deliberately laid down or explicitly accepted', while he uses the term 'meta-legal positivism' to 'refer to theories denying that propositions of law are a species of moral judgment' (pp. 22–3).

Detmold takes as symptomatic of all positivist disorders. We might justifiably query his critique, as Finnis has so effectively cast doubt on many arguments against Natural Law, for attacking a position that not all theorists actually hold. For it is not necessary for all legal positivists to defend the notion that there is absolutely no conceptual connection between law and morality. Hart himself mentions this in his *Essays on Bentham*, in which he explains Raz's opposition to one variant of the law/morals necessary connection argument. Hart points out that: 'It may surprise some that though his [Raz's] theory insists that normative statements of duty have the same sense in legal and moral contexts, the general character of his theory is strongly positivist.'[12]

Thus we may conclude, for the interim, that even if Detmold does succeed in establishing a conceptual unity of law and morality, this, of itself, does not necessarily constitute a refutation of the theses of all who may legitimately claim for themselves the identifying (albeit often indeterminate) label of legal positivist. Moreover, we must be sensitive to the possible ambiguities in Detmold's usage of the term 'unity'. When he talks of the unity of law and morality, what sort of relationship between these concepts is he seeking to establish? Again Hart is helpful, this time in his *Law, Liberty and Morality*, in which he indicates four questions that pertain to the relationship between law and morality. Crucial for our and Detmold's purposes is the second of these: 'Must some reference to morality enter into an adequate definition of law or legal system?'[13] Positivists from Bentham forward have argued that no such reference to morality need be incorporated into such a definition, not denying, however, that there are many significant contingent empirical connections between the two. Detmold chooses to ignore this last crucial rider to the positivist thesis. Significantly, however, it is only such an empirical (and often evaluative) connection and not any necessary or logical connection between law and morality that his thesis defends, and in which, therefore, his unity consists.

For, as we shall now see, Detmold's condemnation of the separation of law and morals thesis is far from conclusive and indeed accords with much that has been suggested in the positivist literature itself. Let us first note the characterization of legal positivism that Detmold adopts. Positivism, in Detmold's view:

disguises the audacity of rules by holding that the logical character of judgment under rules is such that one can make it without being committed to that judgment in any

---

[12] See *Essays on Bentham: Studies on Jurisprudence and Political Theory* (Oxford: Clarendon Press, 1982), pp. 9, 153. See also Hart's *Essays in Jurisprudence and Philosophy*, n. 11 above, pp. 9–10.

[13] London: Oxford University Press, 1963, p. 2.

ultimate moral sense. On this view nothing conclusive is done by our taking a rule: no moral question is importantly prejudiced. But the view is a false one. Rule judgment is not just legal judgment or chess judgment, but ultimate moral judgment; and nothing less than this is the responsibility of those who make it. The normal expression by legal positivists of this false doctrine is to say that rules, including legal rules, are provisional or prima facie, and that for any decision under a rule the full moral question awaits separate answer.[14]

Later, in the opening paragraph of Chapter VII, entitled 'Law-Game', Detmold again summarizes what I take to be the central argument of his book. It indeed leads him to claim 'the unity of moral thought'. He claims that, '(l)egal decisions entail the corresponding moral judgment.'[15] When he talks of 'legal decisions' Detmold is referring to judicial decisions. And herein we find one of the limitations of his thesis: by confining his attention to the judicial reasoning agent, he fails to account for legal reasoning as undertaken by all other reasoning agents such as lawyers, advocates, non-judicial legal officials, legal theorists, legal textbook writers, and even citizens. There seems to be no good reason to believe that legal conclusions reached by these various non-judicial agents necessarily entail any moral judgments. Rather, such non-judicial conclusions are normally products of reasoning processes, motivated by the desire to know what the substantive law on a particular matter is, and involving the application of part of the legal system to clusters of facts. Let us call such conclusions—reached through the application of legal premises to factual premises in a value-free fashion—'legal conclusions'. Let us call the final determinations of judges 'legal decisions'. According to Detmold, the legal positivist erroneously conceives of judges' legal decisions as prima facie in nature as they are simply declarative of the law and always open to moral criticism. Moreover, consistent with Detmold's rendition of positivism, all judges' legal decisions must (logically) accord with their prior legal conclusions. Yet, Detmold asks, how can a judge remain morally indifferent to his legal decisions? The answer, in Detmold's view, is that he cannot. The conclusion to be drawn from this, Detmold asserts, is that there is a unity between law and morality. To this fundamental argument I shall return in the next section. Before that, it is instructive to note that Detmold's thesis is limited in scope.

Detmold can be criticized for concentrating on judicial legal decision-making and adjudication, ignoring non-judicial legal reasoning, and in so doing perverting the positivist thesis. This can be seen in light of the following analysis. Let us suppose there exists an abstract universe of legal

---

[14] Detmold, n. 2 above, pp. 21–2.   [15] ibid., p. 147.

discourse that we call the law—'a legal normative field of meaning', in the words of J.W. Harris.[16] The law is expressed, for the most part, through law-formulations. These are linguistic symbols that are deployed in the formulation of the law. The Acts of Parliament as published by HMSO are good examples of law-formulations. In discourse about the law, we use law-statements. These are existential statements indirectly about the law but more directly about law-formulations. They are second-order statements that detail the meaning-content of the law by describing law-formulations. Law-statements, therefore, have truth-value; the existence of the part of the law being described is the truth-ground of any law-statement. They are one sort of (descriptively understood) deontic sentence. When legal scientists describe the law, when lawyers apprise their clients of the content of the law, when teachers of the law lay it out for their students and so forth, these people all do so in the form of such law-statements. In a sense they are all, to a cruder or more sophisticated extent, descriptive legal scientists. In relation to this, one important aspect of many positivists' theories (and this, in my view, is the separation of law and morals thesis in a nutshell) is that any descriptive legal scientist who makes a law-statement (or draws a legal conclusion) can do so in a value-neutral fashion, regarding neither the statement (or conclusion) as being in any sense morally acceptable or justified nor indeed constituting a moral judgment. A law-statement is simply a description of part of the universe of legal discourse and such a description need not be in any way logically related to the universe of moral discourse. Detmold seems to assert in this context that there is necessarily an intersection between the universe of legal discourse and the universe of moral discourse. This is incorrect if the above analysis of descriptive legal science is accepted. Detmold disagrees with this because he concentrates on judicial decision-making to the exclusion of descriptive legal science. His arguments in favour of the unity of legal and moral thought in legal decision-making cannot successfully be applied to descriptive legal science and his attempt to refute legal positivism is therefore severely limited in scope because proponents of the separation of law and morals thesis are, I believe, as concerned with the latter as with the former. At best, then, Detmold is seeking to

---

[16] See *Law and Legal Science* (Oxford: Clarendon Press, 1979). The above analysis of the law, law-formulations, and law-statements, has been influenced by many jurisprudential writings, but most notably: G.H. von Wright, *Norm and Action* (London: Routledge & Kegan Paul, 1963), ch. VI; Joseph Raz: *The Concept of a Legal System*, 2nd edn. (Oxford: Clarendon Press, 1980), pp. 45–50, 234–8, *Practical Reason and Norms*, n. 6 above, pp. 170–7, and *The Authority of Law: Essays on Law and Morality* (Oxford: Clarendon Press, 1979), pp. 62–5; and Hans Kelsen, *General Theory of Law and State* (Cambridge: Harvard University Press, 1946), p. 45 and *Pure Theory of Law* (Berkeley and Los Angeles: University of California Press, 1967), p. 6.

establish a unity between judicial legal reasoning and morality. Yet, as I shall now show, he does not succeed.

III

In seeking to convince us of his refutation of some positivists' claim regarding law and morals, Detmold introduces the notion of computers replacing judges. The introduction of this metaphor, however, simply highlights the shortcomings of his thesis. Detmold believes that the positivism he rejects 'tends to see judges as computers; as, at least in clear cases, simply certifying what in fact the law is on certain facts, without necessary moral commitment'.[17] In the rest of this chapter, I shall reflect on Detmold's objections to the computer judge in clear cases, and in this way, I think, it becomes apparent that his arguments about the particularity of facts and legal judgment are interesting but not novel, and many of his arguments against the positivist thesis that are not demonstrably invalid are in fact not at all inconsistent with positivism; indeed they have been formulated by other positivists in the past. I shall not discuss hard cases about which Detmold says a great deal of importance with regard to the weighing of reasons and alleged deficiencies of Dworkin's Rights Thesis. For in concentrating on hard cases, Detmold often neglects legal reasoning (not necessarily that of judicial reasoning agents) in clear cases, and, as we have said, overlooks descriptive legal science. (Jerome Frank's warning of long ago—not to concentrate on hard cases to the exclusion of clear cases—still falls on deaf ears.)[18]

Detmold suggests that a state of affairs involving computers substituting judges 'could be instituted'. (In fact, at present, there would be numerous hardware and software difficulties that would prevent the realization of this possibility but we may assume for now—with some magnanimity—that Detmold offers this as no more than a thought experiment.) The conclusions of these machines, he says, would entail no moral justification. Yet this, he argues, would not be sufficient 'to establish the positivistic conception' because the 'single-case responsibility would fall totally to those charged to execute the law'.[19] These people would in turn become the judges and their

---

[17] N. 2 above, p. 257.
[18] Jerome Frank, *Courts on Trial* (Princeton: Princeton University Press, 1940), e.g. ch. XV.
[19] ibid.

legal judgments would, according to Detmold's basic analysis, necessarily entail moral judgment. He goes on:

Legal positivism reduces to this: either one applies the programme of the rule of recognition as the arm, so to speak, of a computer, or one resigns . . . There are no judges in the positivist view; for either the programme is applied without judgment or, one unwilling to do that (unwilling to see himself as the arm of a computer) has no course but to resign. No amount of theorising about judgment and discretion in peripheral cases where rules are not clear can disguise this central fact. So far as the law is concerned judges (in clear cases) are [under positivism according to Detmold] nothing but gas ejectors. Or, more accurately, since there is no judgment in this, there are no judges in law.[20]

Before we evaluate this putative relationship between positivism and computer judges, we should also summarize Detmold's continuation of the analogy in relation to the question of the particularity of facts. The facts of any case are very complex, he points out, and refers us to Hampshire's thesis of the inexhaustibility of description according to which any situation has an inexhaustible set of identifiable features, only the few salient of which we express (or even notice) when explaining our reasons for action. But, as Detmold notes: 'For any described particular, no matter how complex, there stands in correspondence a highly limited universal; and it is a point of some importance to know which of these, the particular or the universal, is at the basis of practical decisions.'[21]

Detmold is not entirely convinced of the relevance of Hampshire's thesis, but he is sure that 'what is ultimately beyond the grasp of a computer is not complexity, but particulars',[22] a point that he makes in passing at the start of his book and follows up at the very end of the study:

. . . it is particulars which stand behind rules. They are subsumed into classes which the rules constitute; so that when a rule decision is made the only question is of membership of the class which the norm of the rule constitutes. (. . . One ought to exercise care towards anyone in front of one's car. Harold is in front of my car. Therefore, I ought to exercise care towards Harold). There is no question here of a passionate response to the particulars of the case, as there would be if I were to make a hard decision: the practical content of the rule decision is given by the subjective determination of the will to apply the norm of the rule . . . Particulars in this sense transcend rules. The rule appropriates the whole universe of discourse on cases to which it applies. It creates an absolute. But beyond that absolute, transcending it, ever present and available for hard decision, are particulars. And so long as there is law not leviathan, as there is so long as I am free to programme myself, single cases are

---

[20] ibid., pp.258–9. Cf. Hans Kelsen, *Pure Theory of Law*, n. 16 above, p. 19.
[21] N. 2 above, p. 15. [22] ibid.

available to reassert these particulars. And it is they which are of ultimate seriousness, they which contain the mystery of the world.[23]

(Notice the metaphysical adjunct.) Detmold asks us to suppose there is a statute which requires the execution of blue-eyed babies, and for those who would be sceptical of the likelihood of there being such legislation, he rightly suggests that these children could equally be Jews at Auschwitz. Under a 'leviathan'—a computerized judiciary—if so programmed, the babies would die, the horrid particulars of the case passing unnoticed. Under law, in contrast, we are not committed to deciding our cases in accordance with the rules, we need not have our wills determined subjectively for we are free, Detmold claims, 'to respond (objectively) to the particulars'. (This of course would involve the contravention of what J.W. Harris terms 'legality'.[24]) Judges are at liberty (although in contravention of legality) 'to abandon the programme (and therefore the assumption of bindingness) and respond to the particulars of the case'.[25] For, as he says later: 'Adjudication, the activity of judging, is what distinguishes law from leviathan. Adjudication is the decision of single cases. Thus a judge's freedom to respond to the particulars of those cases is at the basis of law.'[26]

What are we to understand by this talk of computer judges, programming oneself, gas ejectors, and rule-transcending particulars? I think Detmold is saying no more than this. In any clear case, according to positivists, the judge is committed—perhaps by the value of legality—to making one particular legal decision (or else, we might say, the case is not clear). If the judge wishes to abide by the principle of legality, or for some other reason decides to remain faithful to the law, he has no choice but to make that decision, even if he finds it morally unacceptable. He has no choice because he has classified the particulars of the case before him in a manner that logically requires a particular conclusion. Bearing in mind that if he breaches legality he must resign, in any clear case, where there is no breach of legality, the judicial legal conclusion must (logically) be the same as the final judicial decision (as we defined these notions earlier). As a matter of logic, then, there is no need for judgment in clear cases; there is nothing required other than a conclusion/decision reached through the inexorable application of deductive inference procedures. In other words, Detmold claims that positivism is consistent with the idea of a computer (in principle) performing the judicial task in clear cases and ejecting the enforceable conclusion/decision. Yet if a human being chose to apply and enforce the computer output, he goes on,

[23] N. 2 above, pp. 260–1.   [24] *Law and Legal Science*, n. 16 above, pp. 2–7, 81–2.
[25] N. 2, p. 261.   [26] ibid., p. 263.

there would necessarily be responsibility and moral commitment—thus there is the unity of law (or, more accurately, judicial legal reasoning) and morality.

We can summarize Detmold's thesis in another way: judges, having come to their own legal conclusions (or being confronted with computer conclusions), engage in what might be said to be a subsequent and distinct process of practical reasoning involving (necessarily, in Detmold's view) moral evaluation, and thereafter they come to their legal decisions. If there was not this subsequent process of practical and moral reasoning, and judges simply accepted their legal conclusions uncritically, then, Detmold believes, they would ignore the uniqueness and particularity of each legal problem and evil and atrocious decisions could be delivered. For Detmold, legal reasoning is about classifying particulars and if classifying the particular facts of a particular case would lead to a morally unacceptable conclusion (and, therefore, to an unacceptable decision, on the positivist appraisal, as interpreted by Detmold) then we as human beings, and not computers, can (logically, morally, and as a matter of fact) decide otherwise (notwithstanding legality).

Two major questions emerge from Detmold's thesis. First, is the computer judge analogy useful or desirable? Secondly, does Detmold successfully show that legal decisions necessarily entail moral judgments, and, as a consequence, positivism is refuted, or is the bulk of his argument consistent with what other positivists have said in the past? With regard to the computer judge, it is interesting to note—as an instructive illustration of Detmold's use of the metaphor—that he does not argue for the proposition that particulars are beyond the grasp of computers; he simply states it. He tells us nothing of the notion of computability so that we might decide for ourselves the extent to which computers can cope with particulars. He does not endeavour to clarify why it is that the activity of successfully classifying particulars is beyond the capacity of any computer and yet is within the range of human capabilities. He alludes to none of the remarkable recent achievements in that branch of computer science known as Artificial Intelligence (AI). His attempt to press his thesis home talking of computers and programming is simply uninformed and, in the end, accords with (and is no more effective than) many of the equally unenlightened assaults on mechanical jurisprudence that were launched regularly much earlier this century, fettered as they were by their lack of acquaintance with the intricacies of modern formal logic. In short, Detmold presents yet another familiar assault on the notion of deductive legal reasoning, albeit presented in a different context from those in which his like-minded predecessors offered their arguments against 'formalism'. Of course, computers can be used to mechanize deductive reasoning, and it is this premise that underlies much of the research into intelligent knowledge based systems and expert systems that is currently being undertaken in computer laboratories throughout the world.[27] Yet, in selecting his metaphor, Detmold should have been more cautious.

For in introducing the notion of computer judges and thereby transcending disciplines, he lays himself open to the charge of discussing topics beyond his apparent range of knowledge and experience. Having introduced the notion of computer judges, he should have followed the analogy through. There are all sorts of reasons why computers, at present, cannot replace judges, and it is by no means clear that their alleged inability to cope with particulars is even agreed upon by the artificial intelligentsia, nor indeed is it apparent that in clear cases, particularity is the only stumbling block. It should be noted in passing, however, that not all AI workers reject the possibility of computer judges. Much to his horror (and mine) Joseph Weizenbaum, in his *Computer Power and Human Reason* tells of a discussion with AI pioneer John McCarthy, who had posed the question 'What do judges know that we cannot tell a computer?' McCarthy's answer was 'Nothing' and that the goal of building machines for making judicial decisions was perfectly in order.[28] A detailed study of this matter is sorely needed both to dispel the profusion of misconceptions and to assure the public that while computers will no doubt provide invaluable assistance to the judiciary in the future, it is neither possible now (or in the conceivable future) nor desirable ever (as long as we accept the values of Western liberal democracy) that computers assume the judicial function. In any event, computers cannot yet (if ever) satisfactorily recognize speech, understand natural language, nor perceive images. Judges can. Computers have not yet been programmed to exhibit moral, religious, social, sexual, and political preferences akin to those actually held by human beings. Nor have they been programmed to display the creativity, craftsmanship, individuality, innovation, inspiration, intuition, commonsense, and general interest in our world that

[27] See, e.g., Frederick Hayes-Roth, Donald A. Waterman, and Douglas B. Lenat (eds.), *Building Expert Systems* (London: Addison-Wesley, 1983), Donald Michie (ed.), *Expert Systems in the Micro-Electronic Age* (Edinburgh: Edinburgh University Press, 1979), and J.E. Hayes and Donald Michie (eds.) *Intelligent Systems* (Chichester: Horwood, 1983).

[28] Joseph Weizenbaum, *Computer Power and Human Reason: From Judgment to Calculation* (Harmondsworth: Penguin, 1984), p. 207. See also the comments of McCarthy in Bruce G. Buchanan, Joshua Lederberg and John McCarthy, *Three Reviews of J. Weizenbaum's Computer Power and Human Reason* (Stanford University Computer Science Department Report No. STAN-CS-76-7), p. 19. For a legal theorist's point of view, see Anthony D'Amato, 'Can/Should Computers Replace Judges?' (1977) 11 *Georgia Law Review* 5: 1277. Also relevant are Joseph J. Spengler, 'Machine-Made Justice: Some Implications' and Reed Dickeson, 'Some Jurisprudential Implications of Electronic Data Processing' in *Jurimetrics* (1963) edited by Hans W. Baade.

we, as human beings, expect not only of one another as citizens but also of judges acting in their official role. Research into all these matters—by computer scientists, cognitive psychologists, philosophers of mind, computational linguists and neuro-physiologists, to name but a few—goes on (not with a view to computerizing the judiciary), but they are major and controversial concerns of artificial intelligence that Detmold might have done well to have avoided completely. Moreover, there is also the danger that brief and inappropriate allusions to computers and legal reasoning such as Detmold's bring into disrepute those serious investigations into artificial intelligence and legal reasoning that are currently being carried out, whose goals are not to computerize the judiciary but simply, in the words of this field's pioneer, L. Thorne McCarty, to program a computer to perform 'a very rudimentary form of "legal reasoning" ' (not that of judges) and to learn more of the process of legal reasoning through the computational model.[29]

The second question arising from Detmold's thesis is whether he refutes positivism. In order to refute the separation of law and morals doctrine, and thereby cast doubt on a central tenet of many positivist theses, a legal theorist must show there to be some pervasive logical, or necessary, or conceptual (call it what you will) connection, and not simply a contingent, empirical relationship between the two concepts, that he claims, in the words of David Lyons, 'flow[s] from the very nature of law'.[30] To this end, as we have said, Detmold seeks to maintain that there is indeed such a logical connection between judicial legal reasoning and moral judgment. (The relationship, as we have also noted, is manifested only in that legal activity of judicial decision-making and is sorely absent in that other widespread legal enterprise—descriptive legal science.) It can be summarized thus: a judge cannot make a legal decision without also passing a moral judgment. In support of this, Detmold offers a form of logical argument that is at once both confusing and confused. He asks us to suppose a judge sentences a prisoner to hang, and in so doing follows and applies a Hartian rule of recognition that validates a death penalty rule. Relating this scenario to an encapsulation of the separation law and morals doctrine by Raz, Detmold asks 'Could it be that our judge's following and applying the rule of recognition does not entail that he

---

[29] See L. Thorne McCarty, 'Reflections on TAXMAN: An Experiment in Artificial Intelligence and Legal Reasoning' 90 *Harvard Law Review* 838. For a useful selected bibliography of the AI/legal reasoning field, refer to Constantino Ciampi (ed.), *Artificial Intelligence and Legal Information Systems* (Amsterdam: North-Holland, 1982), pp. 409–22. Also see Richard E. Susskind, 'Expert Systems in Law: A Jurisprudential Approach to Artificial Intelligence and Legal Reasoning' (1986) 49 *The Modern Law Review* 2: 168–94 (republished in this book as Chapter 8).

[30] *Ethics and the Rule of Law* (Cambridge: Cambridge University Press, 1984), p. 62, and see generally ch. 3.

holds it to be morally justified?' His answer is that '(t)his could only be true if the following were non-contradictory: (A) The prisoner ought to hang, but it is not the case (morally) that the prisoner ought to hang'.[31] This, clearly, will not do. In answer to Detmold's question, I think many a positivist would want to retort with a resounding 'Yes'. Certainly Raz once argued (although in his most recent work his views on this matter seem to have changed somewhat) that it is both possible (logically) and not rare (as a matter of fact) for a judge or other official to follow and accept a rule of recognition without regarding it as morally justified. All that is required, on this account, is that the judge accepts the validity[32] of the rule of recognition, which acceptance need not be based on moral approval of the rule but may be based on reasons of prudence, self-interest, or indeed on no reason at all.[33] This is not to deny, of course, that sometimes a judge, in following and accepting the rule of recognition, does indeed make such a moral judgment that holds the rule to be morally justified.

Before Raz, Hart also claimed that it was not necessary to make a moral judgment when following and accepting a rule. In 1958, he warned that: '(w)e must . . . beware of thinking in a too simple-minded fashion about the word "ought" . . . The word "ought" merely reflects the presence of some standard of criticism; one of these standards is a moral standard, but not all standards are moral.'[34] Hart went on to show that a decision under a rule could be both purposive and intelligent without commitment to any particular moral principle. Unless one is prepared to stipulate (as a matter either of dubious logic or crude deterministic psychology) that when judges make decisions they necessarily pass moral judgments, then, I think, from the writings of both Hart and Raz (at least from his earlier, and, in my view, more acceptable, work) emerges the unassailable doctrine that the connection between judicial legal reasoning and morality is no more than a contingent one. As a consequence of this, Detmold's rejection of the separation of law and morality principle can be shown to fail and no important unity between law and

---

[31] Detmold, n. 2 above, p. 23.

[32] Following J.W. Harris's useful analysis of conceptions of validity, by 'validity' I mean here that the rule of recognition '(c)orresponds with social reality' and not that it '(h)as an inherent claim to fulfilment.' See *Law and Legal Science*, n. 16 above, p. 105 and ch. IV generally. Failure to distinguish between these different conceptions of validity lies at the core of Detmold's faulty analysis.

[33] The view attributed to Raz above is expressed in his *Practical Reason and Norms*, n. 6 above, pp. 124–5, 147–8, and *The Authority of Law*, n. 16 above, pp. 154–5. Yet Raz seems to have made some modifications to his position: see 'La Pureza de la Teoria Pura' in *Analysis Filosofico* (1981), p. 74 (cited in Hart, *Essays on Bentham*, n. 12 above, p. 156) and 'Hart on Moral Rights and Legal Duties' (1984) 4 *Oxford Journal of Legal Studies* 1: 123–31, esp. pp. 129–31. For a critique of Raz's argument in this context, see Hart, *Essays on Bentham*, n. 12 above, pp. 153–61, and *Essays in Jurisprudence and Philosophy*, n. 11 above, pp. 9–10.

[34] *Essays in Jurisprudence and Philosophy*, n. 11 above, p. 69.

morality is established. Detmold's shortcomings are surely rooted in a failure to pay heed to the admonition of Hart just quoted. If we do indeed have regard to Hart's warning, it is apparent that the truth of the question Detmold poses need not depend on his '(A)' being non-contradictory: for, as we have said, a judge may follow and apply the rule of recognition that validates the capital penalty rule without passing moral judgment.

This apart, Detmold's willingness to entertain the possibility of contradiction in (A) constitutes an illuminating assumption in deontic logic, a supposition which can be seen even more clearly in his reformulation (attributed to Raz) of (A) as (C3): 'From the legal point of view the prisoner ought to hang, but it is not the case morally that the prisoner ought to hang.'[35] Most deontic logicians would claim that it does not make sense to talk without qualification of logical contradiction, or non-contradiction, between normative statements emanating, as the two statements in (C3) most certainly do, from distinct authorities or sources.[36] The only possible defence to this logical imperfection would be to assert that the two normative statements do indeed pertain to the same normative system, which system would clearly contain a contradiction. This allegation is, of course, at one with the notion of there being a unity between law and morality. Yet this ploy unambiguously exposes the nonsense of the unity thesis, as no one could sensibly maintain that the two parts of (C3) belong to the same system, for this would imply that the legal point of view normativity system is simply a subset of the normative system of morality (whatever its contents might be). This, in turn, would call for defence of the suggestion that every act that we are required to do or forbear from doing in accordance with the law is also required or forbidden by morality. In so doing this would necessarily exclude the possibility of moral criticism of statements of descriptive legal science; a consequence few would wish. Once this mistake of deontic logic is rectified, and it is accepted that a valid statement from the legal point of view can justify a judicial decision without moral commitment, then the thrust of Detmold's central thesis is quashed.

It should be noted that through the above scrutiny and correction of Detmold's work, we were provided with material with which we could forcefully fortify legal positivism. In another respect, Detmold also has close affinities with positivist theorists. We have said that his use of the computer analogy (albeit misplaced) functions both as a critique of deductive legal reasoning in clear cases and of the more general notion of formalism. Hart has said of the charge of formalism that: 'Levelled at the legal theorist, the charge

---

[35] Detmold, n. 2 above, p. 25.
[36] See *Norm and Action*, n. 16 above, p. 16. Cf. Raz, *The Authority of Law*, n, 16 above, pp. 138–9.

means that he has made a theoretical mistake about the character of legal decision; he has thought of the reasoning involved as consisting in deduction from premises in which the judge's practical choices or decisions play no part.'[37] In fact, there is much in *The Unity of Law and Morality* regarding formalism that accords with claims Hart (a self-confessed legal positivist) makes in his 'Positivism and the Separation of Law and Morals'. First, in denying that the 'conception of the judge as an automaton' was proposed and defended by Bentham and Austin (the founding fathers of English legal positivism), Hart makes it absolutely clear that that model of judicial reasoning is erroneous.[38] Hart's automaton is, of course, functionally equivalent to (yet far less contentious than) Detmold's computer judge. Secondly, Detmold's arguments concerning the uniqueness, the particularity, of facts, are also anticipated in Hart.[39] When Detmold argues that 'beyond that absolute, [created by a rule] transcending it, ever present and available for hard decision, are particulars' I do not think he is saying much more than Hart when he tells us that '(f)act situations do not await us neatly labelled, creased, and folded; nor is their legal classification written on them to be simply read off by the judge.' Thirdly, just as Detmold talks of the 'responsibility' on those who make rule judgment, Hart speaks of 'the responsibility of deciding that words do or do not cover some case in hand, with all the practical consequences involved in this decision'.[40]

And so, Detmold seems to joint Hart (and Bentham and Austin) in rejecting various aspects of the notion of deductive legal reasoning. Indeed he goes further by reaffirming many of the other arguments against this model of judicial legal reasoning that can be found in a whole host of jurisprudential (not all positivistic) writings of the past: his ideas about judgment and will were anticipated by Kant; his comments regarding particularity were made by Jensen in 1957 (as well as by Hart); and the possibility of injustice resulting from deduction in law was outlined by Gottlieb in 1968.[41] Yet, paradoxically, his very expression of the positivist case regarding computers, intended as a model for us to reject, constitutes, I think, a particularly lucid vindication of much that has been well said by MacCormick and Sinclair in favour of deductive legal reasoning in clear cases.[42] For despite the many

---

[37] *Essays in Jurisprudence and Philosophy*, n. 11 above, p. 65.

[38] ibid., p. 66.   [39] ibid., pp. 63–4.   [40] ibid.

[41] See Immanuel Kant, *Critique of Pure Reason*, trans. Norman Kemp Smith (London: Macmillan & Co., 1929), pp. 177–8; O.C. Jensen, *The Nature of Legal Argument* (Oxford: Basil Blackwell, 1957), p. 16; Gidon Gottlieb, *The Logic of Choice: An Investigation of the Concepts of Rule and Rationality* (London: George Allen & Unwin, 1968), p. 18.

[42] See D.N. MacCormick, *Legal Reasoning and Legal Theory* (Oxford: Clarendon Press, 1978) and 'The Nature of Legal Reasoning: A Brief Reply to Dr Wilson' (1980) *Legal Studies* 286; and Kent Sinclair, Jr., 'Legal Reasoning: In Search of an Adequate Theory of Argument' (1971) 59 *California Law Review* 3: 821.

weaknesses of deductive legal reasoning in the penumbra, I believe Hart, many natural lawyers, and even Dworkin would agree that in those cases in which there is little doubt that the facts fall unambiguously within the ambit of an undisputed rule of law (including its exceptions, which the full statement of a rule may express, although this may presuppose, for practical purposes, an unsatisfactory theory of individuation), the suggestion that deductive inference procedures are a suitable vehicle by which to arrive at a legal conclusion cannot sensibly be disregarded.

Detmold, like so many other legal theorists (positivists and non-positivists alike), does seem to have overlooked the possibility of allowing for a mere partial rejection of deductive legal reasoning, retaining it as an indication of the deep structure, as it were, of self-consistent and rational legal thought.

IV

Of what school of thought does it transpire, then, that Detmold is a member? He is in no sense, I think, a natural lawyer. He does not suggest there to be any higher law discoverable by reason whose content can be used as a benchmark against which the moral acceptability of human law may be gauged or, again, whose provisions can function as the foundations of an acid test for the truly legal (or non-legal) character of any human laws. Far from asserting the existence of such natural laws, Detmold dogmatically sides with those who deny there to be any objective morality: 'Those who think there are no objective values are right. There is only the world, and no reason to think that objective values are to be found in it (what would an objective value look like, sound like, or feel like?)'[43] This, of course, is a rather compressed version of J.L. Mackie's 'Argument From Queerness'.[44] In compressing it, however, Detmold confusingly conflates the metaphysical and epistemological aspects of this now influential argument in favour of moral scepticism. We can justifiably object that we seem to have no way of perceiving objective values analogous to our methods of knowing through the occurrence of sensory experiences or mental events—the epistemological claim (although J.M. Finnis, in his recent *The Fundamentals of Ethics*, forcefully argues against this argument[45]). It is less easy, however, to sustain such

---

[43] Detmold, n. 2 above, p. 153.
[44] *Ethics: Inventing Right and Wrong* (Harmondsworth: Penguin, 1977), pp. 38–42.
[45] Oxford: Clarendon Press, 1983, ch. III.

bare (again naïve) metaphysical claims as the Detmoldian assertion '(t)here is only the world'. (Perhaps the moral sceptic need not go beyond the epistemological claim and can simply place the burden of proof of establishing any further metaphysical contentions firmly on the moral objectivist.)

In any event, Detmold is not a natural lawyer. Nor does he defend Dworkin's third theory of law. He certainly does not propound any thesis that can be regarded as a fourth theory, for its central principles (those that are not false) differ in no significant respects from the basic principles of many legal positivists. Yet I have to confess that despite its many limitations, with its healthy peppering of classical quotations, its several humorous dialogues, its subtle (if untenable) interplay of the philosophies of law and love, its extract from King Lear and its modular layout—all vaguely reminiscent of the spirit of the much larger discipline—transcending *Gödel, Escher and Bach*[46] by Douglas Hofstadter—in *The Unity of Law and Morality*, philosophers and jurisprudents will indeed find a curiously compelling, unconventional but recommended contribution to their fields. However, legal positivists will no doubt be relieved to learn that one of their central tenets—the separation of law and morals thesis—emerges from *The Unity of Law and Morality* misunderstood, unscathed and, as I have argued, perhaps even corroborated. Indeed, the book might well bear the more apposite subtitle 'A Vindication of Legal Positivism'.

[46] New York: Vintage Books, 1980.

Index

Lightning Source UK Ltd.
Milton Keynes UK
UKOW05f2339180914

238750UK00001B/24/P